THEY CHOSE HONOR

THEY
CHOSE HONOR

THE PROBLEM OF CONSCIENCE IN CUSTODY

by Lewis Merklin, Jr., M.D.

HARPER & ROW, PUBLISHERS

NEW YORK, EVANSTON, SAN FRANCISCO, LONDON

1817

FIRST EDITION

Designed by Sidney Feinberg

Library of Congress Cataloging in Publication Data

Merklin, Lewis.
    They chose honor.
    1. Prison psychology.   2. Federal Correctional
Institution, Lompoc, Calif.   3. Vietnamese Conflict
1961-   —Conscientious objectors.   I. Title.
HV6089.M3 1974   365′.9794′91   74-5794
ISBN 0-06-012939-5

To my family, Lewis, Elizabeth, and Marjorie Merklin, without whom this book could not have been written, and without whom this writing would not have been a book

Contents

PART THREE

The Group

PART FOUR

Afterword

Author's Note

My greatest debts have been acknowledged in the dedication, but no formal statement of gratitude can express my debt to many prisoners who taught me, by word or example, more than they or I realized. Some of them have been quoted in this book, with their permission and their encouragement, and I have tried to protect their anonymity with pseudonyms; others were present in spirit if not in word as this volume took shape, and their example has informed its tone and content. Many prison employees were important in the experience sketched here, both those who "wanted to teach that doctor a thing or two" and those who were more benignly instructive. All of them who appear frequently in the text have also been assigned a fictitious identity.

From the time when this book was no more than a notion to the point when it was no less than a burden, I have been the beneficiary of comfort and criticism from friends and colleagues who may be thanked more publicly. Their help has been considerable, but their listing must be alphabetical. They include Jean Black, Kai Erikson, Tom Farber, Kay Gallwey, Patrick Gallwey, Gene Hoffman, Hallock Hoffman, Joan Kahn, the late Celia Merklin, Perry Ottenberg, Antonia Rachiele, the late Edward Reed, Mary Reed, Melody Rosenberg, Michael Rosenberg, Jane Silver, Lee Silver, Barbara Ten Eyck, Otto Will.

Much of the formulation of what has been summarized in this volume took place during my tenure as a Research Training Fellow of the Social Science Research Council at the Centre for Applied Social Research of the Tavistock Centre, London. I am indebted to the Council for the fellowship and to the Centre staff for their time and interest. I wish to thank in particular John M. M. Hill and Isabel E. P. Menzies of the Centre for their criticism and commentary on early drafts of this work.

It would be a disservice to his singularity of vision if I did not point out in particular that little of this book would have been realized without the benefit of the acuity and grace of W. R. Bion.

Although I have had the benefit of the consultation and support of many, it must be pointed out that sole responsibility for the content of this book rests with the author and that it in no way represents an undertaking of the U.S. Public Health Service or of the Federal Bureau of Prisons.

"All trials are trials for one's life, just as all sentences are sentences of death."

Oscar Wilde,
De Profundis

Preface

THIS book concerns the lives of private men in public custody. The private men were a group of remarkably self-possessed young Americans who refused conscription for reasons of conscience. The public custody was their experience of incarceration at the Federal Correctional Institution at Lompoc, California. As with other prisoners, incarceration provoked many conflicts in these men: between their concern for their integrity and the environmental pressures toward disintegration, between private conscience and official coercion, between individual strength and institutional power. No less disturbing were the tensions within conscience, between conscience and self, and, finally, among the resisters themselves. The primary focus of this book is upon such conflicts and the manner in which they affected the resisters' psychic and political perspectives in their confrontation with themselves, each other, and their nation.

Those conflicts and confrontations took place within the special world that is prison (a world that is becoming more destructively familiar to more and more people), and they were discussed and sometimes actualized in a particular setting: the office of the prison psychiatrist. Since much of the material in this volume was gathered in a series of group interviews with the resisters over a period of two years, and because we were all contained to some degree by the physical and psychic restrictions of imprisonment, this book is concerned not only with my involvement with the resisters, but also with the psychic effects of incarceration on every prisoner—effects that were especially troubling to me since as the prison psychiatrist I was expected to act therapeutically in an institution that could not have been more antitherapeutic without the revival of physical torture.

There is yet a third dimension to this volume. Even though I was aware of—and was initially attracted by—the paradoxical aspects of the resisters' presence in the prison population, I was not prepared for my subsequent realization that their response to incarceration was by no means unique. When compared with the effects of imprisonment on other inmates and prison employees, the resisters' experience was far more similar than it was different, and I came to realize that however disparate in background, circumstance, and temperament they may be, all who live or work in prison are unified by the need to respond to the effects of incarceration. Although this book may be read as an account of draft resisters in prison, it is also an account of the struggle to resist the destruction of the self which prison imposes on everyone who goes inside.

I went to work in prison from 1967 to 1969 in response to my own Selective Service requirements—unsought but also unresisted —as an officer in the U.S. Public Health Service, and a group of draft resisters was organized and conducted within the general group psychotherapeutic program which other doctors and I struggled to maintain. To all the groups I brought the attitudes, conduct, and habits of thought derived from my own personal development and from my professional training in individual, group, and family psychotherapy within the psychoanalytic tradition. I brought many questions as well—clinical, developmental, and social. How do people change in prison? What patterns of character had brought them to custody and what might bring them through it? To people in transit from adolescence to adulthood, could life in a "youth institution" bring growth as well as grief?

In my work with the resisters, these matters concerned me as well as others. In their saying no to the draft, I felt that they might be saying yes to themselves, confirming certain ideals and values important to them and to their inner sense of identity. I wondered whether that yes could be sustained in custody. Could the resisters' needs for integrity prevail over the prison's demands for compliance? What were the effects upon men of conscience of being treated as criminals, indeed of being punished more severely for their exercise of conscience than were other prisoners for their apparent deficiency of it? Nor could I overlook the possibility that their no might be more adolescent than adult, an expression of the emotional conflict characteristic of that period, or an act of impulse or worse which had brought them to a situation that could distort or negate both adolescence and the adulthood that lay beyond it.

As a result of my training and my interests, I also brought with me to prison a concern for the effects, for good or ill, of institutions upon individuals. I had learned a little about "therapeutic communities" from the hospitals at which I had taken my psychiatric training, but the chill of the allegedly rehabilitative prison environment around and increasingly within my patients, my colleagues, and myself soon led me to feel that the institution was the opposite of therapeutic.

Although this is a book about "private men," it is also about the effects of the public custody in which they were immersed: the extreme pressures of incarceration and the severe psychological distortions they promote. It is particularly concerned with the fact that those pressures act not only *upon* the imprisoned but *within* them. The volume and intensity of psychic stress invalidated the prison's announced therapeutic intent, the number of parole violators returned to custody contradicted its claims of correction, and the uselessness of the skills required in its work programs refuted its goals of rehabilitation even in its narrow vocational sense.

But if it did not treat, correct, or rehabilitate its inmates, the prison did punish and confine them. Indeed, punishment and confinement went far beyond chastening and detention to the imposition of dehumanization and the implicit (and sometimes explicit) encouragement of psychopathy to relieve it. It was soon apparent that the effects of imprisonment deformed even those who were not in custody, at least legally, and that going home after a day's work did not usually moderate those effects. Within a constricted physical space and under heightened social and psychic pressure, both prisoners and staff were reduced to a contracted range of mental life and social experience and thus to a painfully narrow identity.

Beyond the general aspects of dehumanization, I began to recognize more specific psychic deterioration in my clinical work with inmates, in my association with prison employees, among my colleagues in the prison hospital, and within myself. The most important of these were the tendency toward categorical and concrete thought, the disturbance of abstraction and of symbolic integration, the confusion of time, the diminution of moral consciousness, the loosening of the inner restraints of conscience when another was not seen as human and oneself as barely so, and—most important— the disruption of contact with one's own inner life and with the lives of others. I doubted very much that I could alleviate the progressive "psychic death" which imprisonment seemed to require, particularly when I was also subject to it.

Thus it was not only the volume of need in the prison clinic or my particular professional interests which affected my work with the people I was supposed to help; there was also my own despair. I do not think it inappropriate to speak of compassion here, not as pity or condescension, but in its most literal sense of bearing with, and of the hope it raised of bearing up. Of whatever value I might have been to those who sought my help, I knew as well that they were of value to me, for I realized that my own self-respect, already challenged by what seemed to be required of me as a prison psychiatrist, depended upon my exercise of concern for others, my responsible involvement with them, my refusal to ignore their humanity or mine, and upon my struggle to remain faithful to my ethical sense as a doctor and a man.

If it was important to be compassionate, it was also necessary to be dispassionate. My training had awakened me to the risks of assumed objectivity and of unexamined subjectivity and to the realization that neither is desirable or entirely escapable. Since I

was responsible for the organization and sometimes the maintenance of the groups with whom I met, to imply uninvolvement
would be to add a distortion greater than that of recognized bias.
It is doubtful whether an attempted synthesis of responsive objectivity and restrained subjectivity (for that was the attitude I tried to
maintain) is long possible for anyone who works in prison and is
sensitive to the pressures and conflicts which flourish there. The
assumptions, goals, and methods of correction on the one hand,
and of psychotherapy on the other, seemed irreconcilable. I had
come to the prison with a commitment to psychotherapy as an ethically informed *ally* process, one relying upon consent and collaboration in *resolving* conflict toward the goals of personal growth
and social responsibility. But correction, as I saw it carried out,
seemed to be a moralizing *adversary* process demanding blind
obedience, *exploiting* conflict, and resulting in stagnation and ostra-
cism.

If the assumptions, goals, and methods of these two approaches
seemed to be at cross-purposes, the conflict between them was
intensified by the divisive psychological effects of the closed and
hostile prison environment. The situation was not one that promoted
balance. Rather, its major effect was to aggravate inherent splits
within and between employees and prisoners and to compel in both
an inner partitioning and reorientation toward an absolute, categorical, all-or-none psychological posture. A major solution to the
difficulties of prison life, for staff and inmates alike, was to accept
one exclusive, simplified identity and its simplistic attitudes, and to
accept them completely, ascribing their opposites to other people
and rejecting *them* completely. The longer one spent there, the
more difficult it was to resist the pressure toward such an inner
realignment. Even—and perhaps especially—for a relatively transient psychiatrist, the problem was not whether to identify with
one group, either staff or prisoners, but with which group to identify
and to what extent.

I felt committed to the prisoners, the people I was there to
"help"; some were more likable than most of the employees, and
they seemed more open to change and growth. But if I was to be

of any value to them or to myself, I had to try to avoid at least the worst extremes of a polarized identification. For example, there was the danger of seeing prisoners as inanimate or subhuman (as did most officials and some doctors), and there was the risk of idealizing them as wayward heroes or patronizing them as helpless victims (as did many prisoners and some doctors). Indeed, there was the danger of thinking of people as a categorized "them" of any kind. But if a complete identification with officials or prisoners was not desirable and a rigorous objectivity was not possible, I felt that it still might be useful to consider, if not to alleviate, the psychic *rigor mortis* which seemed to be the dominant mental state of prison life. Recognizing these dimensions, I was more a thoughtful participant than a sympathetic observer, and therefore this book is based on both clinical and personal experience.

Clinical and personal interests had much to do with my organizing a group of draft resisters and with my choosing to focus upon them in this book. The prison officials conceded, at least in private, that the resisters were not criminal and therefore classified them as "not candidates for rehabilitation." In practice this meant that they were to be immersed in the prison as anonymously as other prisoners but that they were not to be eligible for the few rehabilitative resources the prison offered, such as college correspondence courses or early release to halfway houses. I also thought, at least initially, that the resisters were "not candidates for rehabilitation": I did not think that their draft refusal was criminal or even pathological, and I doubted that they would need the limited help a psychiatrist can provide in prison. In fact, I wanted to meet with them because I thought they might help *me*.

I was interested in the resisters for several reasons. First, I respected their physical and moral courage in confronting the critical issues of the times: the legitimacy of the Vietnam war and the legitimacy of the government's power to define conscience. Second, they were trying, like everyone else there, to survive in an institution that was becoming familiar to a growing number of Americans of every background, an institution which seemed to me to be the most representative of the times: prison. Third, within the prison, they were faced with the most important psychosocial issue of the times: officially sanctioned dehumanization. Finally, I thought that in possessing and exercising the strengths and virtues which brought them to prison, the resisters might be the group least likely to be deformed by incarceration, that they might say something unique about survival in a critical time and place—not only their survival but mine and that of other men I was trying to help. I have chosen to write about them, however, because in disproving this last, naïve assumption, their prison experiences documented the irresistibility of the identity erosion which incarceration imposes on everyone—a psychological atrocity that none of us thought could be so widespread, so pervasive, or so inexorable.

When I reviewed my notes and impressions after the resister group meetings I was surprised to find that the issues and themes discussed corresponded closely to those that characterized other groups—of inmates and of the medical staff. The prison experiences of the resisters were less unusual than I had supposed; when compared with the experience of others, there were more correspondences than there were differences. The resisters were all middle-class and college-educated, but with the imprisonment of increasing numbers of students for drug offenses and other criminal acts the prison population, too, was becoming more middle-class and college-educated. This shift in the population was disturbing to guards, who had become used to the more classically delinquent and stereotypical young inmate known in prison jargon as the "low rider." This change in the population was also disturbing to the low riders still in prison; the first inmate of the new breed to "meditate" in the prison yard was assaulted sexually. Furthermore, what I had assumed to be the relative advantages of well-integrated personalities, supportive families, and good prospects for work or school after prison—not to mention the interest of a concerned psychiatrist—were only marginally helpful to the resisters in withstanding the overwhelming institutional pressures of physical intimidation, social control, and psychological coercion.

If comparison of my notes and impressions was not sufficient to convince me that the resisters' response to imprisonment was not strikingly unusual, their own opinions and subsequent behavior were more than convincing. None of the resisters had come to prison thinking that he was above the law; indeed, they all came precisely because they felt honor bound to accept its judgment. Still, some had felt that once inside they might be special prisoners, not so much privileged as distinctive. Few held that opinion for very long. The pressures against individual distinctiveness and toward anonymity were far too intense and multiple to be resisted. No resister felt that his experience of incarceration was exceptional.

I have written about the resisters in prison, not because they were special but because they were exemplary. They were "model prisoners," not because they were compliant but because their response to incarceration paralleled that of other prisoners and staff; whatever the superficial differences, the basic psychological processes were the same. It was not that they suffered unduly but that they suffered similarly; it was not that they could "take it" but that they took it in; that is, they came to accept the assumptions, perceptions, codes, and behavior that every inmate is required to adopt. There are variations in the situations and pressures of prison life, to be sure, and men respond to pressure in different ways, but those variations I observed among the resisters appeared to be much more in degree than in kind. The experiences of the men who speak through this volume seemed to be far more shared with others than special. In one sense, this is a book about my engagement with private men in public custody, about draft resisters in prison; in a larger sense, it speaks for all prison lives.

As my susceptibility to prison life affected my work, so has it affected the writing of this account. Although prison has often stimulated literary effort, its effect upon me was the opposite. The pressures of the work and the atmosphere, the physical and emotional exhaustion they exacted, and the intellectual constriction they induced forced me to defer—to a later time, a distant place— a review of my notes and tapes and an evaluation of what they contained. To recapitulate and formulate a prison experience is a task indeed, in view of the opposing tendency, fostered by incarceration itself, to regard it as having been a static and ugly thing and to psychologically wall it off and isolate it from further awareness. The best studies of prisons, I suspect, have been done from the outside; the best accounts of prison life, from the inside. Mine, however, was a middle position: I was neither completely incarcerated nor free of the prison regime. This book, therefore, is neither a study of a prison nor an account of prison life but a report from the middle distance.

Reflection has clarified what I had felt more dimly all along: that what happened at Lompoc could not be encompassed—and might be needlessly constricted—by the special vocabulary of the clinical report. In professional publication and discussion, I have considered the particular psychodynamics and social relations of the resisters, but in this book written for the general reader the emphasis is upon the resisters as particular people in a critical situation rather than as subjects for clinical study. But to write for the general reader is not to be merely descriptive or to overlook psychosocial complexities—they were very much in my thoughts as I selected transcripts for this account and they are evident in the text. I have not hesitated to use some technical language to emphasize a particular point or to make a statement that would otherwise be incomplete, but I have seen no advantage in the use of a specialized system of clinical nomenclature in a book whose scope is broader than that specialized system.

Lest my reticence in employing clinical categorizations be misunderstood, let me be specific about a particular matter: it was not my assumption (nor is it my conclusion) that to refuse conscription or to go to prison for that refusal was an indication of psychopathology. Indeed, my bias was in the opposite direction. When the group began to meet, I was well aware that draft refusal and incarceration might possibly be associated with a more pervasive and pre-existing personality disorder, but I did not feel that the acts themselves were necessarily symptomatic. I felt that if the resisters had emotional difficulties, they would manifest themselves in any event and that they could be assessed by other, more strictly diagnostic criteria. I had already begun to realize from my work with other prisoners that whatever their previous emotional difficulties might have been, the immediate problems aroused by imprisonment were more pressing and, in many instances, more serious. I was, of course, interested in why the resisters had come to Lompoc, in *what* they were doing there, but in facing—and to some degree sharing—the narrowed life of prison I was more concerned with what prison was doing to them, with *how* they were doing there.

In any usual sense, the therapeutic dimensions of the group were slight at the beginning: the resisters did not seek me out, I went to them; the group was organized at my request and with their consent. Two of them had seen a psychiatrist before coming to prison, and though a few had asked to see me upon incarceration, the majority did not join the group as people seeking psychiatric help, as patients in the strict sense of the word. That the group subsequently took on a therapeutic aspect, that they *became* patients, was not the result of my desire to cast them into that relationship with me but rather the consequence of the dreadful fact that incarceration can make a psychiatric patient of anyone.

In organizing the contents of this volume, I have chosen to begin with a discussion of the nature of public custody and its psychic effects in order to provide at least an anecdotal and impressionistic context within which the resisters speak in subsequent pages. I must stress that this book is not a study of a social system, nor is there an attempt to advance an ethnology of prison or a typology of group behavior. Part One is an account of the prison atmosphere, but it is an account of that atmosphere as I have sensed it. It begins with a physical description of the prison's environment and of the building itself. There follows a brief sketch of the prison personnel and of the manner in which the institution seemed to be administered more to relieve the anxiety of its staff than to bring about the rehabilitation of the inmates. On the basis of my own observation and experience, I have outlined elements of the personnel code and of the inmate code (both codes being more implicit than clearly articulated, but no less forceful for that) and of the way they interacted to further the dehumanization of institutional life—and to encourage relief from that dehumanization through psychopathic behavior.

The most important effect of incarceration is, in my opinion, that many inmates unwittingly internalize these institutional codes and identify with prison authorities (and with significant prisoners), thereby unconsciously accommodating to a psychic incarceration as narrow and as arid as their physical confinement. In Part One I have tried to delineate the most prevalent form of that psychic incarceration as I encountered it. I have called it petrifaction—a term suggested by the complaints of many men I tried to treat in the prison clinic. This vantage point was a particularly intimate one from which to view the many effects, acute and chronic, of the correctional process. Those effects crowded my days and disrupted my nights, not only with the usual emergency calls but with unexpected nightmares, and both pressed in upon me with such clamorous urgency and mute despair that I could not ignore them even when I wanted to. Just as the effects of imprisonment were observable in my patients, it was not long before they were evident in me. I have, therefore, included an account of how I happened to come to Lompoc, how the prison affected me and my colleagues, and how the group program in general and the resister group in particular came about.

Part Two consists of character sketches of six resisters who personify particular aspects of individual development and remarkable responses to the stress of prison life. I was able to interview a few men individually and in some depth, but the number and duration of those interviews were limited by the demands of my other work. Although it was not possible to interview every resister individually, I have tried to include in this section brief profiles of those who figure prominently in the group excerpts which follow in Part Three. My principal contact with the resisters, however, was in the group, and that contact was limited to two hours a week.

There were other constraints as well. The resisters were "private men" in any case, but in prison they were even more sensitive about what little privacy remained to them. In the beginning, at least, they were particularly sensitive about the questions of a prison psychiatrist. In reporting the interviews of the men who appear in Part Two, I have augmented their concern for their privacy and anonymity with my respect for it. Despite those limitations, I regard the interviews as useful and important, but because of those limitations, I do not think of them as thoroughgoing or complete. Respecting the constraints and the individuals concerned, I have chosen not to substitute conjecture for direct clinical evidence or to replace with speculation the exploration in depth and over time that I would have preferred to undertake in other circumstances.

Part Three is made up of selected transcriptions of some of the resister groups which met over a two-year period. Several months went by before the group was sufficiently cohesive and trusting to look upon a tape recorder as anything but an instrument of criminal investigation, but even then I was reluctant to use one because I did not wish to be identified any more closely with the prison authorities than I already appeared to be. It was only after the men grew weary of my struggles with notes and encouraged me to bring my own recorder that I did so. The prison did not have a tape recorder available, but it is doubtful anyway if the group would have permitted the use of any machine other than my own. Even then, they were not always reassured by the fact that the tapes were kept in my care and under lock and key. For myself, I chose to use a tape recorder, not so much to gather data or to ensure factual accuracy or even to record nonverbal nuances, but simply to keep track of what was happening from week to week. In this group and in others I was expected to maintain continuity by the men with whom I met, but the psychic changes I was undergoing made this task less and less feasible.

Although group discussion was often absent or erratic and the continuity from week to week was tenuous, certain themes recurred and developed over time in what was, for good or ill, a long-term experience. Because the group extended over time and in depth, it provided a better situation than individual interviews in which to observe directly and to explore the ongoing effects of incarceration. In attempting to present both thematic and chronological development, I have imposed some organization by arranging the transcripts topically; within each topical section, they are arranged chronologically. The material is presented so that individual statements remain in context; emphasis, denoted by italics, is that of the speaker. I have hesitated to intrude upon the dialogue with excessive commentary or interpretation, but I have tried to present a few introductory and transitional paragraphs. In presenting these comments I have felt no need to concoct syndromes, to interpret gratuitously, to paraphrase laboriously, or to remind the reader constantly that a psychiatrist is at work.

Having reviewed my notes, listened to the tapes, and read the transcriptions of them—in sequence and in solitude—I recognized two themes that are presented successively in Part Three. The first theme is that of identity erosion, which every prisoner experiences and which results, in extreme form, in the psychic state I have termed petrifaction. In the first half of Part Three the resisters recount those experiences which they shared with other prisoners and which contributed to their identity erosion. The latter half of Part Three deals with the second theme, of victimization, and with an event which was particular to the resisters but which in its basic psychic elaboration was not an isolated phenomenon. This event reflects not so much the psychological cruelty toward the resisters and all prisoners as it does the cruelty the resisters inflicted upon each other; for when they could no longer bear their own sense of victimization and the identity erosion it aggravated, they turned, as did other prisoners, to the victimization of each other.

Part Four begins with a brief summary of what has preceded it. Next is a short epilogue which I do not claim is a follow-up report. How momentary or pervasive, how situational or essential, are the psychic changes of imprisonment is still uncertain. An assessment of those changes now would be mere conjecture; to explore that issue comprehensively will require, I fear, another book. Finally, there is a postscript regarding prison reform in which I note that while prison abolition is a laudable goal it does not appear to be an immediate likelihood. In the interim, I suggest, it would be well to consider the possibility that prisons are now so competent in confinement and punishment that they cannot be converted to agencies of rehabilitation. Sensible rehabilitation can begin only when a clear distinction can be made between the goals of confinement and punishment and those of rehabilitation, and that distinction is not likely to occur in prison or among most prison personnel. If meaningful treatment is to be sought, it must be outside prison walls.

As this book has taken shape it has also assumed a form of its own. The narrative begins, somewhat arbitrarily, with my arrival at the institution, and it ends, for the most part, with my departure. There is some sense of time but no clear chronology. People appear and then recede and no single prisoner sustains a major relationship with the reader for the entire course of the work. At times the material may seem more collected than integrated, more organized than synthesized. These aspects of the text reflect the limitations of the author, to be sure, but they also reflect certain dimensions of prison life. Staff and prisoners arrive and depart under circumstances beyond their control. Time passes or stands still, but it is accounted for with even greater difficulty than it is served. People impinge on each other, but there is rarely a sense of connection, and attachments to those outside become fractional and marginal as well. Days are organized and experiences are collected, but they often are not meaningfully linked; as the exercise of choice over external life is limited, so are the internal processes of psychic integration and synthesis diminished.

It is doubtful whether transcriptions can adequately convey or connote the depth of feeling and its inaccessibility, or the intensity of conflict, both vocal and inarticulate, so palpable in life and still audible on tape. Nor can it impart the silences of grief and anger, the laughter of hilarity and anxiety, or the tears of relief and sorrow. Finally, one can only imagine the textures of tone of voice, facial expression, and posture which do not survive transcription and are often more moving than speech. Nonetheless, I have felt that the eloquence of the men quoted here is more important than my wish to present a more polished account, and I have therefore chosen to retain the fragmentary quality inherent in successive quotation. I have felt as well that it would be unacceptable to present too facile an account of an experience which was essentially one of psychic and social disjunction.

PART ONE

The Prison

The Town

THE road to Lompoc is a dead end. It twists through twenty miles of hilly ranchland from the main highway and stops in a field of commercially cultivated flowers. An Air Force missile, glaring white and obsolete, stands on display next to the field. Beyond that technological scarecrow lies a factory processing minerals into diatomaceous earth. Lompoc depends on all three: the flowers grown in its fields, the missiles interred in its Air Force base, the silica mined in its hills. The town is in an isolated valley near Point Conception, on the coastal elbow of California and at the edge of the continent. It is a place of riptides, shipwrecks, fog, and wind.

The countryside seems different from the rest of America, different even from the rest of California. It is wilder, emptier, and in its way more beautiful. The coastal fogs of morning soon burn off to throw the chalky cliffs and hills above the town into the strong clear light that once must have shone upon all of California. There seems to be far less land than sky, with very few trees to soften their harsh conjunction. The hills which are not bare chalk and rock are briefly green in the spring and then lose their color to sun and drought. The wind blows constantly; it is playful in the hills but relentless in the city on the plain. The light, the scattered scrub oaks, the rocky hills, and the local mistral seem more typical of

Provence than of southern California. Provence, however, is sometimes warm. It is always chilly in Lompoc.

The town was founded as a temperance colony in the 1870s on the broad alluvial plain south of the Santa Ynez River, and at first the land was ranched and farmed. The winds and the soil made the cultivation of flowers profitable, and soon wide fields of rigidly furrowed acreage were planted for the commercial production of flower seed. The hills above the flower fields were mined for diatomite, the accrued remains of plankton. Several companies began to process the raw chalky material into diatomaceous earth, which was used for the filtration of industrial waste and, later, of swimming pools. The town grew slowly. People came and raised their families in white clapboard cottages with bay windows and front porches and in the neo-Spanish bungalows which were popular in the 1920s. Several miles from town, the army built a training site named Camp Cooke, and in 1940 W. C. Fields's *The Bank Dick* was filmed in Lompoc. These intrusions had little effect; in 1950 it was still a sleepy town of about 5,000.

Geography and technology created another Lompoc in the next two decades. The latitude was ideal for launching missiles into polar orbit, and the isolated stretch of Pacific coast, already held by the military, provided an excellent firing position for a western missile-test range. The army base at Camp Cooke and the naval station at Point Arguello, ten miles west of town, were consolidated into a major Air Force base which was to become both the site of the western test range and the western headquarters of the Strategic Air Command. A disciplinary barracks built at Camp Cooke in 1945 as a maximum-security military prison was transferred to the Federal Bureau of Prisons for medium-security civilian use. What enterprise and nature had started, government and geography continued.

The military, the contractors, and the civil service came to Lompoc. Thousands of military men and missile-makers, launchers, and trackers went to live there with their families. By 1970 the town had become a small city with a population over 25,000. The streets—letters of the alphabet running north, names of trees or flowers running west—were stenciled further into the surrounding plain and were pockmarked quickly with tract housing. Absentee land speculators ran up garish shopping centers along the main street. Not a curving road relieved the interlocking grids of streets and furrows until a new suburb was built near the air base. The names of these new streets expressed the changes which had brought them into being: between town and suburb, Tangerine Avenue and Walnut Street gave way to Constellation Boulevard and Milky Way. Upon the old town and its Provençal countryside there has been imposed another town, built, it seems, entirely of plastic. Like objects made of that excessively maligned material, the new Lompoc often appears synthetic, gaudy, ugly, cheap, and impermanent. The bright sun glares on the yellow, pink, or turquoise stucco of the raw new buildings, but there is little warmth. The builders didn't plant trees, so there is harsh light and deep shadow but no shade. Without roots to hold it, what little soil there is slides away with the winter rain. Even the dirt is temporary.

Most of the land along the twenty miles between Lompoc and the main highway has been owned and ranched by one family for a century, but in the town not many people own very much and few stay for very long. There is a constant, anxious turnover of residents. In tacky housing developments or in apartment houses with names like Kimi East and Tahitian Village, they live on month-to-month leases. New schools have been built, but the buildings look transitory. Teachers come, but many stay only until they find better jobs. A palatial library has been erected, but it is thinly stocked. The nearest bookstore is sixty miles away in Santa Barbara. Social life focuses on the many bars in town; on the officers' clubs at the air base and the prison; on the Moose, Elks, or Rotary; on the church auxiliaries; and for teen-agers, on the sidewalk in front of the Foster Freeze on Ocean Avenue.

Many people were ordered to Lompoc by the military, others were transferred there by their corporations, and still others were requested to go there by the civil service. All of them, however, were sent. Although many have been called to Lompoc, few have chosen to live there. Some quietly seek permanence and dignity in their home and work and family. Others boost the town's attractions and put on their cars a poison-green bumper sticker that proclaims, "I Like Lompoc." They are quick to point out that the Indian name of the town is not pronounced "Lompock," but "Lompoke," thus shifting the imagery evoked by the word from lumpish disfigurement to lumpish torpor.

Other citizens are less enthusiastic. They quietly put up with the place, wait for their next transfer, and dread that it might not come. Even less settled are those whose jobs depend solely on defense contracts, who have no seniority or skills, and for whom the next budget convulsion means quick unemployment. Still others merely wait for their retirement to take effect. The older, more permanent citizens have little to do with the new residents who have outnumbered them in the last decade. Small agricultural Lompoc and big technological Lompoc live side by side but they rarely touch. The gritty soil supports grain silos and covers missile silos, but the town is in the hands of absentee landlords and absentee voters. It is a town of reluctant transients, and many have stayed longer than they have liked.

I came to Lompoc just as reluctantly, to serve my military obligation as a psychiatrist with the Public Health Service hospital attached to the Federal prison just outside town. The two general doctors and I would have preferred other assignments, but in some ways we were glad that we had not been sent to even less desirable parts of the country. We learned to put up with the town and its tedium and to enjoy the sunsets when we could see them, the beautiful countryside, the air smarting with eucalyptus, and even the morning and evening fogs, pungent with kelp and ozone.

As reluctant as most of us new arrivals were to be there, some were more reluctant than others. For the military and its civilian employees, one base and its town is like another; for missile men, environment is not terribly important; for prison employees, most prison towns are similar. But there was a group in Lompoc which was there with more reluctance, less comfort, and not even the illusion of choice. This book is about the men who came to Lompoc in chains.

2

Going Inside

W<small>HATEVER</small> his offense, every prisoner is bound when brought to the Federal Correctional Institution at Lompoc. He is transferred from court huddled in the back of a U.S. marshal's car and shackled to one or two other equally frightened new convicts. They travel ignorant of what lies ahead and ignored by the usually silent marshals who drive them. Often traveling in strangely sleek cars, sometimes a Grand Prix or an AMX, they stop at roadside gas stations to shuffle into the men's room, clanking publicly. If they come from Los Angeles, 150 miles to the southeast, it is by Highway 101, turning from the sea through the lovely pass the Spanish named Gaviota for the gulls they found there. If prisoners come from the north it is down 101, staying overnight in county jails along the way. Whatever direction they come from, they quickly skirt the town and drive out through the flower fields to the prison.

Although it has been "in business," as the officials like to say, for years, the prison is not well known in the town. It is always referred to as the F.C.I. or the Institution; it is never called a prison or a jail. There is little official contact between the prison and the town except for a minor work-release program which constantly verges on cancellation by anxious prison officials, and an occasional talk by an official to an interested group. The prison and the town are separated by preference, policy, and the Santa Ynez River.

The prison road bisects the flat fields that stretch to a blank horizon under an empty sky. On both sides the flowers are planted in broad stripes of pink and white and blue and yellow. The only direct access to the prison is by a one-lane bridge over the Santa Ynez. The river is usually dry but it can be torrential after the winter rains. The flower fields press close to the prison grounds, which are screened by a thick stand of eucalyptus. Guarded by snapdragons and three gun towers, the prison sits on a bluff and is surrounded by a ten-foot double chain-link fence topped with barbed wire and a trip alarm.

It is strangely quiet on approach. The only sounds are the rasp of ravens and the squawk of the intercom in the gun tower. The din inside the prison is muffled by the heavy walls. The screech of jets and the roar of missiles from the air base are the occasional sounds of an outside world. The building, brutal and heavy, was built of concrete, and the impressions of the wood pouring forms were left on the dried cement. At first glance, it looks as if it could have been designed by Louis Kahn on a bad day. Fat fingers of concrete—the cell blocks—protrude at right angles from the central building.

The mass seems impermeable to the clear light and fresh air surrounding it. There is a strange contradiction between the massive bulk of the building and the bright skies, the stately eucalyptus trees, and the meticulous landscaping around the main entrance. This contradiction provokes disquiet, resentment at the intrusion of an ugly artificial gray mass into a place so bright with natural color, of such formidable enclosure into the generous breadth of open space. The building is doubly grim: in its own ugliness and in its obscene conflict with its surroundings. Its very appearance announces that this is a place for relentless custody, for unrelieved detention, for containment without restraint.

In the morning fog and in the midnight glare of arc lights, however, there is no contradiction between the appearance of the building and its environment, which becomes equally desolate. And the view from the prison is more oppressive than the view of it. To live or work inside is to have one's life drained of color, brightness, and air; to go inside is to pass through a kind of filter into a gray-brown existence without shades of meaning, into the suffocation of thought and feeling by monotony and despair.

Blinking in the bright light and stumbling in chains out of the marshal's car, new prisoners are prodded down a ramp into a crotch of the building. There they are stripped, sprayed, searched in every orifice, and are given a tan uniform, a long number, and a short haircut. They go to live in a dormitory called "Admission and Orientation" for the first thirty days, where they are told repeatedly by guards and officials that they are being rehabilitated and that the guards and officials are there to help them. They are exposed to a formal program of orientation to the institution, are tested psychologically, and are given routine inoculations. The unofficial orientation, however, goes on in the cell blocks and the mess hall, the unofficial psychological testing in the showers and on the exercise yard; but there is no inoculation against the psychological effects of imprisonment.

Whereas new convicts are hustled into custody, a visitor or an employee has a more difficult approach to the prison. It is even difficult to park. The lot is usually full and it is dominated by the employees' large camper vans. Bumper stickers are ubiquitous: "I Like Lompoc," "America, Love It or Leave It," and the ambiguous "When Guns Are Outlawed Only Outlaws Will Have Guns." If the tower guard does not recognize a visitor, he will order him to stop and will ask if he is carrying arms or drugs. Having figured out an answer and gained access, the visitor first goes into a small building set into the fence where he must wait until the inner steel door is opened by remote control after the outer steel door closes and locks. A concrete path across a narrow lawn leads to the administration building. Inside, another guard sits at a desk with a communications console, and behind him another even heavier steel door opens to a small courtyard. Beyond the courtyard is the prison itself. Another series of electrically locked doors, this time of bulletproof glass, leads to the main prison corridor. To get this far from the outside it is necessary to go through the following barriers: steel door, waiting room, steel door, lawn, steel door, lobby, steel door, courtyard, glass door, antechamber, glass door. Medium security.

This obstacle course does not prevent escape attempts, usually by work crews near the road or by prisoners who make frenzied dashes at the fence while in the exercise yard. The sequence of barriers indicates to inmate and visitor that a considerable boundary has been traversed and that a substantial air lock exists between inside and outside. It reassures the guards that they are secure by emphasizing that sections of the prison can be sealed off in the event of riot. It encourages the belief that the "badness" of the people in custody can be compartmentalized, but the overemphasis suggests a lingering doubt that that "badness" can be completely contained.

The last of the doors leads to the main corridor, which is about a quarter mile long and perhaps thirty feet wide. It stretches the length of the building. From it branch the cell blocks, the isolation block, the hospital, the dining room, the auditorium, the file room, and the case workers' offices. Each of these wings can be isolated quickly with double-locking doors. The hallway is painted a drab Institutional Cream and is clangorous with banging doors and the shouts of inmates. Near the dining room the corridor always seems to smell of coleslaw; along the rest of its length, of sweat and disinfectant.

Like any boulevard, the corridor is used for transport, commerce, and social life. Now that marching in single file is not considered rehabilitating, inmates go to meals in *lateral* phalanxes. Near the center of the hallway is the commissary, where prisoners line up to buy cigarettes, toothpaste, potato chips, and ice cream. ("Buy" is probably the wrong word, since no transaction takes place. Prisoners are not permitted to have cash lest they use it during an escape; all expenses are deducted from their monthly earnings, which are kept on account until their release.) Not far from the commissary is the pill window, where outpatient medication is dispensed and where every prisoner taking a pill is thought by the staff to be malingering or tonguing the pill to trade to another inmate for illicit drugs. Everyone in the corridor is under the supervision of guards walking its length as well as others stationed at the midpoint in a three-sided glass booth which protrudes several feet into the traffic.

Every one of the twelve hundred inmates of the prison goes up and down this hallway several times a day: to and from meals, to and from work, to and from the exercise yard. To reproduce the timetable of an ordinary prison day would probably induce in the reader a stupefaction approaching that which is imposed on the prisoner; to avoid such an event so early in this book, this summary will have to do. Prisoners are awakened by a buzzer at 6:30; they go to breakfast and then to work; they return to the cell blocks to be counted and then go to lunch. Work resumes after lunch and continues until 4 P.M., when everyone is locked in and counted before the day and evening guards change shifts. After dinner there is a "free" period until lock-in and count at 9:30 and lights-out at 10:30. What is more important than the specifics of how the day is spent is that the entire day (and night) is structured, regulated, and supervised by the prison staff.

Rather than attempt to describe every physical aspect of the prison in this brief commentary, I have chosen to confine my observations to those areas with which most prisoners came into contact and about which they spoke most often with me. They are also those areas with which I came to be most familiar in my daily work, and they include the cell blocks, the honor unit, the isolation unit, the hospital, and the dining room. I seldom visited the prison farm and walnut grove or rode around the prison cattle ranch. I spent little time in the exercise yard, but it was enough for me to observe that "hippies" gathered on the volleyball court, that "body freaks" stayed in the weight-lifting area, and that black and white prisoners played basketball at opposite ends of the same court but on mutually exclusive teams in separate games aiming at different goals. I visited the shops where prisoners passed the time braiding cables, finishing garments, or repairing furniture, and it was obvious that they were not the studios of vocational training they were announced to be but were menial make-work areas whose major effect was to bind the worker to the special, narrow realities of prison rather than to prepare him for the larger community outside or to teach him a useful future occupation.

The cell blocks branch off the main corridor, are named alphabetically, and are referred to as "units." One cell block, an honor unit, has inmate-operated cell doors and no guards; the rest have at least one guard who controls the movements of both inmates and cell doors. The doors are opened and closed electrically at the officers' whim and at the numerous counting times during the day. At night, men are counted at ten, twelve, two, and four. "Admission and Orientation" and one or two other areas are laid out like barracks. Although this arrangement appears more benign than the usual cell block, is cheaper to build and maintain, and is easier to supervise, the absence of cells ensures that there is no privacy for the inmate and guarantees that there is no protection against assault, theft, rape, or riot.

Men are assigned to the other cell blocks in rotation as they come into the prison; there is no distinction in housing according to offense, background, or personality. First offenders are housed with accomplished psychopaths, conscientious objectors with bank robbers, drug addicts with drug dealers. Each inmate has his own cell, however. The average cubicle is about five by seven by nine feet; it is built of cinder block and has a concrete floor; it is furnished with a cot, a washstand, and a toilet in full view of any passerby. Each cell has a set of earphones tuned to two frequencies of Muzak. In each cell block about a hundred men share one television set tuned to the programs chosen and enforced by the dominant group.

The cells rise in three-story tiers, with the upper levels reached by a starkly beautiful system of exposed stairways and catwalks. The three-dimensional pattern of cells is repeated in a two-dimensional pattern of cellules of bars on glass in the large windows across from the catwalks. Some of the cell blocks are painted the same dun color as the inmate uniforms; others are done up in electric blue and pink, in a gruesome collision of Disney and Piranesi. As a result, an inmate must either merge anonymously into a background as nondescript as his uniform or he must make a constant effort to ignore surroundings as visually intrusive and as noisy in color as they are raucous with shouts and clanging doors.

Prisoners are officially encouraged to work up from the general cell blocks to the guardless honor unit by their good behavior. Though this policy had the cooperation of some inmates, it was hampered at Lompoc by two facts of life that particularly affected honor prisoners: the excessive, literal use of the rule book by guards outside the honor unit and the prevalence of forced homosexuality within it. Despite his general good behavior, an honor prisoner could be demoted to the ordinary cell blocks for the most trivial offense, such as having his hair uncombed or his shirttail hanging out. This kind of harassment happened so often to the honor prisoners and so rarely to others that it seemed as if some guards could not tolerate their own resentment of the honor prisoners' relative freedom, privacy, and distinctiveness and therefore did all they could to return them to the uniform mass of prisoners.

If harassment by guards outside the honor unit was burdensome, the absence of guards in that cell block imposed its own difficulty: forced homosexuality. To some prisoners, homosexuality was voluntary and congenial, to others even the suggestion of the practice was abhorrent, and for still others it was compelled by pressure and their inability to resist it. Although the rules against inmates visiting each other's cells were not always enforced in the ordinary cell blocks, and though the presence of guards there did not protect the unwilling or impede voluntary homosexuality, its practice did require some circumspection. But neither protection nor precaution was evident in the honor unit: the absence of guards—a condition otherwise pleasing to most prisoners—permitted homosexuality to flourish there as nowhere else, to be both rampant and, as it were, couchant.

The isolation unit, reserved for "behavior problems," is at the opposite end of the main corridor from the honor unit. Known officially as I Block, it is more commonly and accurately referred to by both staff and inmates as The Hole. It is difficult for me to describe The Hole, not only because it is painful to recall it, but also because I found it as physically disorienting to go there as it was emotionally upsetting. The second and third floors are known as Administrative Restriction, or more familiarly as A-Rest. The cells there are a little smaller than those in other cell blocks, but the physical environment, at least, is essentially the same. These two upper ranges are reserved for men who the staff think are in need of light restriction and for those prisoners who seek protective custody.

The downstairs area is known as Segregation; it is reserved for more severely disciplined prisoners and is set off from the rest of I Block by a separate door as well as a difference in floor level. It was hard to tell, when I went there, whether the cells in Segregation were at or below ground level, but in any case the small, windowless cubicles were dark, clammy, cold, and poorly ventilated. There were no beds in them, but rather a concrete ledge on which was sometimes placed a mattress or a black rubber pallet. There was an inner barred door to each cell and an outer solid steel door with a peephole, but the outer door was usually left open.

The cells were only occasionally illuminated by a single light when the guards remembered to turn on the electricity or to replace a burned-out bulb. There always seemed to be water or some other liquid on the cement floor: the daily swabbing was careless, the toilets overflowed, and prisoners sometimes stopped up the toilets or urinated on the floor in protest or frustration. Floating in the liquid there was sometimes food—lettuce and tomato usually—which had fallen off the serving cart at mealtime or had been angrily dumped there by guards or inmates. Prisoners often stood about naked or in their underwear: sometimes the laundry was late or the guards were slow in distributing it; other times inmates refused to wear the uniforms or ripped them up.

Prisoners in Segregation were allowed one or two books, but they had to ask for a pencil and they couldn't keep it. The odor of sweat, urine, garbage, and disinfectant was sometimes overwhelming, but nothing expressed the utter emptiness of this dungeon so well as its silence. Every other cell block, even A-Rest upstairs, was noisy, and the noise was not so loud as it was unremitting. Segregation was quiet.

If the honor unit was less attractive than might be supposed, The Hole was more popular than might be anticipated. The presence of these ultimate cells, the prison within the prison, was valuable to both staff and prisoners. The Hole figured prominently, as threat or refuge, in the lives of everyone at Lompoc. A tour in Isolation was often recommended by the staff as protective custody. To inmates who complained about any aspect of prison life, from the food to homosexual threat, a standard staff response was, "If you don't like it, go to The Hole." This variation on the love-it-or-leave-it theme was only the most extreme physical expression of the general psychological tendency of the staff to wall off rather than to face and resolve problems (as the prison itself was walled off from the outside) and thus to avoid further contact with the problems and the men presenting them. There were indeed a few repetitively violent prisoners who had to be restrained, but most people in The Hole were there through staff encouragement, as the consequence of an impulsive act, or voluntarily.

Although sending prisoners to The Hole saved the staff the bother of making substantial improvements in the institution, for the inmates it was an event which always showed up on their disciplinary reports when the parole judge came around. This double bind (you can always go to The Hole, but you'll stay in prison longer if you do) intimidated some prisoners, but others went there often and a few stayed. Indeed, it was difficult to ignore the paradox that going to the honor unit meant for some prisoners an increase in staff harassment and homosexual pressure, but that by accepting the "dishonor" of going to The Hole, they could actually achieve some peace and quiet. Although The Hole was feared for its isolation, degradation, and monotony, some prisoners felt that there at least, at rock bottom, they were free at last, that nothing more could be done to them. Many men went to The Hole in desperation, on advice, or on impulse, but others went in search of safety, privacy, and what remained of their self-respect.

Whatever advantages The Hole afforded staff and prisoners,

the sensory and social isolation presented an extreme psychological threat. Transfers there were often sudden and not always listed on the daily announcement of housing changes. The grapevine was usually a good source as to who was there, but it was not reliable as to their mental state. If only to keep track of the patients I was already seeing, not to mention the new ones The Hole would provide, I tried to go there every day. But I too was intimidated by the silence, the smell, the cold, and the wet, and not least by the dread of the living wreckage I might find there.

I didn't go to The Hole every day. Indeed, it was as easy to ignore The Hole as it is, on the outside, to ignore prisons. I was grateful for those many busy days when I was too caught up in immediate problems to go. When I was less busy, I sometimes had to force myself to make the trip. Going to The Hole was on some days an act of commitment, but on others it became an act of responsibility, or an act of duty, or an act of will. And on more days than I like to admit, it was avoided by an act of omission.

The hospital, across the corridor from The Hole, did not seem to be a great deal better. It was difficult to tell if it had been converted from a cell block or only modeled after one, but it was clear that it was, first, a wing of a prison and only secondarily a hospital. There was a guard at the door from the main corridor and admission was by written pass only. The guard made regular hospital rounds at counting times, day and night, and every patient —even if he was bedridden or unconscious—was resolutely locked into his room. No registered nurse would work in the prison and few inmates wanted to work in the hospital once they found out that it was difficult to steal drugs. Retired military medical corpsmen who worked there as medical technical assistants selected the inmate staff and forced out those they didn't like. Conscientious objectors asking for hospital assignment were refused because the prison executives wanted them to work on the farm or in the factory, where they could be relied upon not to escape and to keep up productivity (and, presumably, the officials' own productivity ratings). As a result, some very unreliable people worked in the hospital; simple but vital duties such as pulse-taking after surgery and rudimentary cleanliness were ignored. For psychiatric patients, there was no such thing as occupational therapy or even diversion; except for television and limited time with the psychiatrist, there was nothing to occupy them but their difficulties.

Those men who are not in The Hole or in the hospital take their meals in the dining room. It is a large room off the main corridor and the food is served cafeteria style. The cosmetics of rehabilitation have done away with long wooden tables and tin cups, and now the men eat in "conversational groupings" at little white plastic tables, but they are still under the direct gaze of guards ranged about the room. The intermittent-meat-and-high-carbohydrate diet was at the minimum level for institutional food and not very carefully prepared. Most new prisoners were assigned to the kitchen until they were given permanent jobs, and as a result of their indifference or frank hostility, the kitchen was an unhealthy place. When evidence of infection among the inmates required bacteriological testing, the pathological organisms E. coli and Proteus were regularly cultured from the kitchen utensils.

After having worked in the kitchen and become aware of the hazards of eating the food, many inmates went to the dining room only for the change of scene and the company of men they might not see elsewhere. It was not unusual for many to eat as little as possible of the prison food and to fill up instead on ice cream, candy, and potato chips at the commissary in the hallway. This practice was based on the objective evidence of displeasing and possibly infected food as well as on the fact that to some prisoners the food symbolized, however unconsciously, the bad aspects of the prison, particularly the poor nurture it provided. The officials were understandably apprehensive about the heightened possibility of riot in the mess hall, and it seems likely that the frequency of dining-room demonstrations in many prisons has as much to do with the hateful dependency symbolized in the food as with the fact that the food itself is bad or insufficient or that there are many tense men concentrated in a closed space.

It was true that there was bad nurture and bad food, but it

was also true that some prisoners unwittingly endowed many aspects of the prison—of which the food was only one—with their own repudiated attributes. But what was symbolic and unconscious to most prisoners and staff was very concrete and all too painfully conscious to men who became psychotic in prison. In such circumstances repudiated parts of the self could often be felt to be coming back with every swallow, and with murderous intent. Nearly every psychosis I was called to treat was predominantly paranoid, and most of these men were afraid that their food was poisoned or drugged.

Although some prisoners thought that living on commissary food was childish and self-indulgent, there were often important psychological gains to balance the nutritional losses. Many prisoners sought the relative freedom of choosing and buying their own food, even though the cost was deducted from their prison earnings. To some, it also represented symbolic contact—communion, really—with the outside world as well as a chance to balance the bad prison diet with good food which had come in already wrapped and was not contaminated by bacteria or by the "bad vibrations" of prison life. Though eating the ice cream or candy was pleasurable in itself, it also stood for the memory and the hope of a better life than that being lived in prison. "Little packets of home" was the way one man, by no means disturbed, described his daily potato chips. When eating them he was momentarily *at* home and, above all, tasting freedom.

3

The Prison Staff

ALTHOUGH it was built by the military as a maximum-security institution, Lompoc is operated by the Bureau of Prisons as a medium-security prison for men under twenty-five, the only such "youth institution" west of the Rockies. It draws its population from men convicted in the Federal courts of California, Oregon, Washington, Idaho, Montana, Nevada, and Arizona. I was told by the officials that there was no census of prisoners according to offense, but by following the "rap sheet" (the daily announcement of new arrivals and their offenses) over a period of months, I was able to learn what acts had brought what men to Lompoc. Approximately a third of the twelve hundred prisoners were there for interstate car theft; another third were imprisoned for marijuana smuggling or other drug offenses; the remaining third were made up largely of men convicted of bank robbery, frequently related to drug use; interstate fraud; offenses committed on Federal property, such as Indian reservations and post offices; and Selective Service violation. Neither was there a census according to race, but perhaps 40 per cent of the prisoners were black, Indian, or Chicano. The average time served by most men was two years.

All twelve hundred prisoners were under the control of about two hundred prison employees talking rehabilitation and practicing custody. Managing the day-to-day existence of prisoners were about 150 guards, six case workers, several work supervisors, and several senior officials. Trying to be more directly therapeutic were five medical technical assistants, two general doctors, two dentists, one psychologist, and one psychiatrist.

The guards tended to appear middle-aged. It was difficult to tell if many were a young fifty-five or an old thirty-seven. They wore gray uniforms with gray caps and gray shirts set off by a maroon tie with their choice of stickpin. The most popular stickpin comprised two little silver handcuffs. Close behind in popularity were pins of little silver guns or little silver keys. There were no little silver scales of justice.

In my daily rounds about the prison, or when talking over the problems of an inmate I was trying to treat, or while standing in line waiting to check in or out the massive ring of keys we all carried, I was able to strike up (and to continue over two years) some conversations with a few guards, despite the unwillingness of many others to have even the most superficial contact with a psychiatrist. I never formally interviewed any guards, and still less did I "analyze" them as we talked casually. Nor, of course, did I treat them. (A few guards sought my professional help for themselves or for members of their families and I was willing to provide it if I was able, but I was advised by Washington that my "constituency" was the inmate population and that my "mission" was their rehabilitation only.) Nonetheless, I was able to begin to get some idea of how a few guards thought and felt about themselves and their work.

One guard I got to know was middle-aged both in years and appearance. Like many others he was rather pale, somewhat overweight, slightly bald, and more than a little resigned. He had grown up on a tenant farm in the South and had left it eagerly to join the military. He had gotten his high-school diploma while in uniform and had stayed in the service for twenty years. At retirement, he had taken his first prison job because there was a prison near his last duty station and he and his wife had not wanted to move right away. He had had no interest in prison work before, but some of his military friends had transftrred to prison jobs and it had seemed to him to be the easiest thing to do. Besides, he pointed out, there were no other jobs available at the time. He was also attracted by the regular hours, the retirement benefits, the job security, and the relative ease of the work. Having been with the prisons for several years when we talked, he had gotten the routine down and was now putting in his time toward his second retirement.

There are probably any number of reasons why so many prison employees are former military men (that is, former noncommissioned officers), but at least one is the ease with which the transition can be made, both physically and psychologically. About half the Federal prisons are close to military installations. There are several bases within sight of Alcatraz (now abandoned), and there are bases within easy reach of Federal institutions at El Paso, Texas; El Reno, Oklahoma; Englewood, Colorado; Leavenworth, Kansas; Petersburg, Virginia; Tallahassee, Florida; and Terminal Island, California. And like the prison at Lompoc, there is a "correctional facility" in Florida that is completely surrounded by a military base. This propinquity provides a steady flow of retirees to the prisons, and it attracts men who can continue to stretch their incomes by shopping at a saving at military commissaries and by having their families cared for at no cost in military clinics.

But if the physical transfer from military khaki to prison gray is easy, the psychological transition is easier. Many guards spoke of the similarities between their prison work and their former military duties. It often seemed, in listening to them talk about their work, that they had changed jobs but not careers, that to change from noncommissioned officer to correctional officer required only minor alterations in attitude toward two systems of wearing uniforms and accepting and imposing uniformity, of giving orders and taking them, of accepting a place in a clearly defined hierarchy where there was always someone above and always someone below, of being licensed to use weapons against an enemy in time of crisis, and of processing papers, equipment, and men. Many guards no more thought of themselves as practicing rehabilitation or contributing to the "war on crime" than they had, in the military, seen themselves as vitally necessary for the defense of the nation or as personally making the world safe for democracy. Nor did they think of themselves, in prison, as brutal sadists or exploiters of inmates any more than they had felt they were, in wartime, killers. Rather, they were doing in both situations the day-to-day thoughtless processing, the moving of men and things from place to place and then moving them back, which seems to characterize a kind of life in both organizations. In considering the connections and attractions between the military life and the prison life, it would be an error to overlook the appeal of the opportunities for sanctioned violence, but it seems that even more important are the weight of inertia and the need for continuity.

But at least until recently a military career brought with it a certain pride, something which is not so common in prison work, particularly at the guard level. The guard I have spoken of had few illusions about his choice of work, and he clearly acknowledged that it had been, as far as he was concerned, the best he could do. If he was not exactly ashamed of what he was doing, he was not terribly proud of it, either. When his son had asked about taking a summer job in the prison, he had discouraged him from applying. When I asked him why, he answered: "I want him to do better than me, not just take what's available. I did what I could, but I want him to do better. Let's face it, Doc, would you want *your* son to be a prison guard?"

I have no idea how typical or representative this guard was, but he was different from others I knew at Lompoc in at least two respects: he felt no need to conceal from himself or from anyone else that his work was mainly custodial, and he had no need to decorate what he was doing with claims of rehabilitation. He had no pretensions about "liking to work with people"; he had not expected to be more than a watchman when he signed on, and that was what he felt he was. Indeed, he guessed that those who insisted the loudest that they were practicing rehabilitation might be those who were actually doing the most harm; and it was he who first pointed out to me that to the extent that the prison staff (at all levels) believed they were being therapeutic, they were protected against the full realization of the effects of incarceration —upon the prisoners and upon themselves.

Some guards saw inmates as children, others saw them as animals, but they most commonly treated them as inanimate objects. Although many guards were capable of compassion, many more had little idea of treating inmates as anything but property to be watched. It was routine for guards to refer to prisoners by their numbers, and I never was able to get used to the kind of calls I got: "I have number 1234 here, Doc; when can he see you?" The attitude of some of the guards seemed to resemble that of a butcher toward carcasses in his freezer: they merely pass through his storage vault, they are to be handled fairly roughly but not publicly bruised, they have no life of their own, they are indistinguishable from each other, they are destined to be butchered or ground up sooner or later.

This indifference was best expressed in the common attitude toward a prisoner who made a gesture of distinctiveness, any personal statement of complaint, sadness, or—rarely—exuberance. The usual guard response was, "He's just asking for attention." Although it was tossed off as a quick dismissal, the phrase comes close to epitomizing the guards' view of rehabilitation. Prisoners are to have no attention, are not to be recognized as having needs or abilities, are not to be thought of as having an inner life of desires, feelings, thoughts, or aspirations. Rather, they are to be processed through the institution with as little attention, particularly from the guards, as possible.

Although the guards' predominant manifest attitude toward prisoners was that they were nonhuman, many also felt, and not always unconsciously, that prisoners were both subhuman and superhuman. That is, they were seen as bestial, as uncontrollably aggressive and in need of constant external restraint; at the same time they were thought to possess extraordinary strength or cunning which must not be confronted. There were indeed many prisoners who were notably aggressive or clever, but the attribution of base and aggrandizing qualities to all prisoners as a group and without distinction among them expressed the unconscious displacement onto the prisoners of repudiated ideas and feelings of the guards themselves rather than their accurate assessment of specific qualities of individual inmates. But the anxiety aroused by such ideas and feelings could not be tolerated for very long, and they were inevitably neutralized by the psychological defense of thinking of prisoners as neither subhuman nor superhuman but as nonhuman. It was as if the dominant philosophy were: "If we're running a warehouse, it is best that the materials in storage be inert rather than combustible."

Some of the more usual comments about inmates (from all members of the prison staff) were "no damn good," "never amount to anything" and "all alike." The frequency and fervor of these observations, and the treatment of prisoners which accompanied them, suggested that they expressed the idea that prisoners were not only inanimate, but also immutable and without individuality. Far from being mere observations or passing ideas, this triad of perceptions formed the basis of the staff's pattern of dealing with their own anxieties. To the extent that prisoners embodied—in addition to their own qualities—repudiated and projected aspects of staff members, it appeared that the staff had a psychological need to perceive prisoners as unchanging, lest the evil attributes they were felt to contain be released. And to the extent that the staff could not tolerate ambiguity, uncertainty, and diversity, it was similarly necessary for them to distribute their anxieties equally and totally throughout the entire prison population, thereby perceiving prisoners as without individual distinctiveness in a way far more pervasive than the superficial loss of individuality achieved by the imposition of prison numbers, uniforms, and haircuts. In these ways—unconscious for the most part—the anxieties of the staff were neutralized, stabilized, and equalized; and as a result prisoners were thought of—and treated—as inanimate, unchanging, and interchangeable.

By evolving this dehumanizing attitude, the staff was simultaneously using it inwardly as a psychological defense against anxiety and translating it outwardly into action, not only as the basis of a system for social control and the management of the prison but also as the nucleus of an institutionalized social system as a defense against anxiety. Some prison employees were indeed remarkable—whether for their genuine interest in prisoners or for their blatant paranoia, moralizing self-righteousness, or jovial sadism—but the predominant emotional tone among them was that of numbed, plodding dullness. They often appeared, and indeed some felt, to be as lacking in individuality as the prisoners they oversaw. In uniform clothing and jobs, they were often treated by high officials in the Bureau of Prisons without regard for their particular skills or needs, as interchangeable parts within the same job assignment.

Most of the guards at Lompoc were concentrated on the daytime shift, but they rotated shifts and job locations every three months. These frequent moves were usually a welcome change to most prisoners and guards alike, but they undermined the announced rehabilitative interests of the prison by preventing any meaningful contact between individual guards and inmates. For the occasional guard with the concern and the intelligence to become interested in an inmate, the pressures of time, policy, and numbers were against the beginning, let alone the growth, of a fruitful relationship.

Indeed, a fruitful relationship was about the last thing desired between guard and inmate. There is a long prison tradition of absolute detachment between guards and prisoners based on the fear that any "fraternization" could only result in corruption. There are, to be sure, some guards who are corrupt and some prisoners who are eager to exploit that potential. But the tradition of absolute detachment seems to derive from the assumption that not just some but all guards are gullible or corrupt and that all prisoners are wily and clever. This tradition (at least in its aims) substitutes absolute detachment for judicious contact and, like many prison traditions and the policies derived from them, is based upon *a partial truth made universal.*

Prison officials often said that the guards represented the prison's greatest resource for the practice of rehabilitation, and in a very few instances that was at least potentially true. But the practice of containment at the expense of contact prevents the development of the mutual relationship (and it need not always be a positive one) upon which any system of rehabilitation, whatever its theory, depends. Of course, anyone entering a rehabilitative relationship with another person must learn to exercise reasonable detachment, to avoid untoward involvement, to resist manipulation and unprofessional conduct, and to respect the person he is trying to help. But it was exactly this kind of discretionary relationship that guards were neither expected, trained, nor trusted to develop.

Some guards have become work supervisors who are responsible for the operation of the prison farm, the ranch, landscaping, and the prison industries, which use men for printing, welding, furniture repair, garment making, and cable twisting. Though some of the work supervisors have been guards, a worthwhile relationship may occasionally develop between them and prisoners, particularly if the job is one which the inmate enjoys or at least does not hate, and if the supervisor is a reasonably open man and does not insist on a master-slave relationship. If prisoner and supervisor feel united in a common task, even if it is only doing time, they may meet on other grounds as well. A supervisor may occasionally (certainly more often than does a guard) address a prisoner by his last name and, in private, even by his first name. This intimacy does not work both ways. Work supervisors prefer to be addressed as "Boss."

Case workers are usually addressed by their own names. They have sometimes been to college, though they often have no particular social-science or psychological training. They process the files of inmates, each case worker carrying a load of about two hundred dossiers. With such a case load, any kind of personal contact is impossible; merely to keep up with the paperwork is a full-time job. In addition, the case worker controls the prisoners' visits and correspondence; both visits and letters are officially limited to family members and to one friend of each sex. All other visits and correspondence are by dispensation only. The case worker also corresponds with the Board of Parole about the inmate and places parole applications before the parole judge, who visits the prison every two months. Since getting out is uppermost in the mind of most inmates, the case worker is commonly known as the "parole officer," even though he does not supervise parole and has only a limited, advisory influence upon its determination.

Some of the case workers at Lompoc were marginally less insensitive than most guards, but usually they had been with the prison system for a shorter time. They viewed most inmates as bodies but at least saw them as having flesh and blood. Some case workers even referred to prisoners without mentioning their numbers. But the use of names did not imply psychological sensitivity.

Case workers' evaluation of prisoners' "progress" in the institution is mainly secondhand. It is based on behavior reports written by guards, and little thought is given to individual character structure or particular psychological or social needs. Although there is intensive formal and informal orientation to the prison for arriving prisoners, there is none at all for those departing. Every inmate must work out his own parole plan from inside the prison, and there is no referral to specific helping agencies on the outside. The "individualized treatment" and "case work" are based on guards' disciplinary reports and the case workers' minimal involvement. Despite their professed concern for "the whole person," the interests of most case workers were limited to two kinds of inmate behavior: sufficient misconduct to justify a recommendation against parole, or the appearance of the narrowest kind of conformity—the only kind convincing enough to recommend release.

It would have been reassuring, somehow, if the case workers felt that since they could not make meaningful contact with prisoners and thereby try to rehabilitate them, they could at least put together a good file. But that was not the case. Prisoners were tabulated, classified, and stored away as though they themselves were the files, and their dossiers were tenderly assembled, anxiously checked for completeness (but not for accuracy), and dutifully nurtured with memoranda with all the watchful care of a nervous mother for her problem child. It was difficult to escape the impression that far more energy and interest were lavished on the records than on the men. Because of this grisly confusion of the human and the inanimate, the file keeping was not conducted as an alternative to rehabilitation; it *was* the rehabilitation.

Like other prison employees, the retired military medical corpsmen who worked in the hospital as medical assistants ranged from decent to bumbling to paranoid. One medic was incapable of executing simple written orders. Another reported the contents of every confidential medical staff meeting to the prison officials, along with his editorial comments. One man spent much of his time decrying the soft regime running the Bureau of Prisons and yearning for the good old days back at Alcatraz. Whatever their individual qualities, the medics were united in their intense fear of being outwitted by the prisoners whom they screened in the outpatient clinic. There was a fair amount of malingering and duplicity among the prisoners, and a prudent concern for such activity was indeed necessary. But the medics' fears of inmates' deviousness went so far beyond the exercise of reasonable doubt that genuinely, if mildly, ill prisoners were often assumed to be faking and were sometimes refused access to the clinic until they returned in sufficiently convincing distress.

It was not so much compassion as it was the eventual realization that sicker patients meant more work for themselves that led some medics to moderate their suspicions, but when we discussed the "real" malingerers, few medics could believe that malingering might have psychological dimensions other than the obvious pleasure of putting something over on them. We on the medical staff repeatedly stressed that we preferred to assume the occasional risk of being fooled to the greater one of endangering prisoners' health. Our willingness to assume the risk relieved the medics' anxious watchfulness, but hardly enough to influence their inner identification with the policing aspects of the prison rather than with the therapeutic aims of the hospital.

There was one medic, however, who worked reliably, didn't deny mistakes or blame them on someone else, or hate all prisoners as a group. He was consistently refused promotion. He not only trusted some prisoners; he knew how to talk with them and how to help them. He combined psychological sensitivity and a bluff manner of scatological banter to promote open communication, brief psychotherapy, and decent treatment for the many men with whom he worked and to whom he dispensed medication. One official, who could not tell the difference between decency and "fraternization" or between shrewd badinage and angry insult, repeatedly denied him promotion or even transfer with the assertion that he lacked the milk of human kindness.

The prison executives have less contact with inmates. They often bear the pallor of flesh and mind which is the mark of a career with the Bureau of Prisons. They usually come up through the ranks, starting as guard or perhaps case worker, and following the same route of transfer from prison town to prison town. Perhaps a tour in a junior post at headquarters in Washington has relieved the tedium of long stretches in the provinces. Most of the senior officials began work in what was called, by a high official in the Bureau during a talk at Lompoc, "the Rock 'em and Sock 'em Period." This same official went on to describe, chuckling, the new emphasis on rehabilitation: "When you guys are draggin' someone down to The Hole, I want you to lean over and ask how he's doin' on his problem with his father—if he knows who he is." Although these men owe their careers to the proper articulation of the managerial line at the proper time, their advocacy of the current mode of rehabilitation is not particularly convincing.

Whereas the guards referred to prisoners as numbers and the case workers saw them as bodies, the higher officials called them "cases." This connoted a nonhuman status as well as a detached and scientific "professional" attitude. The chief concern of the higher officials seemed to be the unimpeded processing of every "case" through the institution, its file in order, its time accurately computed, its commissary allowance duly paid, and its civilian clothing and bus ticket ready on the day of its release. This careful attention to "flow-through" seemed to assure them that their system was in order if their charges were not.

Indeed, the regular operation of the system of admitting, numbering, classifying, counting, housing, feeding, and discharging prisoners seemed to be the *sole* concern of the officials. Because of their preoccupation with the procedures of this system and with the details of their application, they were virtually unaware of its human costs. Because of their inner insensitivity and their emotional detachment from others, they were protected from the censure of their own consciences and freed as well from conscientious restraints upon their treatment of other men. Of course inmates did not exist as other men; they existed primarily as integers on case reports, as units to be counted, as items to be processed, as elements in an aggregate called "the population"; as the means of the system, not its end.

Thus it seemed that at every level of the prison staff, from guard to executive, inmates were seen—and treated—as nonhuman, as incapable of change, and as indistinguishable one from the other. And at every level, the prison was administered to reflect and reinforce those shared perceptions. Although the announced goal was rehabilitation, the actual practice was containment. The stated aim was individualized treatment, but the dominant attitudes were that the prisoner was not human and not individual, that he was devoid of an inner life, that he was defined only by his behavior—and solely by his criminal behavior at that. It is perhaps unnecessary to point out that these attitudes are the very reverse of rehabilitative.

By calling their program rehabilitation, prison executives have mollified reformers ready to believe that the official prohibition of physical punishment and a veneer of professionalism are automatically therapeutic; they have satisfied the general public, which is interested in prisons only when they intrude themselves into the public consciousness through escape, scandal, or riot. But even more important, by perceiving prisoners as inanimate, unchanging, and interchangeable, by becoming emotionally detached, by immersing themselves in the procedural aspects of their daily work, and by genuinely believing that their program of social control without meaningful contact is therapeutic (many employees truly believe this, while for others it is a cynical pretense), prison employees at every level have been protected from the full realization of the impact of this program on prisoners and themselves.

This dehumanization of the staff is reinforced by the fact that as a result of institutional policy, social pressure, and individual preference, many employees find their personal lives restricted to the prison community almost as completely as if they were on the job twenty-four hours a day. And as the contiguity of personal and occupational lives reinforces this adaptation, it also isolates many employees from the outside world, leaving them insensitive—indeed hostile—to innovation.

Many of the guards, case workers, and officials live on a government reservation a few hundred yards from the prison gate. It is an enclave of semidetached and prefabricated bungalows winding uphill to a summit of single homes in lock step with the organizational hierarchy. The commuting is quick, the rents are low, and the housing is as good as that in town, but those are not the only reasons employees want to live in the compound. They know that at least there they will be socially acceptable. Employees often encounter local distaste for a prison and its staff even in areas where the institution has been established for years; and the stigma attached to prisoners by the public affects, to a lesser degree, those who are in close contact with them. What is more, the policy of frequent transfers within the prison system discourages the growth of local ties. The loyalties of many employees are far more intense to the Bureau of Prisons, with which they must live all their working lives, than they are to the town in which they temporarily reside.

As a result, contact between the prison and the town of Lompoc was minimal and was characterized by a mutual distrust reminiscent of the worst kinds of town-gown conflicts in academic communities. This tension would have been no more than a minor cause for regret if it had not also seriously undermined an innovative experiment in rehabilitation—the work-release program. The idea of preparing inmates for release by allowing them to work in town and sleep in the prison had been suggested for years, and it was finally implemented by officials of the Bureau of Prisons with at least as much genuine interest in rehabilitation as in their public image. Under the best of circumstances such a program requires the support of prison staff, intelligent evaluation of candidates, careful job placement, good relations with the community, public education, and the expectation that there will be some failures. None of those factors seemed to be operating at Lompoc.

Though at least one official was wholeheartedly in favor of work release, it was evident that several others would have preferred to forget the whole thing. But since the program was initiated over their heads, they were torn between their need to follow orders and their distrust of all inmates with its concomitant wish for the illusion of absolute security. Consequently, the program was conducted in a manner that guaranteed its failure. In the absence of any systematic approach, candidates for work release were selected by the case workers' intuition and were then subjected to a final decision according to the officials' prejudices. There was no black prisoner on work release while I was at Lompoc, and when an Indian was proposed, one official vetoed him with the remark that he "didn't want any drunken Navahos running around downtown." Though the prison psychologist and I offered to help evaluate work-release candidates, our offers were never taken up. The decision on those few who were considered eligible depended on the case worker's ability to wheedle, flatter, or cajole the officials into agreement. The inevitable embarrassments that followed the slipshod selection thus confirmed the officials' assumptions, fulfilled their negative prophecies, and increased the tension between town and prison. It was not long before a mayoralty candidate campaigned to abolish the work-release program.

Encapsulated at work and at home, the prison community is cut off even from the limited stimulus of a town such as Lompoc. It is possible, even likely, for employees to spend their lives in the shadow of the walls. They blandly accept the personnel directives, the reorganizations, the transfers, the boredom, and the status quo. Expediency seems to be their only value, efficiency their only virtue. This life may meet deep psychological needs, and some employees may find it satisfying. But in their inner identification with the operations of processing and custody demanded by their jobs, in their acceptance of dehumanization as both a practice and a fate, they have become themselves as gray and cold as the coastal fog, as rigid as the concrete that forms their prison.

4

Getting with the Program

THE most common advice by officials to people at every level was "get with the program." To prisoners, that meant "stay in line or you won't be paroled"; to guards, "no direct physical violence"; to case workers, "keep your files in order"; to doctors, "stick to the hospital and don't ask too many questions"; and to the officials themselves, "keep the pipeline open." It also meant that every inmate and employee was required to accept the implicit assumptions and explicit policies by which the prison was governed. Though many policies were determined in Washington and were related to the prison's primary task of containment, wide discretion was granted to the executives of each prison. In the course of my work, while talking with guards, conferring with case workers, and attending meetings with executives, it appeared to me that within the limits required for the performance of the primary task, the manner of operation of the prison seemed to be closely related to the psychological needs of the employees.

Those psychological needs were, principally, for protection against the full experience of anxiety, guilt, hate, and uncertainty. The staff was able to meet those needs at least partially through the intrapsychic processes that led them to perceive prisoners as inanimate, unchanging, and interchangeable and themselves as rehabilitative. But the further need for support against anxiety led to the development of interpersonal socially structured defenses in an attempt to externalize and substantiate objectively the particular inner psychic defenses of the staff. Thus the less visible realities of the inner lives of the staff were translated into patterns of social control and institutional management which shaped the more visible realities of daily prison life.

The rigid structuring of the day, the obsession with the maintenance of absolute order, the concentration of discretion in the hands of the executives and their refusal to grant it to guards, the emphasis on detachment, the prohibition of contact between staff and inmates, the preoccupation with the mechanisms of processing, and the denial of human feeling were some of the more striking managerial concerns in effect at Lompoc, concerns which were equally necessary as social defense mechanisms limiting the anxiety of the staff. To integrate one's individual psychic life with these institutionalized social defenses was the task for every employee; to submit to them was the requirement for every inmate. This task was a far greater one than merely following directions and learning the rules: it required the redefinition of one's self in prison terms—the cultivation of attributes that would coordinate with the demands of the institution and the comparable suppression of attributes that would conflict with them.

There were, to be sure, people at every level of the staff who were aware of the antirehabilitative and demeaning aspects of many of these practices and attitudes, however valuable they may have been in defending against anxiety. Some employees spoke openly and movingly of the pressures of conformity, of their own frustration and exhaustion, of their loss of discretion and judgment, and of their disappointment at having to become merely file keepers, watchmen, or processors rather than putting to use their original genuine interests in rehabilitation. But as dissatisfied as these employees may have been, their adherence to the predominant psychic and social systems of defense against anxiety was greater than either their ability to confront and work through their anxiety or their freedom to leave the prison system: they were unable to act other than oppressively. They did not fully recognize this discrepancy between their inclinations and their behavior because of their unconscious identification with the prison organization, because of the close alignment of personality structure with institutional structure. They had indeed gotten with the program, and they had been gotten by it.

There is nothing unusual about the existence of anxiety and the need to defend against it. Neither is it surprising to find anxiety and its defenses heightened among people who work in prison; it is an anxiety-provoking situation. Nor is it remarkable that individual and social defenses should articulate with each other to allay anxiety and to further the everyday tasks of the organization within which they operate. What *was* remarkable about the way Lompoc was run was the degree to which the concordance of individual and social defenses distorted and undermined the official goals of the institution as defined by the Bureau of Prisons—its "mission" to reduce crime through deterrence, custody, and correction.

There are, to be sure, many tough prisoners, and they are tough to take. They lie, steal, and cheat, and they can be vicious and assaultive. They can enrage and disappoint the most compassionate men. But at Lompoc there were even more prisoners who were not so dangerous or threatening, and it was this distinction which the staff was unable to make. The existence of such a situation, one of both danger and diversity, required all the more the exercise of careful evaluation of each prisoner rather than stereotyped labeling of them all, the practice of astute judgment about the individual rather than paranoid distrust of the mass. But because of the concordance of their individual and social defenses against anxiety, because they had "gotten with the program," staff members were psychologically unable to recognize differences, make distinctions, or exercise discretion. Indeed, they were far more likely to identify all prisoners equally and totally with attributes they themselves had rejected, and thereby equate all prisoners with each other. And because the staff tended to identify prisoners with each other, they were unable to discriminate among them sufficiently to recognize who was dangerous and who was not.

The degree to which thought and conduct were affected by irrational elements, the degree to which the staff pursued their unconsciously projected impulses in addition to the manifest behavior of prisoners themselves, supplied what may be termed the "persecutory increment" which further poisoned the atmosphere of the institution. It was not so much the presence of this element of projective identification but its *predominance* which supplied the critical difference between careful distinction among inmates and arbitrary discrimination against them all, between reasonable regulation and stringent deprivation, between prudent, responsible security and the ceaseless, zealous pursuit of an illusory perfect seal.

Because of the predominance of projective identification, the individual and social systems of defense were insufficient as a means of containing anxiety. Because the justifiable concern for security in the prison was exaggerated by the anxiety of the staff, the result was not a reasonably stable institution but an increasingly violent one in which there was a particularly vicious circle of excessive order provoking disorder evoking further oppression arousing more disorder. This self-defeating pattern was manifest in three particularly impressive aspects of prison life: the prevalence of physical violence, the inconsistent rule enforcement, and the persistence of smuggling.

It is made clear to the inmate, from the moment he leaves the courtroom in chains, that he is not merely "in the custody of the Attorney General" (the official euphemism for Federal incarceration), that he is not only subject to the government's authority, but rather that he is in its power. That power is symbolized in the prison building and realized in its function of containment; it is exercised through routine prison administration and is applied by direct physical force. The tower guards at Lompoc were armed, as were the search parties which went after escaped prisoners. The guards inside the institution were not armed lest their guns be seized by prisoners, but it was not lost on prisoners that they were contained by force and controlled by coercion. Though the incidence of official violence was low, the threat of force was constant, and it was with this threat that each inmate had to live.

But force was not the exclusive prerogative of the staff; it was also the principal medium of psychological and physical exchange between prisoners. What could not be settled between inmates by coercion and intimidation was achieved through direct assault. The prevalence of fighting was so great that it seemed that the staff, having been forbidden to exercise direct physical punishment, had implicitly commissioned prisoners to do it for them. And violence was not only condoned; it was openly advocated. At the first meeting of the Adjustment Committee (the disciplinary board) which I observed, two of the three staff members advised the inmate who was appearing before them to settle his difficulties by fighting it out with the prisoner who was bothering him. The third member of the Adjustment Committee concurred and added that the fight should take place near a guard, who would then break it up and send both men to The Hole for a few days and thereby settle the dispute. As a result of this kind of advice, Lompoc was a very violent prison. During my two years at the institution there were five crippling stabbings, one murder, thirty fractured jaws, innumerable fist fights, and two major and several minor riots.

In addition to directly advocating violence as a means of resolving conflict, the staff did nothing about the small number of men who by past history, prior criminal record, and present behavior were extraordinarily violent. Among the twelve hundred prisoners, there were perhaps fifty unusually violent men who were a clear threat to the safety of the other prisoners and the staff. Yet, except for occasional confinement in The Hole after an assault, these men were not housed separately, nor were special precautions taken in regard to them; there was no thought or planning given to their particular needs or problems, or even to the best method of physical containment. Instead, the entire prison population was managed anxiously, since all twelve hundred were equally identified with the violent lowest common denominator. Because of this identification, all prisoners were expected to be violent, and the violent ones were then treated as "ordinary" prisoners. This practice of punishing all for one and one for all provoked, by its harshness and manifest injustice, precisely the aggressive behavior the staff most feared and most needed to justify its increased control.

The same self-generating cycle could be seen in the pattern of rule enforcement. Although absolute detachment was both the tradition and the rule, it was not the practice. "Eternal vigilance is the price of liberty" has been a watchword since the time of Jefferson. It is the motto of both the American Civil Liberties Union and the North Atlantic Treaty Organization. But at Lompoc, the guiding principle seemed to be "Eternal vigilance is the price of custody." This vigilance, however, was more pose than practice; surveillance was only selectively exercised. Since the guards could not supervise all inmates all the time, they were in a difficult position: they had to both oversee and overlook.

To obtain the cooperation of prisoners, guards had to make many accommodations; they were not quite so absolute in their detachment as tradition and policy required them to at least appear. Prisoners were allowed to share minor, if menial, guard duties, such as mail distribution; homosexuality and modest transvestitism were permitted; light violence (without weapons) was advocated; certain rackets were not interfered with. The most obvious of these rackets was the sale, for cigarettes or sexual favors, of specially starched, bleached, and pressed "bonaroo" uniforms, which gave a particularly spruce appearance to men who wore them to the visiting room.

Although the guards had to moderate their at least theoretically complete control, they had neither the encouragement of the executives nor the inner flexibility to exercise their own judgment. Instead, many guards fell back upon the use of the rule book, not as a guide to be interpreted in the light of current conditions but as a literal arbiter of conduct. But the rules were enforced neither flexibly nor absolutely; some were applied constantly and harshly and others were ignored completely and flagrantly. The selectivity and intensity with which many trivial rules were enforced and the manner in which seemingly more important regulations were overlooked, the degree to which some rules seemed to have a life of their own—as litany rather than principle—beyond their immediate supervisory utility, suggested that, in this respect as well, the prison was managed more for the emotional security of its staff than for its announced goal of correction.

The inconsistent and contradictory rule enforcement, the apparent confusion of the trivial and the important, would have been almost comical if it had not also been apparent that these practices promoted the dual goals of harassment and humiliation of prisoners and of reassurance of the staff. For example, the surreptitious trade in "bonaroo" uniforms continued, but prisoners were disciplined for not tucking in their shirts. Transvestitism and homosexuality flourished, but men were sent to The Hole for embracing their wives too avidly in the visiting room. Marijuana and other drugs were circulated in the institution, but toxic drugs which were growing wild on prison land (the officials knew they were there because I pointed them out myself) were never removed. By condoning connivance, perversion, and drug use as they condoned violence, the staff could actualize their negative stereotypes of prisoners and thus permit them to personify and confirm "objectively" what had already unconsciously been attributed to them. By niggling over minor regulations, the staff could express contempt, reinforce social distance, and still convince themselves that they were carrying out orders to the letter.

The zealous pursuit of institutional and personal security went beyond the concern for internal order and the physical retention of prisoners within the walls. The authorities were not only worried lest anyone get out, they were fearful lest anything get in. The preoccupation with smuggling, in contrast to a reasoned concern for its risks, was a response to a clear but limited threat. But it was a response augmented to an intense overreaction.

The hit-and-miss attitude of emphasizing the trivial and overlooking the dangerous was expressed in both the definition of contraband and in its ineffective regulation. The definition was as broad as the anxiety that demanded it and as narrow in its recognition of the needs of inmates as the minds that fashioned it: any object that was not issued by the prison, sold in its commissary, or specially approved for educational purposes was considered to be contraband. It is true that much of what was smuggled was either weaponry or drugs; there was a proud collection in one of the prison offices of sinister weapons and little vials that had been intercepted over the years, and no one would deny the necessity of eradicating such traffic.

A considerable amount of contraband, however, had nothing to do with harm but a great deal to do with human need. Much of it served the same purpose as the commissary food: symbolic connection with life outside and momentary relief from life inside. Indeed, many of the contraband objects could have been bought at the commissary. For instance, one man tied his shoes with smuggled laces indistinguishable from those available in the prison; another wrote his letters with a contraband pencil, although one could be had from the guard for the asking. Some contraband was not smuggled in by the user but had been handed down within the inmate population for years. Cheap wrist watches could be bought at the commissary, but few articles were more prized than the contraband Bulova which was passed along—as much a talisman as a timepiece—from departing to remaining prisoners. One should not underestimate the pleasure that can come from keeping something when everything has been taken away, and particularly something which has never belonged to the prison, something which has been given in love or friendship and not dispensed in resentment and contempt.

The excitement of secrecy was of course highly important, if only as a means of feeling briefly alive, but the prevalence of innocuous smuggling had as much to do with privacy as it did with secrecy. Many prisoners came to feel that their thoughts as well as their bodies were in Federal custody, that their feelings as well as their persons were under constant scrutiny, that they were losing not only their privacy but their private selves. To possess something in fact reinforced one's possession of one's thoughts; to keep something *for* oneself meant that one could keep something *of* one's self.

Fear and anxiety influenced even the management of those instances when the material smuggled presented a clear threat to the safety or the health of the institution. Men who smuggled drugs or weapons were often known to the staff; when they were apprehended they were segregated briefly and their visits were suspended. After their period of discipline, the known smugglers were returned to the general population and to the ordinary visiting routine. In this routine, all visits were supervised by a guard and afterward all prisoners were searched in every orifice. There was no thought given to separating the visits of known smugglers from the general visiting program or to instituting a more stringently supervised program for them and a more realistic program for those who had demonstrated their reliability. To do so would have required the recognition by the staff that some prisoners were reliable and —a far greater psychological shift—that some were more reliable than others and therefore distinguishable from them. Though the talk of individualized programs was loud and frequent, the conduct of the visiting program, like every other prison routine, was based on the assumption that all prisoners were interchangeable.

This situation did not reflect a deep commitment by the staff to basic equality; it revealed, rather, that the need of defense against anxiety by identifying all prisoners with one another overruled thoughtful evaluation of direct experience. Therefore, all prisoners, whether they actually smuggled or not, were presumed to be smuggling and were required to bend to the degradation ceremonial of routine physical inspection. With regard to smuggling, as in other matters, there was no considered distinction between the dangerous few and the innocuous many, but fearful and hostile discrimination against all.

These unconscious processes and ritualized activities helped to diminish staff anxiety, but they did not diminish smuggling. The attitude of eternal vigilance was more important as a psychological operation than as a practical one, and in any case such scrutiny could never be as absolute as the wish that prompted it. To the extent that members of the staff were unconsciously projectively identifying themselves with the prisoners—to the degree that they were in effect policing their own impulses—they could anticipate the prisoners' smuggling only in ways in which they themselves might smuggle. As a result, only the most obvious routes were controlled and only the most careless smugglers were apprehended. Since not all of the staff were lacking in imagination in other respects and since few prisoners were really very clever, it was remarkable to see how incapable the staff was of learning from their experience or of modifying their supervisory behavior.

Marijuana was widely smoked in the prison. At the Saturday-night movies (one hundred straight weeks of violence during my two-year assignment at Lompoc) the air was thick with its aroma. Although the use of the drug helped to relieve the pain of imprisonment and to enliven the "psychic numbing" which was the principal defense against that pain, it is doubtful that such relief was the intent of the staff. It seems more likely that they ignored the drug use in order to ignore their inability to control drug traffic and to conceal from themselves the worthlessness, in practical terms, of their attitude toward contraband. Although this situation was pleasing to many prisoners, it made even greater fools of the staff and was a further mockery of the marijuana laws—for the violation of which fully a third of Lompoc's inmates had been convicted.

Nor were all the highs imported. Jimson weed (*Datura stramonium*) grew wild on the prison grounds. The active chemical agent in its leaves is a belladonna alkaloid similar in effect to the widely used medicine atropine. The vapor of these leaves has been used historically in the treatment of bronchial asthma, but when taken internally in high concentration, jimson weed induces a minor high; in still higher concentrations, a terrifying, hallucinating toxic psychosis. The jimson weed was taken by some prisoners in every possible form and with every possible effect. The leaves were swallowed and smoked, chewed and brewed. They induced some pleasant effects, from mild giggles to sexual arousal, but they also induced almost every known form of atropine poisoning, from dry mouth and racing pulse to intense thirst and painful swallowing; from slight mental confusion to flagrant hallucinations and, in one instance, mania. The prison officials were well aware of the existence and location of the jimson fields and of the use of the leaves by prisoners, but for the pleasure of some and the terror of others, the weeds in "Jimson Gully" were never removed.

5

Deprivation and the Code

By their attitude of constant vigilance and their practice of inconstant enforcement, by their ceaseless checking up on appearances and their regular neglect of serious misconduct, by patrolling the boundaries of the prison and ignoring the interior, by concentrating on what was peripheral and overlooking what was central, the staff seemed to be reassuring themselves by magical thought and ritual behavior that if they did those things well, the deeper psychic threats did not exist. But because these practices were administratively ineffective, the prison was managed incompetently; and because these attitudes were derived from developmentally primitive defenses against anxiety, the staff generated an atmosphere of rigid tension and hateful distance. Though prisoners were regarded as inanimate, unchanging, and interchangeable, and were treated as such; though the prison was managed to facilitate processing; and though that management was festooned with claims of rehabilitation, the hatred assaulted every sense. It stared from hard eyes, chilled in tone of voice, snarled in harassment, stank in vicious personal and racial slurs, and embittered the experience of deprivation which is the fate of every prisoner.

The most notable of the institutionally mediated deprivations at Lompoc were those of physical liberty, personal contact, sexual choice, and personal autonomy. Though to overemphasize the importance of this system of deprivation would lead to formulation of the principle of "depraved on account of deprived," it is nonetheless true that the imposition of deprivation is a major element in the psychological deterioration of men in prison.

The obvious deprivation of liberty is compounded by the deprivation of name, customary physical appearance, material possessions, and the slightest amenity. Having been shaven and shorn on admission, many inmates had difficulty recognizing themselves in the mirror, and this was only the most superficial element in the erosion of identity which incarceration effects. One prisoner expressed his feelings of what he called "mistaken identity" this way: "When I look in the mirror, the face I see isn't the one I know."

Deprivation of personal contact is enforced through control of mail, by the geographic isolation of the prison, and by the supervision of visits. Prisoners' correspondents are officially limited in number. Outgoing letters are censored and often are returned for editing; incoming letters may be returned if the sender is not on the approved list. It is difficult for friends and family to get to the prison, particularly if they do not have a car. The institution is 150 miles from the nearest large city and sixty miles from an airport; there is one bus a day into Lompoc in time for visiting hours; there is no railroad service to the town and no public transport within it. All visits are held in the visiting room under the direct gaze of the guard on duty, who sits on a little dais. A certain amount of chaste embracing is allowed, but an embrace which lasts too long is publicly interrupted and the offending man is disciplined on the spot before his family and other prisoners.

Deprivation of customary sexual choice is accompanied by homosexual pressure. There were, of course, many prisoners to whom homosexuality was a lifelong and pleasant pursuit, but because of coercion and commerce they very often could not choose or keep their own partners. Others who had not previously been homosexual were raped or were coerced into compliance. Although a direct verbal approach could be avoided, it was not so easy to avoid an assault. Still more difficult to avoid was the anxiety aroused by the open homosexual practice and by the atmosphere of constant pressure. For many ordinarily heterosexual prisoners, what had been taken for granted as an established, inherent aspect of themselves—their sexual identity—became a matter of conscious concern, chronic anxiety, and repeated redefinition. One man put it this way: "The first thing you have to decide in prison is what sex you're going to be. If you don't decide, and keep on deciding, then someone else will."

The most significant deprivation—of a sense of personal autonomy—is the most pervasive and the most subtle. A prisoner may not exercise choice about any major aspect of his daily life. He is dependent on the institution for the essentials of food, shelter, and clothing, for the organization of his day, and for his release. This reinforcement of dependency hardly encourages young men toward responsible adulthood. Rather, it forces regression toward ever more immature thought and action, toward immediate gratification through fantasy or impulsiveness. Not only does prison life induce regression, it discourages resolution of that inner situation by psychological means other than those which are themselves regressive: compliant behavior is rewarded; the capacity for inner automatization is maximized by the routinization of daily activity; inherent dependency wishes are gratified; the exercise of judgment, discretion, and choice is prohibited. This inner reorientation seals men into prison and prison into men. Moreover, this gradual psychic inactivation often leaves many men helpless in the face of new tasks or problems and is responsible for the sense of bewilderment and panic many prisoners feel when they return to a less organized life outside—and thus for their early return to prison.

It is excruciating to be dependent on those you hate and cannot trust, but in prison the anger and impotent rage evoked by such a situation can rarely be openly expressed. Some prisoners are able to remain in touch with their anger despite the pressures to repress it from awareness; they may even embrace it rather than feel nothing. Others, fewer in number, are able to put their feelings on paper—in letters, essays, or fiction—in language so direct and accurate in its intensity that it can seem tendentious only to those who cannot imagine the oppression of prison life and the inner revisions it requires. But for many more prisoners, much of the anger which cannot be expressed is taken up by conscience and turned back upon the self as intense, guilty depression. The hostile outward supervision by the staff is often matched by hateful inward scrutiny; the lack of physical privacy is often accompanied by the belief that one's thoughts and feelings are also being supervised, that mental reservation is impossible. And as the outer supervision is harsh and punitive, so does the inner surveillance reflect it.

These feelings find an ally in the universal human capacity for exaggerated guilt which is the residue in adult psychic life of the inherent inequality between every child and his parents. The exploitation by the prison staff of this basic inward disparity brings about in many prisoners a feeling of being totally bad, not only for their offense but as persons; not for what they have done but for what they are. Even the Mosiac law of talion imposes restraint as well as retribution: it exacts an eye for an eye, not decapitation for an eye. But the psychic effects of incarceration go far beyond such limits. The guilt evoked and reinforced by incarceration is often so intense that it arouses, in defense against that pain, an unconscious process leading to a denial of having done anything merely illegal. One prisoner, contrasting his day-to-day suicidal self-loathing with his attitude toward his crime, said it succinctly: "I feel so bad, I don't feel guilty."

Many inmates denied their offense outright ("I didn't do it") or attributed their incarceration to conspiracy or externally contrived parole violation ("I was framed" or "I was violated"). Though some of these remarks were outright lies or mere excuses, in other instances they often represented an extensive psychic realignment, an unconscious revision of reality which was as truly accepted as that revision which led many prison employees to believe sincerely that they were being rehabilitative.

In insisting that "I was violated," many prisoners were affirming their sense of helpless passivity and were also saying, in effect, "If I am irresponsible, then you, 'Society,' are responsible for my irresponsibility." It is by the evocation of this psychological process that incarceration fails most subtly and completely as both punishment and rehabilitation: for in inspiring pervasive guilt it forecloses the possibility of considered regret for a specific offense, and in encouraging global rationalization in defense against that guilt, it prevents the recognition of limited culpability.

If the staff—in order to manage their own anxiety, hatred, and guilt—saw prisoners as subhuman and superhuman and then nonhuman, if they distributed their anxieties and fears equally and totally throughout the prison population, thereby perceiving inmates as unchanging and interchangeable as well as inanimate, then similar psychic operations were also present among the inmates. Because much that was hateful in themselves was unconsciously projected by prisoners onto the staff, the prison employees came to be seen as more evil than their own actions; and because that evil was spread equally and totally throughout the entire staff, each member of it was seen to be utterly bad. If high turnover of the prison population and frequent housing changes within it combined with the imposition of numbers, uniforms, and haircuts to reinforce the staff's perception of prisoners as without distinctiveness, then the quarterly job rotations of guards, their own uniforms, and their acceptance of the institutionally required attitudes of detachment and impersonality reinforced prisoners' tendencies to equate the guards' physical similarity with psychic uniformity. It thus became most difficult for prisoners to recognize guards and other staff members as individuals; to distinguish between the completely hostile group and the occasional single figure who was earnestly trying to do his best.

If the prison staff saw the inmates as constantly threatening, the prisoners saw the staff and the institutional environment as intensely persecutory. Just as the staff's psychic defenses were reflected and reinforced by the socially structured defenses which influenced prison management, so were the prisoners' needs to contain anxiety, hatred, and guilt translated into a socially structured defense known as the inmate code. That the code flourishes in most prisons (as well as in the criminological literature) attests to its survival value. Like the intrapsychic defenses from which it is elaborated, the precepts of the inmate code often reciprocate the guards' attitudes, and both codes are rigid, suspicious, and isolating: "Never Snitch" versus "Report Every Infraction," "Never Notice Anything" versus "Eternal Vigilance," "Do Your Own Time" versus "Absolute Detachment." Although the inmate code is adaptive to prison life, indeed because it is so valuable for survival, its acceptance brings prison into the prisoner, imposing its own deprivations, setting up internal bars and augmenting inmates' inherent capacities for rigidity as surely as the steel rods which reinforce the concrete of the prison walls.

The first principle of the code (as it was applied at Lompoc) is "Never Snitch." This attempts to maintain a firm boundary around inmates as a group and specifically interdicts any but the most superficial contact with employees; any such contact is assumed to be heavy with snitch potential. Moreover, the acceptance of this precept and the boundary it imposes reinforces the assumption by prisoners of the debased identity of the convict and augments the tendency of the staff to view all prisoners as indistinguishable. Although this precept clearly demarcates prisoners from guards, it does not ensure unanimity or a sense of solidarity among inmates except as they are defined as belonging to a single group who are not prison employees. Though there was much talk of unity and fraternity among prisoners, there was not much friendship. This is not to say that there were no loyalties between prisoners or that no friendships were formed, but rather to emphasize that the number of black eyes, bruises, stab wounds, and fractures was convincing evidence of extensive conflict, pressure, extortion, and violence.

The second principle of the code is "Never Notice Anything." It might be restated as "Eternal Vigilance Not to be Seen Noticing Anything." Although it is impossible to ignore something that happens right in front of you, it is possible, even necessary, to appear to ignore the event and, more important, your own feelings about it. To give compassionate attention to another prisoner in trouble would only place you in jeopardy yourself. Since all prisoners are at some psychic level equated with one another in the minds of the staff (and frequently in the minds of other prisoners), the inmate who appears to notice something wrong is often assumed to be the culprit. And since someone must be punished and the actual culprit may not be identifiable, the reporter of an event or the witness to an irregular procedure is therefore punished as the perpetrator. It is here that the specifics of the code reinforce the limitations on conscience imposed through the more general psychological pressures of incarceration. For to act compassionately, to be, however briefly, your brother's keeper, renders you suspect to your brother's keepers—and frequently to your brother.

The third principle of the code is "Do Your Own Time." Emphasis is placed on repression of all feelings, especially anger, from public notice and private awareness. The inmate is encouraged not to weaken by displaying emotion; he is told to "hold your mud." This attitude helps him to "maintain," to cling to his sanity, dignity, and self-respect. It encourages the active effort to hold together and to avoid response in kind to provocation. Acceptance of this precept diminishes perception of anger, fear, and anxiety, and inhibits the spread of these and other common, intolerable, and highly contagious feelings. Whatever one's emotions, they are not to be shown or shared. This is the most difficult task, but one learned with time.

It hardly seems accidental that the inmate and staff codes are similar. Both have evolved as psychosocial responses to a situation which would be even more difficult without them. The inmate code reflects the staff code not only in the rigidity and isolation of its precepts but also in the peremptory tone in which it is transmitted and in the authoritarian manner with which it is enforced. Because it is *enforced* and not merely taught, it is internalized and not merely learned; its precepts gradually become one's own—they are adhered to and not merely obeyed. And because the code is internalized, its inner psychic coercion takes over where the outer rule of force leaves off.

6

Petrifaction and Perversity

B_Y the demands of the rules, the social structure, the codes, and the necessary psychic responses to them, the prisoner's sense of being fully alive is eroded. It is a rare man who has the perversity to act in his own interest no matter what, the insensitivity to ignore what is happening to him, or the integrity sufficient to transcend incarceration and to maintain a personal sense of continuing life while in prolonged custody. For many prisoners, incarceration changes perception as it reduces it, alters experience as it narrows it. Some men may take refuge in inward preoccupation or daydreaming, and a few are unable to recognize that they *are* daydreaming, thereby exchanging one prison for another. Others may succeed in walling off the entire prison experience as they compartmentalize their inner lives while in custody: they may go through prison only dimly aware that anything is happening; each day is crossed off and dropped away, and when the time comes to leave it may seem as if the whole thing has been left behind, as if it never did happen.

But the longer many men spend inside, the less access they have to their own capacities for emotion, memory, reflection, or anticipation. Like a prism in reverse, the effect of incarceration is to constrict the broad spectrum of ordinary mental life, with all its color and variety, to a colorless mental state in which fine distinctions are lost, shades of meaning are obliterated, and abstraction is condensed, in which imagination fades and concentration fails; thought becomes cliché and feeling mere sensation.

Prison is most obviously painful for men who have just arrived or are about to depart. In these terribly uncertain times of boundary crossing, anxiety is most intense and change is most abrupt. The inner state of many men new to prison can only be described as one of shock. Though the shock may be delayed for a matter of weeks after arrival, it is no less intense. The initial complaints of many arriving men were not so much those of the deep-seated terror they later poured out but of a sense of physical slowdown, of sluggish thought, of homesickness, of sudden episodes of laughter or tears unrelated to immediate events, of wild swings of emotions, and of no emotion. Some men described feelings of unreality, of "this isn't happening"; others felt that everything was all too real. Many spoke of feeling trapped and controlled, and of being unable to exercise control over their own thoughts or emotions. To put it schematically, the most common complaints were those of deceleration, enclosure, and explosion.

If arrival can produce a state of shock, departure often arouses panic. The prospect of leaving prison after many months inside—without preparation, with the mental faculties of anticipation and planning having been impaired by imprisonment, and with no specific place to go—is often more frightening than arrival. The dread of leaving was sometimes expressed in agitated mood and posture, racing thought and speech, and outspoken fear of being unable to master the demands of ordinary life which seemed to be pressing in from all directions. As some men approached release from the prison environment of narrow space and regulated traffic, of stunted mental life and broken connections to the outside, they developed clear symptoms of agoraphobia—the fear of exposure in an open space—and would not go out to the exercise yard after having done so every day for months. Other men desperately threw themselves into futile escape attempts a few days before their scheduled release.

Here is what one inmate wrote to me, months after his departure: "I didn't realize how institutionalized I was until I got out. I am still ill at ease when I am out in the open, away from buildings. I was walking in [an open space] a few days ago, and I felt really panicky. There was too much space there, and no guards to direct traffic. Jesus X. Christ, I made a good convict." The panic prior to release is a compound of emotional agitation, a sense of vulnerability, and fear of the onrushing outside world. The problems of release may be summarized, again schematically, as those of acceleration, exposure, and implosion.

Between the deceleration, enclosure, and explosion of prison entrance and the acceleration, exposure, and implosion aroused by return to the streets, there is the long middle period of doing time. For many prisoners, the psychic state of that long stretch is one of, well, arrest. It is experienced as a period of emptiness, of routine, of boredom, and above all of stasis. During this middle period, the codes, the rules, and the psychic changes in the prisoner interact to keep feelings, both comfortable and distressing, at a distance. Since direct expression of emotion is discouraged by the code and aborted by unconscious psychic defenses, the pain of imprisonment is often more real than apparent.

Because feelings are numbed and the ability to conceptualize and articulate them damaged, the chronic flat depression, unhappiness, and misery are most often expressed in physical terms. Many prisoners spoke of their insomnia, loss of appetite, and lethargy, and of specific concerns with their bodies. Some men got headaches, others had paroxysms of rapid breathing that sometimes ended in coma. A few men complained of strange gases in their bellies, others felt that they were losing contact with their limbs or genitalia; still others said that parts of their bodies were missing, inoperative, or decomposing. Many spoke of a more general sense of mental and physical paralysis; they complained that they were becoming robots or zombies, that they were drying up, freezing, or "turning to stone."

The men who spoke this way were not docile but dazed, not submissive but stunned. Their complaints could be accounted for easily (and narrowly) as "depressive equivalents," as statements in physical terms of an inner state not completely accessible to awareness and not expressible in other terms. Beyond mere depression, these statements of numbness, disintegration, disarticulation, decomposition, automatization, and immobilization—sometimes voiced in fear but more often in the flat dissociated tones of apparent unconcern—constitute the points of reference of the fundamental experience of incarceration: psychic death.

The psychic milieu of the prisoner reflects the psychosocial climate of the prison: there is timelessness without permanence, enclosure without security, quiet without peace, life without vitality. By reawakening infantile fears, perceptions, ideas, and ways of dealing with them, by stimulating infantile experiences of isolation, helplessness, and terror, and by reinforcing them, imprisonment leads the inmate to feel that his deprivation is not merely a lack of gratification but an annihilation; that the monotony, isolation, and inactivation of prison life are experienced unconsciously as death.

Condensing as it does images of terror, hardening, and stasis, the descriptive term "petrifaction" can stand for both the process of psychic adaptation to prison and for the mental state which is its most serious result. Widely variable among prisoners, the process of petrifaction may lead to nothing more than a diminution of feeling or to nothing less than the end of feeling; to a narrowing of the range of affect or to emotional exsanguination; to a slight decrease in vitality or to utter exhaustion of initiative; to moderate constriction of attention span or to complete impairment of concentration; to momentary lapses in thought or to inability to conceptualize; to slight sadness or to black despair; to a longing for others far away or to disbelief in the existence of a social universe.

However severe its effects, petrifaction is at once a response to imprisonment and a defense against it, and every prisoner is "petrified" to some degree; that is, to paraphrase Webster slightly, confounded with fear and amazement. Dostoevski described his reaction to imprisonment as "we need all the unconcern we can muster to get used to it," but the apparent unconcern which many "petrified" prisoners exhibit is not so much indifference as the silent statements "If I notice nothing, then nothing is happening," and "If nothing is happening, then nothing is happening to me."

Something less than catatonia and far more than boredom, petrifaction represents the unconscious choice of a lesser evil: of a waking trance rather than a living nightmare, of the desiccation of consciousness rather than a deluge of pain and suffering. To speak psychodynamically, petrifaction may be viewed as the manifestation of the impact of incarceration upon the unconscious lives of prisoners. As its symptoms suggest, this impact is one of immobilization of psychic energies in defense against their extreme arousal, of a disarticulation, regression, and recombination of mental agencies into a new configuration which is more primitive, tyrannical, and rigid.

In addition to various phenomena of dissociation, depersonalization, and derealization, and beyond the affective blocking and other manifestations of psychic immobilization, the clinical aspects of petrifaction include three major entities: somatization, thought disorder, and time disturbance. Worries about their bodies were the most common form of initial complaint among prisoners who came to the psychiatric clinic, but these somatic concerns occurred in some degree to everyone. The intensity of these concerns varied from increased awareness to obsession to delusion, and their locus from limbs to organs, fluids, and functions—sometimes elaborating into the conviction that the entire body was felt to be different in form, shape, or color. Somatization has been described as the symptom presented primarily by lower-class people, but this was not true for many prisoners at Lompoc who could be considered middle- or upper-class by any standard.

The origins of somatic concerns are multiple, but their high incidence at Lompoc seemed most directly related to their expression of the intensified physical emphasis of every aspect of prison life, to their value as body language when abstraction and conceptualization were impaired, to their statement that something—physical or psychic—was being maimed, to their assertion of a sense of immobilization, to their indication of an altered identity (as a change in self-representation), to their declaration of the threat of death omnipresent in prison, and to their representation—in a persecutory environment—of an inner sense of decay at the hands of invisible (because internalized) persecutors.

Closely related to somatization is the thought disorder which comes with prolonged imprisonment. There is a tendency for concreteness to prevail over abstraction, for the literal to confine the imaginative. The impairment in the ability to think and speak abstractly, the loss of perhaps the most specifically human of attributes, is the most significant result of incarceration and perhaps the most enduring. The disturbance in abstraction is most notable in the disruption of the faculty of symbolic integration, leading to impaired conceptualization, to the inability to recognize or use imagery and metaphor, and therefore to the loss of the capacity to represent to oneself one's own experience and thereby to endow it with meaning.

For many prisoners who complained that they were turning to stone or were dead, it was no longer "I feel as if I am turning to stone" but rather "I am turning to stone"; it was not so much "I feel like I am dead" but rather the paradoxical "I am dead." To reach this point in concretization is to be unable to recognize paradox, to be inaccessible to inherent contradiction, to be unable to appreciate a statement of imagery *as* imagery. This is more than depression. It is more than depersonalization or derealization. This is a process of desymbolization which leads to the most profound form of desocialization among those still biologically alive. It creates—through successive removals from feeling, person, reality, symbol, and society—an inner state close to the ultimate removal of death.

Unable to link a significant past with a meaningful present, many prisoners live without imagining a future. But if time is not recognized as an abstraction, it is also deformed in the perception of its daily passage. It is not long before days begin to feel like weeks, weeks like months, and months like years. But before years become decades, the sense of time passing is distorted into an eternal present. Although the atmosphere of prison is felt to be timeless, days and months are often dealt with as if they are solid objects. If time can be considered a fluid, it becomes more viscous; if it has a velocity, it slows. Time is less a dimension than an object, not a variable but a constant. It is not something that "passes" or "flies" but, in the words of one prisoner, "it is something that you *do*."

Time is indeed "done," "pulled," or "served"; it is "hard" or "short," but mostly it is "flat." It may be heavy with depression or it may be relieved by the manic excitement which is often taken for good spirits; it may be rancid with anger or yellow with fear; it may weigh one down or seem to be enveloping; it may sometimes appear as a discrete entity which can be thrown away each day, "like toilet paper." Or it may not be "there" at all: the psychic arrest of incarceration is often accompanied by a sense that time is standing still, that one is not changing but is in a kind of suspended animation, that those outside the prison are not changing either, and that everything will be the same after release, no matter how long the interval. However it is experienced, time is an imposition; it is an external entity, something to be enumerated, calculated, manipulated, or ignored; it is without personal significance to a life of one's own. And when time becomes external, one exists outside time.

There were moments when I wondered to myself (though I never uttered such thoughts) why more prisoners did not escape. It is true that some inmates who have nowhere else to go are happy to have the shelter and the regular meals, that some are genuinely penitent and wish to "pay their debt to society." It is also true that some prisoners are intimidated by the physical and legal consequences of recapture and that others realistically perceive that the possibility of a permanently successful escape is unlikely and that the shortest sentence lies in being the best prisoner. It is not to diminish the importance of these matters to point out that the psychic imprisonment of petrifaction also affects the relative infrequency of escape attempts.

With the recapitulation in prison—though in a far crueler key—of the inherent inequalities between parent and child, the inner tensions of dependency and guilt are amplified and distorted into apathy and terror. Having "gotten with the program," having accepted the psychic limitations which accompany physical detention, some prisoners became so dependent on the institution that their apathy smothered the initiative, ingenuity, and purpose necessary to escape. Other prisoners were caught up in their own dependency but were also terrorized by an irrational, infantile guilt which prohibited even the thought of escape, not only because it would be wrong but because it would be a desertion.

Besides disrupting thought processes, the psychic effects of petrifaction interfered with their effective integration with feeling and action, so that some long-term prisoners were psychically unable to conceive, plan, and execute an escape. With the loss of such faculties and of a sense of connection with a larger world, escape was not only impossible, it was literally unimaginable. Finally, if the stasis and timelessness of petrifaction brought the reassurance that "If nothing is changing, then I am not changing," then its corollary was "If I am not changing, then I need not escape."

If escape was unlikely, many prisoners found relief from petrifaction through three principal activities: drug use, self-mutilation, and psychopathy. Marijuana was in constant and widespread use and was prized by many prisoners for its sexual arousal, its stimulation of pleasant feelings, interesting fantasies, and at least the momentary impression of good-fellowship—in brief, many of the pleasures of ordinary life erased by imprisonment. But when marijuana was not available there were other drugs. Besides the local supply of jimson weed, which brought more pain than pleasure, prisoners frequently got drunk on various home brews, or sniffed themselves high (and sometimes into coma) on the fumes from paint thinner, mimeograph fluid, printer's ink or, most frequently, glue. However self-destructive this behavior may have been, it was also sometimes self-affirming, an attempt not so much at intoxication as to feel *something*, as if to say that relief from petrifaction lay in getting stoned.

More serious than drug use, yet still a relief from petrifaction, was the practice of self-mutilation. The most common form of self-mutilation at Lompoc was superficial cutting about the arms, torso, or legs. This practice is not rare in prisons and it frightens everyone. Prisoners who witness it fear that they may be driven to act similarly, and guards are reminded by the act of the cruelty which they impose. Despite its frequency at Lompoc, cutting was not responded to by competent or sympathetic treatment by guards, or by improvement of the situation which induced it, but rather by loud insistence that it was "manipulation" or "trying to get attention." Like so many other official generalizations, it was sometimes quite true: cutting could be a deliberate attempt to bargain for a new job or better privileges. But in other instances it could be a suicidal gesture, a hateful attack on the self, a gratifying form of the masochism which is aroused in many prisoners, an effort to peel off "dead" skin to reach the tissues of a living self, or a concrete, physical attempt, as one man expressed it, "to get out all the evil that's in me." This particular man had indeed done some evil things, but his incarceration had brought him to a sense of personal evil far beyond anything associated with his actual behavior.

But in the many variations on the theme of spontaneous self-mutilation there was a common note of attempted self-definition. In an atmosphere where a man is subjected to sensory and social as well as sexual deprivation, where he is regarded as inanimate and comes to think of himself that way, he has difficulty remembering who he is, what he is, and *if* he is. Losing touch with their emotions, and sometimes with their senses, some men become confused between internal and external realities, between what is "me" and "not me." When petrifaction reaches this point, cutting could be an assertion of being, an effort to know that where a man cuts, he feels; that where he bleeds is the border between himself and the outside world; an attempt to prove that if he bleeds he lives, that he has not been "turned to stone."

But men in this extreme state do not think this, for they lack the ability to construe it; nor do they say this, for they cannot speak what they do not know. They act quickly and silently, and then stand, shocked, in mute incomprehension. For the psychic death of imprisonment leads some men to so disbelieve in their own existence that they must confirm it by the testament of their own blood; it leaves them also in wordless terror, gripped by the earliest of fears—older than speech—of being overwhelmed by their own impulses; it leads them often to desperate action, to express their unutterable despair in an unspeakable act.

However useful drugs or self-mutilation may have been in

ameliorating the affective, cognitive and kinesthetic aspects of petrifaction, the most common and probably the most serious escape from this living death was psychopathic behavior. Neither psychotic nor necessarily criminal, psychopathic behavior is usually referred to as "manipulative"; that is, exploiting others for profit, pleasure, and aggrandizement. Psychopaths themselves have been described as given to immediate pleasure and lacking the capacity to form attachments or loyalties to others, to groups, or to codes of living. In the psychiatric literature the delineation of the psychopathic character is an issue which is as vexed as some psychopaths are themselves vexing.

It has been well argued that only the flawed psychopath is apprehended, that he is betrayed by his own need for others; that the true psychopath is so immune to human attachment and yet so artful that he never sees the inside of a prison or of a psychiatrist's office unless he sits at the warden's desk or in the psychiatrist's chair. Nonetheless, there were many prisoners at Lompoc—glib con artists all—who could be said to have something of a psychopathic character, and they flourished in the prison as did no one else.

Whether these men were suave or brash, voluble or terse, roving or sedentary, they did not internalize the prison codes any more than they accepted the laws of the outside world or of ordinary human decency; rather, they exploited the prison world to their own immediate advantage as they had attempted to do outside. Because of their superficial charm and intelligence they were sought out by the officials as clerks and orderlies, and they were liked by guards and prisoners for their seeming self-assurance and mesmerizing facility, even envied for their apparent ability to control their environment. These men did not, of course, come to the psychiatrist except to size him up; still, there was no lack of opportunity to observe psychopathic behavior, for some of the most accomplished psychopaths worked in the hospital, and psychopathic behavior was widespread, though less concentrated in single individuals, throughout the prison population. (The reader who wonders how the most blatant psychopaths could work in a hospital job which would seem to require a high degree of reliability is probably unaware of the power relations which prevail between permanent medical assistants, who select the inmate staff, and transient doctors.)

After observing the more classical psychopaths, after listening to other prisoners and to the prison staff, after thinking over our own behavior and impulses, it seemed to us on the medical staff that the perverse, capricious, and manipulative behavior we saw and were tempted at times to join was the dominant means of survival in prison. It was becoming apparent that psychopathic behavior provided at least a temporary defense against the immobilization and inactivation of prison life. To adapt oneself psychologically to imprisonment meant to be diminished in every respect. As the effects of prison flattened many inmates into sullen despondency, they often turned for relief to petty thievery, bribery, and "games," as if to say that the way to adapt by acting upon the environment was to act psychopathically. The deals, the hustling, the petty intrigue, the endless conniving and contriving provided at least the momentary impression of motion in the face of stasis, of life instead of slow decay; this equation of psychopathy with life often elicited perverse behavior in defense against the fearsome realization that one was slowly ceasing to exist.

Perversity seemed as much a relief from incarceration for the staff as it did to the prisoners. Harassing inmates and sometimes each other seemed to be the principal diversion of prison employees. And diversion it was. Both staff and prisoners viewed the other group as entirely bad and themselves as wholly justified in their perceptions and their behavior. The unconscious partitioning that imprisonment demands of both inmates and staff temporarily relieved both groups of guilt and ambivalence, enabling each to act perversely while enjoying a brief magical impression of freedom. Every successful hassle brought fleeting sadistic triumph at having power over others and the illusion of having the ability to make things happen. During this soaring pseudo life, the despair and emptiness were forgotten. As difficult as it was even to observe this behavior, it was also difficult to overlook the desperate attempt at freedom which it represented.

7

"Part of the Institution," or "Prejudiced Against Us"

THERE were questions I frequently asked myself while I worked at Lompoc. The words were always the same, but the emphasis depended on whether I was thinking of how little I was accomplishing or if I was feeling sorry for myself. The questions were, "What was I *doing* there?" and "What was *I* doing *there*?" The reader may by now be asking those same questions, and the following is an attempt to answer them.

When I was an intern, I knew that I was going on into psychiatry, so I decided to continue my training if I could. The inevitability of military service for young doctors had been clear to me, and not particularly welcome, since I entered medical school, but I never seriously questioned the fact. The virtually compulsory two years of military duty had seemed to be merely the last phase of the long indenture that is medical education, almost its logical culmination. It never occurred to me not to go. In the mid-1960s there was a minor skirmish in Vietnam, and I was aware of it, but I never thought about it. I looked into the various deferment plans offered by the armed services which would free me of the doctor draft during the period of my psychiatric training in return for my promise to serve two years once that training was completed.

The Public Health Service also offered a deferment plan which assigned psychiatrists to posts at its hospitals and clinics, to the National Institutes of Health, to drug-addiction centers, to Indian reservations, and to prisons. Since I was not attracted to military life, I felt that if I had to give the government two years, that time would be more interesting in the Public Health Service. I was glad that I passed the examination and was accepted for deferment, and I thought little more about it over the next three years while I concentrated on my learning and growth in psychiatry.

Early in 1967, I was notified by telegram that I had been assigned as staff psychiatrist to the Federal Correctional Institution at Lompoc. I had no idea how I had been assigned to the job. My training had included a course in forensic psychiatry, but I had no experience with prison work and indeed had never even visited a prison. In psychiatry as in law, it is considered not quite nice to work with criminals, and I was not free of that prejudice.

Lompoc was not so prestigious an assignment as, say, a desk job at the National Institute of Mental Health, but I was interested in how institutions affected the people in them and I thought that at least in that respect it might be interesting. I was dismayed at the prospect of professional isolation and more than a little doubtful as to how good I might be at "correctional psychiatry." I was reluctant to leave the hospital where I had trained, but I anticipated a natural, as well as an imposed, change in my life that I thought might be good for me. I was looking forward to working more on my own and to living in a part of the country different from that in which I had grown up. It was in this hopeful yet doubtful frame of mind that I drove across the continent, hearing "Ode to Billy Joe" on the car radio all the way from the Delaware River to the Donner Pass. And all along the way I encouraged myself with the same deception I was to hear from so many others at Lompoc: "If nothing else, I can finally catch up on my reading."

The reading never got done. Lompoc had the largest volume of "study cases" in the country. These men are sent to prison for sixty (or sometimes ninety) days of psychiatric evaluation after conviction but prior to sentencing, usually when the courts feel that a psychiatric opinion may relate to sentencing. The volume of these study cases never diminished; even when I interviewed five and six men a day there was always a backlog. Many such men had little or no discernible psychopathology. After a while it seemed that they were being sent for evaluation in order to be shown what prison was like before being placed on probation; in fact, a large number of them did not return to prison. However, a large number of those *with* clear pathology did return; evidently the courts felt that the prison really was a therapeutic institution and that one psychiatrist for twelve hundred men was enough to effect a "cure."

In my first naïve weeks at the prison, I also took seriously the announced concern of the officials for rehabilitation. Acting on the suggestion of one official who was fond of describing his own work as "following the medical model" and who kept emphasizing to me that "you're part of this institution," I visited each cell block, introduced myself to the guard in charge, telling him of my interest in working with him and his inmates. A few guards were interested and open, but most of them told me in no uncertain terms to mind my own business and stick to the hospital. Soon becoming aware of the volume and degree of psychological stress in the prison, I hoped to interest the staff in general in the group work I was instituting, either by helping them conduct their own groups or by working with them as a co-therapist. I offered to consult with other programs, such as prerelease planning and work-release, although I was not yet aware that such programs barely existed. All my offers were turned down.

At about the same time, still naïve and still as unknown as an individual to officials and guards as they were to me, I mentioned an employee to an official and called the third man, matter-of-factly, a guard. The official flew into a rage, asserting that the man I had mentioned was not a guard but a correctional officer, and insisting that my use of the word proved that I was irremediably prejudiced against correctional officers. I was dazed by the intensity of the outburst and amazed at the alacrity with which he assumed prejudice. At the time, "guard" seemed to me to be a word which was both appropriate and inoffensive. Guarding was what the correctional officers were doing, and I did not see anything insulting about saying so. It is one thing for administrators to want to improve the image of a job by giving it a more professional-sounding title, but the intensity of the official's response seemed far out of proportion to an honest error in a simple matter. Like the use of "rehabilitation" to deny the practice of punishment, the insistence upon "correctional officer" instead of "guard" was another example of the prison practice of denying reality by changing the vocabulary. I soon realized that I had not only committed a breach of etiquette but had also blundered into the semantic area of what was to become the more extensive battlefield between treatment and custody.

But there were differences between the administrative and medical staffs other than their conflicting ideas of what constituted rehabilitation. Although we on the medical staff strove mightily (perhaps too mightily) to avoid personal conflict with the officials, there were elements in the situation which made for difficulty. There was no denying that some permanent and possibly trapped prison employees resented the presence of younger men who would move on in two years to what could seem to be enviable jobs and lives; the prison hospital was under the administration of the Public Health Service and therefore not directly controlled by the prison executives—and this lack of complete control made them anxious; the medical staff was providing skilled attention to inmates, but the administrators disliked their dependence on our skills and resented our attention to inmates; the medical staff were all under thirty, the officials were all elderly. The differences were thus not only philosophical but were also situational, organizational, professional, and generational.

Beyond these differences, the longer I worked at Lompoc the more I was impressed—and distressed—by the fact that some of the officials tended to see any difference as opposition, any diversity as danger; that they often responded intensely to more opposition than was externally there. You were wholly with them or wholly against them: "part of this institution" or "prejudiced against us."

Whatever the officials' commitment to rehabilitation, a psychiatrist was still necessary to interview the very obvious volume of study cases and to deal with the less obvious but even more pressing volume of mental illness among the resident inmate population. By far the most common theme I heard from prisoners and guards was their fascination with insanity and their fear of it. It was a rare inmate who didn't ask early in an interview with me whether he was going crazy. It was not always an inappropriate question. Many people come to prison severely disturbed, and the stress of prison life maximizes the chances for initial or further psychotic deterioration. The fear of psychosis—and sometimes just plain fear—brought to treatment many men who might not have sought it otherwise, and it held together many psychotherapeutic groups in the most immediate kind of self-defense.

The fear of the effects of prison life and the guilt for their part in it aroused intense anxiety in the prison staff at all levels. The daily presence of a psychiatrist was a physical reminder that there was a need for one, but the occasional absence of a psychiatrist aroused a deeper fear among the staff: that they might be vulnerable to prisoners animated by forces that only a psychiatrist could control. Although there was no complaint about my work, there was intense concern, particularly among the guards, about my presence. And even though I was in the prison every day and on call every night, many staff members were upset if I did not adhere exactly to the same time schedule of arrival and departure as they. It was as if, magically, I had to be omnipresent as well as omniscient, to be as limited as they by rigid time schedules and thinking, to be equally incarcerated, to have neither the fact nor the appearance of distinctiveness or freedom, to be wholly with them lest I turn out to be "prejudiced against them." I had to be physically as well as functionally "part of this institution."

Between the superficial support for treatment and the deep fear of psychotic chaos lay the middle ground of ambivalent resentment, which had the effect of making it very difficult for a prisoner to actually get to the psychiatrist even when he wanted to go. Prisoners' time with the psychiatrist was seen by many guards and supervisors as an evasion of custody or work: even the written form used to request an interview was called a cop-out. Many guards and prisoners shared the assumption that one saw a psychiatrist only for psychosis, that to actually go to his office meant impending insanity. Consequently, many men didn't come to the clinic until their fears—or those of the guards—reached that point. Moreover, to see the psychiatrist often required great courage, for to do so meant a public admission of weakness. Many prisoners would have scorned the elaborate protection of patients' privacy undertaken in private psychiatric practice, but no such protection at all existed inside the prison. The list of my appointments was circulated routinely to every office and cell block, and to appear on it meant embarrassment and shame, a forfeiture of the identity of a "right guy," a strong prisoner, for that of a "ding-a-ling lame," a mental case.

When the officials felt that a prisoner could not be handled by the usual institutional means of compartmentalization or extrusion, such as transfer to The Hole or to another prison, I was sometimes asked to see if there was "a psychiatric dimension." One administrative answer to a problem with psychiatric dimensions was transfer of the inmate to a prison-hospital in the Ozarks (the Medical Center for Federal Prisoners, Springfield, Missouri), which is operated as a backup facility to the psychiatric services in the various Federal prisons. Medical and surgical care is provided there as well, but the principal function of this institution is the tighter custody and greater pharmacologic control of men who cannot be contained in other prisons. Although the doctors there perform a worthwhile service in their evaluations for the courts, the lack of staff and the necessity of the doctors' frequent travel to court means that the men who are incarcerated in this prison-hospital usually receive less direct attention than that provided in smaller institutions. The existence of this even more isolated place—and the rumors about it—struck fear into many men, and some guards would threaten them with, "If you see the psychiatrist he'll send you straight to Springfield." Having seen Springfield myself on a visit, I was unwilling to send any but the most extremely uncontrollable person there.

There was continual pressure, particularly from the guards, to transfer prisoners to Springfield. Though many inmates were very irritating, few were so vicious or assaultive that they required the maximal physical restraint and literally stunning doses of tranquilizers that Springfield provided. Yet such was the legend that it was necessary for me to tell every person, when we met for the first time, that I was not about to send him on a trip to the Ozarks.

The officials were quite happy as long as I kept up a steady flow of study case reports, for which they did not request more than a diagnostic statement in the way of information. But one official was particularly angry that he had no access to what I heard from prisoners in treatment. That was the only information over which he had no control. Confidentiality is mandatory for any kind of psychotherapy, and that is triply true in prison. (It would also be naïve to expect confidentiality to succeed in prison. The files in the hospital office were regularly rifled or broken into, and copies of my dictation and that of other doctors were made surreptitiously and circulated widely. As a result, I dictated very little and very vaguely.) The attitude I adopted seemed to me to be the only workable one: that I would divulge information only if some third person would be harmed by my withholding it. The officials didn't like this attitude and many of the inmates didn't believe it. It would be naïve to expect candor without the promise of confidentiality, but even with this promise, genuine treatment was balked by the facts of prison life.

Far more frustrating than the organized difficulties undermining treatment was the psychic distortion which imprisonment evokes. It seemed that I was required not only to *be* fully identified with one group, either staff or inmates, but to *appear* to be fully identified with it. If I was not felt to be absolutely and totally a member of that group and the unquestioning acceptor of all its assumptions and stereotypes, I was seen not only as its opponent but as its devil. To the extent that I was not entirely a prisoner, I could appear to prisoners as an agent of the staff, as an expert interrogator, and as a perpetrator of brainwashing. To the extent that I was not fully identified with the officials, I could seem to them to be lifting the lid on all sorts of demons and to be using confidential information "to build an independent power base"—in the words of one official. Both staff and prisoners attributed to me awesome skills and magical powers, and both groups seemed to resent that I stood for and sometimes made contact with what the staff most feared and tried to ignore, with what prisoners most prized and tried to maintain, with what prison does most to efface: the inner lives of men.

Those inner lives were sufficiently troubling to so many prisoners who came to the clinic despite the deterrent tactics of both the staff and the other prisoners that the pressure of need and numbers made group work a necessity. The prison psychologist and I each started several groups. The general doctors and one of the dentists, out of their interest and concern, also started one group each, under my supervision. We met in our own group weekly, first to talk over our patients but later to discuss how we were doing and how we were feeling. We found it increasingly difficult to follow a humane profession in an inhuman place. Our work with our patients was difficult enough but we soon realized that we and they were doubly frustrated by the prison organization. Although the prison called itself rehabilitative, its custodial obsessions undermined treatment at every turn. What minor gains we perceived in the groups was soon eroded by prison life. It never ceased to amaze us that more people did not become more dehumanized. We were impressed with the resolve, however wavering, of many of the men we saw to make the constant effort to keep themselves together and to somehow get themselves through this period of their lives. We were certain that, if we had been in their position, we would not have done as well.

Indeed, there were times when we wondered if we weren't in the same position already. It is doubtful whether anyone can work in prison for any length of time and not feel that he too is incarcerated. This feeling need not stem from a pre-existing idea such as "life is a prison anyway," or from a tendency to identify excessively with prisoners. In my own case I was told that I was in prison long before I was ready to believe it. In my first week at

Lompoc, I was waiting in line to use the hospital's only outside telephone line, which was located on the desk of the medical director. I was muttering quietly to myself about the inconvenience and lack of privacy when I was interrupted and roundly lectured on a number of prison affairs by one of the medics; he concluded by saying that we were lucky to have an outside telephone at all, that it was a privilege which could be summarily withdrawn, and that I had better not forget that "you're in prison now."

From ten paces away, the tan Public Health Service uniform was identical with that of the prisoners. One doctor, taking a short cut home through the rear field and not wearing his officer's cap, was nearly shot when the tower guard mistook him for an escaping prisoner. Soon after this, the entire medical staff grew mustaches, sideburns, or beards. We thought it was for the fun of it, but it also relieved our anxiety. Moreover, it helped to distinguish us from the prisoners (they were forbidden facial hair lest it be used as a disguise in an escape), who seemed so much like us already, and from the guards, whom we did not wish to resemble. Though well within PHS regulations, this dangerous break in conformity, this daring statement of individuality, bothered the prison officials; one of them complained to Washington that the psychiatrist had "influenced" the other doctors to carry out this hirsutism.

Although we had tried to distinguish ourselves physically from the prisoners, it was impossible not to sympathize with them. Given the meanness and hypocrisy of the prison staff, it was difficult even to be coolly formal, much less to accept ethically what seemed to be their expectations of us: keep these men well enough for torture. Alternatively, it was difficult to remain forbearing when faced with so many prisoners who could be whining, demanding, perverse, and threatening. It was tempting to deal with our conflicting feelings by the extreme measures of denigration or whitewash: condemning them as inferior or idealizing and patronizing them as either helpless victims or picaresque heroes. The existence of a middle ground seemed doubtful, and its maintenance, if that were possible, questionable; it was a comfort to become judgmental and a burden to remain judicious. It was as tempting to us as it was to everyone else in prison to deal with anxiety by deep partitioning; to compartmentalize our feelings, thoughts, and perceptions; to discriminate arbitrarily rather than to distinguish carefully.

Nevertheless, the only course seemed to be for us to concentrate upon those qualities of our own which would help us through prison, and to try to ally with those in our patients which would do the same for them. The problem was that we were feeling as helpless, as persecuted, and as unjustly treated as everyone else.

Even worse than the helplessness, persecution, and injustice was the realization that the emotional and intellectual constriction which incarceration imposes was beginning to affect us. Like everyone else, we were becoming, literally, unfeeling. It became harder to laugh, harder to think, and harder to heal. Anger came more quickly, only to yield more quickly to fatigue. Simple things took unusual planning and concentration. Going home at night seemed slight advantage over going to a cell, and sleep no easier. It was a struggle to maintain the subtlety of thought and the suppleness of response necessary not to give up. We had to exert ourselves to keep alive the acuity and the compassion to be of value to anyone, to remain open to the people who sought our help, when that meant being open to the mind-splitting and heart-rending conflict in the situation. How could we be of value in a human relationship, use it therapeutically, when human relationships, in any usual sense, were against the rules *and* the code?

"The reading never got done" because we were too numbed to do it. As we settled into the routine, the routine became most important. Beyond mere routinization, we slowly lost the capacity to think critically, to distinguish carefully, to consider our work in any context wider than the purely utilitarian relief of pain. We lost interest in the scientific literature of our respective fields, we felt no impulse to read seriously, and as our thought became more concretized we were less able to grasp what we did read and relate it to our own experience. And as we lost interest in reading, we also lost our attachments to professional concerns beyond the prison and, more gradually, to a world beyond the town.

It was not just the volume or the difficulty of our work that was getting us down. On the contrary, we were learning how to work well in prison: we were learning not to care. We began to see the attraction in the preoccupation with regulations, the mindless processing of cases, the blindness to Hippocratic tenets which is the life of some doctors who spend their careers in prison. It was tempting to ignore what was happening around us and to us; to adopt, like everyone else, the individual and social defenses of "getting with the program": to convert a partial aspect of our work and of our selves to a sole concern; to diagnose and to prescribe and to dispense with further considerations; to take refuge in narrow professionalism, or worse, careerism, perhaps to grind out a series of papers on interesting syndromes for the right medical journals; to concentrate exclusively on matters of technique; and above all to emphasize clinical acuity and ignore ethical sensitivity.

The knowledge that our patients needed us—and we them—made this callous course difficult, but so did our clashes with the staff. After every trivial argument, after every puerile conflict between treatment and custody, we had to resolve again—harder—that they weren't going to wear us down. What kind of people were we becoming? Neither feeling deeply nor thinking hard, we were losing touch with ourselves, not only as doctors but as decent men. Could we meet these changes in ourselves as in our patients, learn about them, and find, perhaps, corresponding truths?

8

Why Resisters?

ALTHOUGH we on the medical staff were at Lompoc for accepting the draft, a number of men were there for refusing it. In my ordinary errands around the prison I had met a few draft resisters working as clerks or typists, and their efforts to stay alive while living in prison impressed me. I often wondered to myself how they had chosen to come to prison, how they responded to it, how it responded to them. What, I asked myself, is custody like for someone who is certain he has done nothing wrong? What was there about the draft resisters that provoked anxiety in other prisoners and the guards? Once they had made their decision and gone to prison, what were the psychological consequences? Were their ideals enough to get them through prison? What happened *after* conviction? Could a resister resist prison?

From my own experience and from my work with other prisoners, it was becoming apparent that ordinary ethical behavior was incompatible with life in prison. I suspected that the resisters' lack of criminal behavior and the predominance of their ethical sensitivity would be a hindrance to their survival in prison, but I hoped that I would be proved wrong. In more imaginative moments, I thought of the resisters as occupying a middle position in a highly artificial spectrum between other prisoners and the doctors. That is, other prisoners were criminal and incarcerated, resisters were not criminal but were equally incarcerated, and we doctors were not criminal and still less incarcerated. Later I was to realize that such artificial distinctions were useless and that we were all caught up in a vicious environment, but at the time I thought that the resisters' experience in prison might illuminate what was happening to the rest of us. I suggested to the few resisters I knew that we meet in a group to talk about what prison life was like for them. They seemed interested and tried to get in touch with the other resisters in the prison population.

Since inmates were not classified by offense, there was no way of finding out who the resisters were except by word of mouth. They were housed in different cell blocks and they worked on different crews. The library, where some of them had met, was being closed and converted to a Material Resources Center, whatever that was; some of the books were being thrown away and others were distributed to the separate cell blocks. Although they were scattered anonymously throughout the prison population, resisters, because of their offense, were categorized by the officials as "not candidates for rehabilitation." (But they were still very much candidates for the draft. All other prisoners were exempt from the draft because of their felony convictions, but that was not true for resisters. All of them, after the expiration of their sentences, could be reclassified and sent subsequent induction notices.) This information did not get through to the guards, who still talked to them of rehabilitation, but it did upset several case workers, to whom each resister was a milestone of the outer limits of rehabilitation and a living reminder that prison was still for punishment and that they, the case workers, were doing the punishing. Although this classification had no effect on the resisters' job assignments, quarters, or daily routine, it debarred them from the few fringe benefits available to prisoners who were "candidates for rehabilitation." These benefits included college courses by mail, work release, and early release to halfway houses. Denied these benefits yet fully submerged in the prison population, resisters were to be ordinary prisoners with a vengeance.

If resisters were ordinary prisoners, the group in which we

met was, as far as I was concerned, to be as much as possible an ordinary group. Like all the other groups, this one would meet for the same period, two hours; with the same frequency, weekly; in the same place, my office; and under the same ground rules of confidentiality. Though the group's beginning was offhand, its organization was not underhanded; though unofficial, it was not secret; like other groups its meetings were announced weekly, its membership was published in the daily announcement of appointments with the psychiatrist, and its existence was as widely known as that of all other groups.

We met in my office on Thursdays at two. The room, the size of a cell, was paneled in scruffy plywood in a halfhearted attempt at soundproofing, and it was crowded with nondescript furniture from the prison workshops. Everything was brown: the paneled walls, the dark chair and sofa, the armchair, the battered wooden desk, the chipped plastic veneer of the coffee table, the painted bookcase, the uniforms we all wore. The only chromatic relief was the gray tape recorder I started bringing several months later, but even its tapes were brown. When the fog lifted, the fierce light glared through brown window bars. The office was neither comfortable nor colorful, and it was never quiet. Speech and silence were often obliterated by the shrilling of Air Force jets and always punctuated by the snickering of snotty crows.

However much I saw this group as similar to the others with which I met, I could not ignore the differences. At our first meeting I told the resisters what I felt: that going to prison was obviously more than important to them, that the struggle over the draft had been a deeply meaningful one, and that I had no wish to treat them as if draft resistance was itself a symptom of psychopathology. I said that I would make no charts, draw no diagrams, give no tests; that I would plot no curves or throw any. I tried to make clear that my goal in this group, as in others, was not to promote passive adaptation to prison but to try to discover, preserve, and strengthen those human qualities, vital and mortal, which would encourage survival with dignity, then and later.

As with the other groups, I hoped that this one would be

voluntary, confidential, and, if necessary, therapeutic; not only a series of interviews but a shared experience through time. The course of all our lives led through prison, with many differences in circumstance and attitude among us. We would explore our lives behind bars as we lived them, and I hoped to see, through a kind of interliving, through a kind of bifocal vision, if the experiences of the men in this group were parallel with those of others—inmates, employees, and doctors.

I spoke with the resisters of my interest in the problem of survival in prison—my own and that of the people I was supposed to help—and of my concern for what seemed to me the severe psychic distortions which that very survival required. I wondered aloud to them, as I had to myself, whether the ethical concerns which had brought them there would bring them through, and if they changed, how would they change? I felt that the challenges of prison life were at least as great as those which led up to their decisions and actions; that although the legal issues might have been settled in the courtroom, the psychological and moral issues might be approaching their crucial test; that though their trials were over, their time of trial was just beginning.

But my reservations and apprehension more than balanced my interest and concern. I thought the war tragic, the draft iniquitous, and the prison barbarous, and I said so; but I had, after all, protested little against the first, cooperated with the second, and there I was working in the third. I admired the resisters' courage for doing quietly and naturally what I doubted I could have done. I asked myself whether I had the right to impose on them, let alone the temerity to seek their cooperation and help. I could do nothing with these conflicts but discuss them, and I was more than relieved when some men answered encouragingly that my remarks were the first straight talk they had heard in prison.

Although the group began meeting, it was much slower in forming. The resisters were not men of great combining power; most had never done anything in groups. Few had belonged to any organizations; most had refused the draft as they had lived: as private people, acting alone and sometimes in isolation. There were problems of confidentiality and trust in every group, not only between the groups and me but also among the members of the groups themselves, and this problem was greater in this group than in others. Of course the resisters did not know me, but they did not know each other either, and I think I was the only member of the group who did not fear that someone else in the room was a government agent or a prison informer. I don't know how, except through exposure to each other, the resisters resolved their reservations among themselves, but I do know that I didn't like my own position in the group. However interested I was in them, I was still an employee, if not an agent, of the government they had opposed and which had them now in custody. If my situation did not seem moronic, it was at least oxymoronic: I was, after all, a government psychiatrist. Why should they trust me?

They didn't. They knew nothing of me personally, so they closely watched not only my behavior but my conduct. Back in the prison population, they quickly checked my reputation for decency and reliability with other prisoners and, significantly, with guards. Indeed, it was the negative confirmation from the guards which seemed to be the most important. Here is how one resister came to his own conclusion that I was reliable: "I think it was because we brought back different comments from the officers here, what they feel about you; and when we compared the comments they were all the same. They would say to me, 'Going to the nut-doctor, eh? He needs a session himself.' They all said things like that. If the hacks don't like you, you can't possibly be one of them. And it came from such obnoxious creatures that I had to review it myself. I felt you were OK anyway, but because the policeman that was on the gate was a racist and the officer in the truck out to the farm was stone-crazy—he just wanted to shoot people all the time—I guess I added three and three. Besides, you drive a foreign car. I immediately took that down because there aren't too many officers that drive a foreign car. Not Swedish ones, anyway."

So a group did begin to form. The wish and the need for one overcame the initial doubts. The group meeting offered a chance for privacy; an "escape from prison for two hours," if only to talk about prison. Equally important was the deeper longing to relieve the dispersion, isolation, and suspicion of prison life. But this movement toward trust and community was usually hesitant. With time, the fear that I might be a government agent or a prison interrogator subsided, but it did not disappear.

The theme of betrayal was rarely absent from conversation. Although most resisters had acted on their best instincts and in many ways in their best personal interests, few had not also wondered how much they were risking of themselves and their future. This inner concern had been intensified by accusations of cowardice or disloyalty from friends, lawyers, judges, prisoners, and guards. In prison, they were viewed as deviants by the deviants around them. I was asking to invade further what little privacy remained; for people already hounded, the statements or silences of an unknown psychiatrist could easily be taken as attempts to force them to betray their private selves, and particularly those qualities of which they might not be proud. Although the odium of the guards and my choice of automobile allayed some early suspicion, the consistency of my interest, attitudes, and conduct was continually scrutinized. Finally, though I did not always articulate them very clearly, my own needs for such a group were not entirely opaque.

The early meetings of the group were taken up with discussion of the attitudes toward the resisters of both prisoners and guards, and of the general idiocy of prison regulations. Like other prisoners, the resisters were rarely noticed as individuals, but when they were, their "beef" of draft refusal evoked additional comment, similar in content, from prisoners and guards:

"This guy I work with in the pot-and-pan room thinks that all people who refuse to go into the service should be lined up against a wall and shot. But the thing is, he has moral values. That is, he distinguishes between a crook and a thief, and between who you want shot and who you don't want shot. A thief is someone who takes something whether he needs it or not; a crook is someone who takes it from impersonal things like a savings and loan or a giant company that won't even notice it."

"Mr. X [a guard] thinks they should put all the resisters in a battalion in the service and have them run across mine fields and explode the mines."

"There was this old hardened criminal in a detention cell and we looked at each other for a while. So the guy said, 'What are you in here for?' I said, 'Refusing induction.' He said, 'I don't give a shit, but you'll find your average inmate has three kinds of dogs: a child molester, a rapist, and a draft dodger; and they lump 'em all together, you know, they lump 'em all together.' "

"Mr. Y [a guard] says that a lot of the hacks don't know if COs are worse than baby rapers or better than baby rapers, but they're just right in line, right at the bottom." (Mr. Y made the same observation while in the hospital corridor one day, and I took the opportunity to ask the connection between resisters and baby rapers. He immediately answered, straightforwardly and humorlessly, "Neither one is man enough to rape himself a woman.")

"Some guys wanted to kill me one night over in J Unit. They wanted to throw me off the third tier. They were Indians! They knew I was a conscientious objector, and when I told them I wasn't a Jehovah's Witness, I don't think they could understand; they thought I was a Communist. If I had been a JW, they said that'd have been all right, I'd just have been dumb, a stupid person. If I was something other, I was subversive. They tried to take me up to the third tier and I wouldn't go up. One guy shoved me and said, 'What if I hit you now?' And I thought if he hit me now I'd hit him back, so I told him. They asked me if I was scared and I said I was and that satisfied them. It shook me up; I can get very upset, my adrenalin gets going. I don't think I was really too scared, one of my bigger friends was standing fairly close to me. Turned out to be rather amusing, but it kind of shook me up."

Correspondence and visiting were subject to more than the usual petty harassment:

"This guy wrote me a letter saying he wanted to visit, and I went to the officer and applied for a visit. First I applied to get him put on my [regular] visiting list and that was denied; then I applied for a special-purpose visit and the officer told me that *I* couldn't apply and that the other guy had to write and give a specific date. I said, 'OK,' and then I applied for a special-purpose letter to write the guy to tell him to write to me, and the man said I couldn't write a special-purpose letter, the guy had to write to *him*."

The resisters' intelligence, so far as it was measured by the standard testing given on admission to prison, was far higher than the institutional norm. They depended greatly on the meager supply of books and they were deeply affected by the closing of the library. It was possible to have relatives or friends send in books, but the request had to be approved in advance and its propriety was judged by highly selective criteria:

"Mr. Z [an official in the education department] told me today that I couldn't have paperbacks, but that I could have hardbound books. A hardbound is either a reference book or an educational book, and a softbound book is fiction. That's *his* rule. I couldn't have a novel that was in a softbound book, but if I could find a compilation of them in an educational book, and educational book means hardbound book, then I could have them. So he says. I said, 'Now, well, hold it. Fiction is fiction, what's it got to do with the cover of the book?' After a while I couldn't think of anything to say to him. He said that if a teacher sent an official letter that I should read such-and-such books, then he'd see about it. I've been getting the runaround ever since I came here. He did say I could read any trade manual I wanted."

Equally important were the magazines and newspapers to which the resisters subscribed, but the policy of the prison officials toward publications can only be described as capricious. I could not comprehend any reason for the proscription of certain periodicals, but some of the excuses were ludicrous. For example, *Playboy* was forbidden, according to a prison employee, "because it would stimulate masturbation." *The Guardian*, which describes itself on its masthead as an "independent radical newsweekly," was allowed in, but *The New Republic*, which is not exactly radical, was forbidden. I could not resist asking the employee responsible for such decisions how this had come about. He said he had read neither publication; when I asked him whether he thought *The Guardian* was the British newspaper of the same name he answered, "We don't allow foreign material in here." When I asked how he had reached his decision, he answered, "Well, *The Guardian* sounds protective; *The New Republic*, now that sounds like they want to overthrow something."

However much they may have differed in background, offense, and intelligence, the resisters, like the rest of the inmates and staff, were living in isolation. They were separated from each other in the prison, from their families and homes, and were shut up in a concrete compound hidden even from a remote town in rural California. And the problem for these men of conscience in prison was the same as for everyone else: how to stay alive. Threatened by murder, rape, assault, and extortion, each had to preserve his physical integrity. Faced with homosexual pressure, sensory deprivation in The Hole, boredom, and loneliness, each had to preserve his psychological integrity. If sensory deprivation was a threat, moral deprivation was a fact of life. Vilified by guards and inmates, expected to act like a criminal, traitor, or coward, the resister found his primary task was the maintenance of his moral integrity.

PART TWO

Six Resisters,
Six Resistances

A Word of Introduction

MERE idealism is not sufficient to account for the resisters' presence or persistence in prison. Matters of conscience
were indeed primary, but their resistance to the draft and their
readiness to go to prison were reinforced by a special sense of their
own distinctiveness and worth and by their capacity for social
disengagement. Their attitudes and actions were part of their characters—their habitual ways of harmonizing their inner needs and
the demands of the external world—and those characters were
formed within their families and within wider social groups, and
were influenced by their times. These men made their decisions
quietly and privately, slowly and sorrowfully, reluctantly and—it
seems—inevitably. Even more important, they made them at a
critical time in their own lives and in the life of their country.
Called to prosecute what they believed to be an immoral war, they
chose instead to be prosecuted. Opposed to bearing arms and killing, they refused induction into a society which required them to
do both. Unwilling to accept the limitations of an officially defined
conscience, they sought to define themselves by exercising their
own.

The resisters were as diverse as a number of young men can be,
but they were similar in that they were all in prison for reasons of
conscience. As they varied personally, so did they differ in their

thoughts and feelings about the decision and act of refusing induction. Many had been in deep and sometimes severe conflict over the decision, but for each the ethical aspects had been most important. Every one had agonized over the conflict between the demands of the draft and his own need and right to act in accord with his beliefs. Each wished to preserve active control of his life and to maintain consistency between his acts and his values. Going to prison was a personal, expressive act, and a statement of that consistency. The resisters went to prison not only at the behest of conscience but also to preserve their view of themselves as acting harmoniously with it; to retain that unity of what they believed and what they did which defined who they were.

For the sake of that integrity, they were to risk the dehumanization which is the fate of every prisoner, and the full weight of prison was all the more difficult for the anomalous circumstances of their incarceration. They would not destroy others but would chance destruction in custody. They would not corrupt themselves by violating their consciences but would risk corruption in prison. They would not be exploited by a "technostructure" but would face the daily exploitation of prison life. They would take the action of draft refusal but would endure the subsequent inactivation of imprisonment. Appalled by a government they felt to be monolithic and insensitive, they placed themselves, paradoxically, in the control of its most monolithic and insensitive agency. They had refused military service only to find themselves incarcerated in an institution which was not only surrounded by a military base but which was itself operated on paramilitary lines by a staff composed of men who had spent their adult lives in the armed forces.

Men of several faiths or none, the resisters were committed to various forms of secular humanism independent of traditional religious modes but requiring a basic commitment to principles of nonviolence and, in some instances, absolute pacifism. A few had applied for conscientious-objector status and had been refused; two had been exempted from the draft on conscientious grounds but later gave up the exemption, feeling that the government did not have the right to determine the validity of conscience. The rest had simply refused. Their manner of resistance varied from not taking the step forward at the swearing-in ceremony, to not reporting for the induction physical, to returning or burning their draft cards. None had participated in violence in connection with his resistance. Though their resistance was political in the sense that it involved them with the government ("My draft card was the first notice the government took of me," one man said, "and that was the first notice I took of the government"), the majority of these men had little interest in foreign policy, questions of national interest, or ideology. Five of the seventeen in this group were concerned with ideological matters, and the same five were the only ones who belonged to any kind of political organization.

However important were the issues of conscience, however primary was their abhorrence of war in principle and of violence in practice, many resisters also refused conscription because they didn't like being pushed around. They saw the draft not only as the agency of an immoral war but as coercive in itself, as too great an intrusion into their personal lives, too much of an interference with their sense of their own distinctiveness, too extensive an encroachment upon their sense of their own worth. It was not just that they were opposed to the war on conscientious grounds but that they were opposed to the draft for the blind compliance it demanded, the anonymity it threatened, and the moral diminution it required. At the same time, their opposition was, for the most part, concentrated on the war and the draft; it was not directed against all law or the entire government. For the most part, theirs was not impetuous, adolescent, or pathologically indiscriminate "rebellion against authority" but carefully considered adult choice of the inner authority of character over compliance with authoritarian demands. If in their refusal they were saying, "Here I stand, I can do no other," they were also saying, and no less forcefully, "Don't tread on me."

On the path which brought them to Lompoc, some resisters ambled, others strode; some hesitated, others marched. One man, clear about his refusal to bear arms and unclear about nearly everything else, seemed to have wandered into prison; another, still less certain and riven by emotional and family conflict, appeared to have leaped into custody. But to many others, the choice of prison seemed (at least in retrospect) a natural one, both logically and psychologically. Indeed, for some resisters the question was not so much whether as whither. Some had considered exile, and a few actually had gone to Canada for a trial—or more correctly a pretrial—run. None could accept this solution; they all returned to go to court. In the deepest sense, exile was impossible for these men who loved their country and what they felt it should stand for. "It's just not in me to go away," one man said. "It's foreign to my nature," said another; he did not recognize his pun but he felt all too clearly the deep psychological truths it expressed.

What these men emphasized was that those psychological truths —and the acts which derived from them—were their own, the products of their particular growth and their unique response to the issues they faced. Although some felt that to go to Canada was to take evasive action, most did not feel superior for having acted out of psychic necessity. Indeed, most felt that other men with other perspectives could go into exile for healthy and respectable reasons—an opinion I shared. If the impossibility of exile is reiterated in the following pages, it is not to impugn those who have gone but to emphasize the psychic impossibility of that solution for the men who appear in this book.

These resisters could not leave the country, but they were not eager to go to prison, either. Their goal, as they stated it, was integrity, not incarceration. They sought a hearing for the voice of their consciences and a trial for their actions; they would face imprisonment, but they did not demand it. Most would have accepted an acquittal or a suspended sentence. The patterns of their character development, their deep attachment to their families and their values, made foreign exile impossible, but certain aspects of their characters made domestic exile to prison at least conceivable. They were a group of men for whom prison was unattractive but not, in some ways, unthinkable.

Though their conscientious objection to war and their refusal to be coerced by the draft had much to do with their resistance, the decision to go to *prison* arose in no small part from the capacity of many resisters for extended solitude. By choice or by chance, many had spent long periods of their lives alone or in a limited range of social engagement. More self-sufficient than reclusive or asocial, they were reluctant to admit more than a very few to their circle of intimacy. They saw imprisonment far more as isolation than as punishment. As a result, the prospect of that isolation was not as intimidating to them as it might have been to others: having made few attachments, they had few to break; having made deep attachments, they felt these would persist. In contemplating prison, it was not only that, having broken one law and respecting law in general, they felt they had to accept the consequences; it was also that the consequences themselves were psychologically appropriate. For if to refuse conscription had been to do the right thing, then to go to prison was the right thing to do.

Though they all shared some character traits—a predominance of conscience, a more generalized sense of specific distinctiveness and worth, a capacity for solitude—in varying degrees, the resisters were very different in appearance and in manner. They were pale and florid, swarthy and black; slender and stocky, athletic and sedentary. They were coolly rational and sublimely mystical, brutally frank and beguilingly fey. Some wore their consciences lightly, saying almost nonchalantly that coming to prison was merely a practical response to an unacceptable demand. Others were more conscience-ridden, concerned not only with their principles but with their way of holding them, infusing the slightest aspects of their lives with a moral density which transmuted acts into deeds, behavior into conduct. Many were laconic and diffident. Others were voluble and forceful, giving astonishing life to Oscar Wilde's epigram that "conscience makes egotists of us all."

The resisters' backgrounds were equally varied. They came from large cities and small towns, places whose names are known to most and those known only to their neighbors. Fifteen resisters were white, two were black. Their ages ranged from 20 to 27, their sentences from eighteen months to five years. In religious background, fifteen were Protestant, one was Jewish, another was Roman Catholic. Three were married, one was divorced, the rest were single. All had attended college and three had graduated; the colleges included Berkeley, Chapman, Los Angeles City, Occidental, Portland State, and Reed.

Most of the resisters had worked while in school. Their jobs had included farm labor, store clerking, and selling used cars. One man had worked in an electronics plant assembling components for the very missiles he could see, from the barred windows of his cell block, blasting off from the nearby air base. Some had known urban or rural poverty (one had known both) and racial or religious discrimination. One man had the special burden of inherited wealth and family tradition.

Twelve of the resisters came from intact families. The mothers of two were widows, the father of one was a widower, and two sets of parents had been divorced. The fathers were teachers, factory workers, engineers, city employees. Most of them were veterans of World War II or Korea. Two fathers had been conscientious objectors (as had one grandfather), but none had gone to prison. Most of the resisters' mothers worked; they were secretaries, clerks, nurses, social workers. The majority of the parents supported their sons' resistance, many with initial reluctance and continuing concern for their safety.

In the following pages, six men discuss themselves, their resistance to the draft, and their responses—if not their resistance—to imprisonment. Like other inmates, they were exposed to the essential anxieties aroused by incarceration: the fear of being overwhelmed by their own impulses and of being persecuted, by their persecutors and by themselves; and like other inmates they met those anxieties with the basic psychic responses to incarceration: inner partition and projection. Yet each man also brought to Lompoc his own way of responding to stress and of organizing his experience, and each met the challenges of imprisonment in a manner most consistent with his own character. Mark Henley responded by intellectualization; Nick Manos by losing himself through blending into the woodwork and finding himself through concentration on good workmanship; Ralph Lombardi by keeping his wit about him; Ben Post by sitting alone with his conscience; Wayne Foote by social activism; and Calvin Jones by experimenting with violence.

9

Mark Henley, 23

Youth Corrections Act, Six Months to Six Years

FROM his sandy hair to the collar of his tan uniform, Mark Henley's prison pallor was so advanced that when he leaned back in his beige chair he nearly disappeared. But Mark was rarely so relaxed and he was never colorless. He spent most of his time during group meetings and in our private talks leaning forward, listening intently, speaking forcefully, and clenching and unclenching his fists. Nor was there anything anemic about Mark's intellect, his scathing humor, his determined refusal of conscription, or his adamant insistence on his privacy.

Mark went west for his asthma and to Lompoc for his freedom. After several years of illness and anguish during his childhood, his parents moved from their native Midwest to ensure his survival in a healthier climate. Freed from the sickbed and the anxious night watches, he soon recovered completely. He began to breathe and to argue, to grow and to fight. As he discovered his temper, he became aware of his intelligence; both were considerable. Having endured the gasping breathlessness of asthma and the terrors of possible death before he could comprehend them, Mark grew up to be fiercely committed to living his own life—and a rational one. Having been confined to bed or chair, limited by illness and his parent's worries, he was acutely sensitive to restraint or limitation of his freedom, particularly his freedom to stand alone.

Like many other prisoners at Lompoc and like several other resisters, Mark was sentenced under the section of the Youth Corrections Act which imposes an indefinite sentence of six months to six years. Known to its recipients and their comforters as the "Zip Six," this sentence provides that one is eligible for parole after six months in custody and "any time" thereafter. It also provides that a felony conviction may be expunged after satisfactory completion of the balance of the sentence on parole. No one at Lompoc was known to have been paroled after six months, but everyone hoped to be the first; no one was known to have served the full term of six years, either, but many feared that they might be the first.

The Youth Act was intended to be a humane sentencing procedure, but in its execution it was just the opposite. As it was applied, the Youth Act first raised the hopes of prisoners that their good behavior could reduce their period of incarceration significantly—and then it dashed them. In granting further discretion to the prison staff in recommending parole, it ensured that any inmate who did not meet the staff's narrow standards of conformity could be kept in indefinitely prolonged custody. The combination of the cynical promise of early parole and the blatant threat of extended imprisonment aroused further anxiety in men already struggling with the psychic burdens of incarceration. Imposition of the Youth Act did not reduce "adverse behavior," nor did it promote rehabilitation: it only fostered sullen conformity. The disillusionment and bitterness of prisoners subject to the excruciating ambiguity of an indefinite sentence was intense; they envied the men with "straight numbers" (fixed sentences) who knew they could not be kept beyond a definite date.

Mark was one of the few resisters with a clear or coherent interest in politics. The apparent cohesion of Marxist theory led Mark to its study and later to its advocacy; its social goals were important to him, but not so much as the certainty he saw in its world view. The demands of ideology provided stimulus to his growing intelligence and organization to the emotional complexities of his adolescence. Mark's refusal to take the induction physical, however, had less to do with ideology than with his personal insistence on privacy, independence, and responsibility. He was opposed to the war, but he was even more opposed to the draft. He saw the demands of the government, through conscription, as far too great a claim on his personal and conscientious liberty, too great an encroachment by an implacable outside force—"a juggernaut," in his words—into what he regarded as an inviolate area. Rather than yield to such a force, he felt he had to exert control over his life by refusing induction, even if that meant going to Lompoc. A prison term, though unwelcome to him and unsettling to his parents, seemed the only responsible course.

Mark's intellect did not desert him in prison. For several months, he remained only dimly aware of what was happening to him while he studied the prison life around him and, as he said, "observed the local folkways." It was common for new inmates, or "fish," to stand off from prison life, even to study it as a phenomenon unrelated to themselves, and Mark was one of the most thoroughgoing and successful of such anthropologists. He was acute and facile, and he helped turn many resister group meetings into seminars and the rest of us into his research colleagues. But as his sentence crawled on, as he was absorbed into prison and as he absorbed it, his face and hopes became paler, his fingernails and mood more hard-bitten. "I can see how tight I am just from my fingernail index, and now it's at its lowest point in the entire time here. I've gotten down to the quick. That means *I'm* at the lowest point, too. There's a definite correlation. I can graph it: so many millimeters of fingernail, so many months of pain."

The less he was an anthropologist and the more he experienced of prison, Mark felt the parallel between the stringent prison life and the rigidity of a life devoted to pure ideology. At Lompoc he was forced to contemplate a rigidity more intransigent than his own, and to question the ethical aspects of both. The practical need for day-to-day survival in prison brought him to an uncomfortable confrontation with the limitations of a life subject to one particular and exclusive logic:

"In one way, I think I've become a little more human here. I used to believe in a philosophy that might be called Marxism. I still think it's a good basis for social analysis, but it was like having given up on religion I searched for another god. Another icon to worship. I gravitated towards Marxism because that was an acceptable substitution. When you're 18, it's easy to get involved in a cause. Probably the best soldiers are, I imagine, in their late teens, because they can be successfully indoctrinated and are unstable enough, don't have enough experience, so they can't counter the indoctrination rationally. They'll go for any banner that's presented to them and do whatever you want. 'Get 'em young, you got 'em.' *I* was never recruited; I always joined. Eagerly. Usually I was the most outspoken person involved. I couldn't join *anything* now, not as a true believer. I'm more rational about it and not dogmatic. I'm dogmatic to a great extent, let's face it, but I think I'm more aware of my dogmatism and can hold it in check. I can say to myself, 'You're being dogmatic, you really aren't rational,' and I can backtrack somewhat.

"I've seen too much brutality in this prison. It's not so much physical as it is mental brutality. Now, if a revolution were in the offing, I'd choose sides reluctantly and if I shouldered a weapon it would be reluctantly. It would be something thrust upon me, not something that I would welcome. If there was a violent upheaval in this country—or even a nonviolent one, in which case there'd still be great changes, great deprivation—there'd be a lot of suffering. Physical and mental suffering. I've seen too many people here in prison become disheartened, become brutal, become afraid, or become bold as a compensation. I've seen too many people change adversely to want to see it happen in a whole country, have two hundred million people going through that kind of change. Just living *here* you see what happens to people when they're oppressed. It's not a pretty sight; it's a waste of people, a waste of life.

"I think a revolution would impose a prison regime like this one on everybody. That's what I'd be afraid of, exactly. Before I saw what prison was like I could easily talk about the dictatorship of the proletariat, a temporary austere regime with a relaxing to follow. I can't be so glib now. It's just too . . . too awful to do glibly. If it ever comes to the point where things are so polarized that the

Left has to fight for it, I'll probably choose fighting with the Left, but I can't say I'd do so gladly because I don't like to see the suffering that would be caused. After it was over I'd be afraid there'd be a very harsh regime. The thing that haunts me is Stalin. I can't get him out of my mind. Any revolution on the Left is Stalin coming forward. The purges and all that went on in Russia should make one wary."

By the time we talked together, Mark was beginning to realize that the brutality he observed had also come to him:

"I don't think I defended myself from becoming brutal and in-sensitive very well. I remember we brought this up in the group one day. If someone were standing ahead of me in chow line, I wouldn't see it, you know, if a dead body fell in front of me. I'd walk over it and get my tray and go through the line. By the stand-ards of outside the prison, that's, that's an abomination! But that's what I would do in here. So in that sense I've adopted the rules of the prison completely.

"And my usage of language! I've adopted the prison language to a great extent. It came out subconsciously. I was walking around in the yard and I used a joint [prison] word that I didn't mean to use. It just came out. I'd never heard the word used that way on the streets. It was 'righteous.' It just came right out! I was thinking that some guy was really a righteous dude. I was thinking of him, describing him to myself, as an inmate would. And I realized then that I was really in prison.

"I learned to ignore responsibility as well as to not notice or report violence. I think you become, you become callous. You get some of these people coming in here with these six-year Youth Acts, a great majority of them anyway, and I feel, 'Big deal, six years, so what?' A really callous attitude. You tell someone, 'Don't worry, you'll make parole, even if it's eight months ahead.' It's pretty callous when you can tell a person 'Don't worry, it's only eight months or a year,' because that's a percentage of their life gone.

"I think you do that as a defense, because you're getting the same thing, you're getting so much time yourself. And if his time that he has to do is bad, your time is bad, so you tell him, 'Don't worry about that time, that time goes by like nothing, it's easy to do.' If *he* does bad time, then *you* do bad time. You don't like to hear somebody complaining about his time. If there's such a thing as manners in prison, it's a display of very bad manners to say, 'Well, they gave me a year set-off [deferral of parole consideration].' There was a guy in the office where I work to whom they gave a year's set-off and he was moaning and groaning and whining and everybody got really disgusted with him because it's gross bad manners, that's what it is, to complain about time like that. It's gauche, I guess that's the word.

"I was sitting in my house [cell] wondering if, let's say, they [the Board of Parole] gave me a flat denial. I'm pretty sure of getting a [parole] date now, but at the same time you can never tell because it isn't all logical and it isn't all rational, and there is a possibility of getting turned down—it's not probable but it's possible—and I was thinking, 'Now, I've got almost two years in, and it's gone very fast, and I *could* do up to four years.' When I first got here, the thought of four years was appalling. I can remember this guy who went home after doing twenty-one months and I was thinking, 'Twenty-one months, God, that's a terrible amount of time; I don't think I could ever do that amount!' I had twenty-one months in awhile back and it wasn't anything. So I've become more callous to myself, too. And not aware of mental brutality.

"Another two years here would be doubling the measure, but perhaps it wouldn't actually be a double. It might take six or eight months to lose a lot of your sensitivity. What I mean is, your first six or eight months here, when you learn to think like a convict, you become a little bit more brutal, a little bit more callous, less sensitive, less susceptible to kindness; less likely to give, to be kind to another person. After that no really big changes occur. After that amount of time there are none of these really big drastic changes that make the difference between a really free person and an incarcerated person. After that the foundation has been built.

It's like a pyramid and the first half is done after that. The wall's been built.

"It's funny but I don't remember much of what's happened here. I can remember so much, looking back, and remember things that happened when I was younger, and yet things that happened in here a year ago are really hard to recall. I had a tremendous temper when I was younger, but I seldom experience bad temper any more. When I don't feel well is the only time I can become enraged. As soon as I got into high school all that just disappeared, so I don't have much of a temper any more. I'll get angry and argue, but it's very superficial. I mean when I'm really irrationally angry, just furious, where I really just want to knock someone's teeth down their throat, that happens so seldom any more, and any time it happens I'm rational enough to say, 'Hey wait a second, that's a stupid way to settle things.' "

Many of Mark's pre-adolescent fights had erupted when he felt he was being interfered with or unduly restrained, when the narrow terrain of his hard-won sense of inner autonomy was being challenged, when he felt threatened by an intolerable dependency which might place him at the mercy of others and their possible abandonment of him, or when that dependency might render him vulnerable to the full force of his aggression in all its frightening intensity. Fighting was both an involvement with others and an effort to keep them at a distance, an expression of anger and an externalization of it. As Mark grew older, the aggression and fear of abandonment which had characterized his childhood were gradually modified by maturing sexuality and social involvement. Much of his energies were absorbed into and expressed by a stringent conscience, a highly prized intellectual life, a devastatingly ironic sense of humor, a scrupulous rationality which often congealed into dogmatism, and a range of interpersonal attitudes which often seemed exquisitely calibrated to precisely the proper degree of detachment.

"I know how to socialize very well, but I really don't like it too much. I'd rather be by myself. I guess it's because of all the years I *spent* by myself that I really prefer not having people around. Maybe because I didn't have people around, or couldn't have them around, or 'What you can't have you don't want anyway' —maybe that was my attitude. I can remember many times friends calling up and saying, 'There's a party, do you want to go?' and I'd be reading and I'd say, 'No, I'd rather read a book.' Some other friends didn't like it, didn't know if I was snobbish or just weird. That's the way I am to this day; I'd just rather not be with people. I dated a lot but then it was just one other person. I was the first one in my group to date and to go steady, but I wasn't terribly emotional. If someone was standing you up or something like that, it wasn't the end of the world; I was serious yet I wasn't involved.

"I've often wondered, in any kind of relationship, if something should happen to break that relationship, what would happen to me. I mean if the person died, what might be my reaction to it? To me that's sort of the test of something beyond an acquaintance-ship. If anyone I know, including my family, were to die, I don't know how broken up I'd be over it. It's like I've purposely built perfect barriers around myself (and now it's a matter of breaking them down myself) because I, I don't want anybody to be close to me. Just up to a point and no further. And this doesn't seem quite right. I have friends, but I only go so far. I would say there are very few people I've ever admitted beyond a certain point. I've always locked them out. And locked myself in. Superficially we can be very good friends, but beyond that point you might consider it off limits. I don't want to know them beyond a certain point, and I don't want them to know me beyond a certain point.

"I don't even know what I'm afraid of, because obviously I'm afraid of something. I guess it's because if the walls were down I could be harmed by people, either by their removal or their change, or their reacting to some changes of mine. I've often gone back and tried to understand, how can I be harmed by people being close to me? Why am I so great that I wouldn't want anybody close to me? I think of small things but nothing really great except the fact that I was sick for quite a while and didn't have, or couldn't have, anybody around. Maybe that's it, maybe I started building it up then. I was sick for a couple of years, but I rarely went to the hospital because the pediatrician didn't believe in putting children in hospitals unless they were absolutely in a life-and-death situation. Instead of that, either my mother or my father would take shifts sitting next to my bed when I was asleep to watch my breathing. They left the light on to see if I showed signs of lack of oxygen and that sort of thing."

Rather than in the hospital, the life-and-death situation seems to have been set up in Mark's bedroom, and eventually in Mark. His early childhood was one long life-and-death situation rather than the usual pattern of attachment and gradual separation. Mark's first and most basic experience of intimacy and dependency, his childhood, was permeated with anxiety and the fear of abandonment and death. Almost from the beginning, his relations with others were felt to be precarious, and the strength of this early perception led him in later years to concentrate his energies upon his inner life, to stand apart from others, to be serious about others yet remain uninvolved.

But the fact of Mark's childhood illness is less important than its effect on his adult psychic life. However much he "outgrew" his asthma, he did not entirely transcend his childhood, so that even though he was pained by his adult detachment, there persisted a preference for inner realities over external ones, an overvaluation of intellect, an underlying fear of abandonment (and therefore of involvement), and, most important, an unconscious equation of intimacy with death.

Mark's capacity for isolation prepared him for imprisonment, but he had had his doubts about his courage for a long time prior to taking the final step of draft refusal. A distant relative of Mark's had gone to Lompoc for draft refusal several years before, and Mark had visited him in prison and talked with him extensively before making his own decision:

"I knew what it looked like here and I knew basically what went on, so I wasn't too surprised. I interrogated him, that's what it came down to, you know, for many, many hours. We talked a lot about the language (that was the thing that fascinated me), and how you were treated, whether there was violence on the part of the hacks, whether they beat you up in The Hole. I didn't think of psychological violence. It was evident just by observing him that he was very uptight about the whole thing, and for a long time afterward, but it's the type of thing you don't know about until you've been through it. I don't think I could sit down now and explain it. You can easily describe someone getting beat and thrown into a cell, but how do you describe anguish?

"I felt he did the right thing, and yet I didn't know whether *I* could do it. Whether I could do the right thing as a moral issue. I knew it was right, yet I didn't know whether I'd just go to pieces in prison, I didn't know whether I was that strong. I agreed that he was right in what he did. He knew I felt it was so, and if I didn't do it, it would be the type of thing where he and I both knew I took a cop-out. After he got out, he made it very plain that he could understand if I decided not to go to prison. After being here awhile, he could say, 'Prison? Are you nuts?' It was then that I realized there could be a legitimate *choice* for me and I felt, 'Good, it's strictly up to me. It's on *my* shoulders.'

"I was very depressed just after I refused the draft. It was just after I'd been released on my own recognizance in the custody of my parents, and I couldn't ever cooperate with the draft, and I couldn't take the physical, and yet the thought of going to prison! There was the choice of going to Canada and I knew I couldn't do that. I was so depressed over the whole thing I sat for many hours thinking, considering the alternatives.

"Well, finally, it was common sense coming to the aid of stubbornness; because I get very stubborn when I'm pushed, and feel, 'God damn it, you *won't* make me do this, you *won't* make me leave the country, you're *not* going to force this on me!' I was just holding my ground and saying no. Because when I feel I'm right, I get pretty damn stubborn. Canada is just as much a compromise as Selective Service. My reason is purely pragmatic. After a while, how much of a life do you allow them to take away? I have friends here, I have relatives here, my interests are here, this is where things are easiest to do whatever I want to do. But if they're going to demand that I can't even do what I want to do for years and years, then the time has come when you say, 'Maybe I'd better go somewhere else (to prison) for a while, or be partially functional for a while, rather than be out and be completely afunctional.' "

Mark's preference for seclusion and self-sufficiency made the contemplation of prison possible, just as his stubbornness and patriotism made forced exile unthinkable. However much he might protest that his decision was essentially a practical one, it was the inner necessity of conscience which brought him to the point of action. He preferred to be "partially functional" in prison for exercising his conscience to being "completely afunctional" in freedom for compromising it. What would have made him "afunctional" was the inner criticism he would have felt, the tension between conscience and self which would have prevailed if he had compromised. Still, he could not finally act until he was sure that he was in control of his decision, that the choice was up to him. As long as he felt subject to his relative's judgment he was not free to act; he could do so only when he could truly *exercise* his conscience and actively choose what was necessary. It was this inner sense of active choice, the cohesion between conscience and self, that made his decision feel so natural and seem as clear, in the end, as common sense:

"As I've gotten older I've liked fewer and fewer restraints, and wanted no one to tell me what to do and what not to do. I become easily irritated if someone says, 'You shouldn't do that,' the idea that they're telling me instead of advising me. The only times recently that I've ever become angry, really furious, is when someone has told me what to do. I like to ask for someone's advice, that's something else, but I don't like anybody to have the arrogance to assume the responsibility of interfering with my actions. I'm responsible, and solely responsible, for my actions. I blame no one for anything I do and I credit no one for anything I do. I mean, I sink or swim on my own. It's still my responsibility for the things I do.

"I think the thing that bothers me most is how this place fosters a *lack* of responsibility. People get to the point where they will blame everyone else but themselves. The best example I can think of is the word 'violated.' People here never violate parole, they're always violated. Every guy that comes in the gate says, 'I was violated.' He says it wasn't his fault, he didn't do anything, he was violated. That struck me; that irresponsible attitude sums up the attitude of the people here. I think maybe a lot of them came here in the first place because they weren't responsible. I think this place just worsens it."

Mark's fiercely independent stand didn't seem to coincide with his two years of cooperative residence in complete custody of the government. The prospect of such a situation of forced compliance may well have contributed to Mark's depression between his trial and his incarceration, but how was he made into a cooperative convict?

"I think I worked that out a lot when I was still the anthropologist. In other words, being told what to do was just a curious act that the natives went through and I followed it, not wanting to upset the routine. By the time I ceased being an anthropologist and became an inmate, I was so used to being told what to do that there was no big conflict. Any contradiction between my not wanting to be told and being told didn't occur, as I said, because by the time I was ready to be an inmate I was *already* an inmate. My resentment at being told what to do? I was already so used to it that it wasn't slapping me in the face. Most of the resisters in here haven't refused anything. Once they have been locked up they go along with it. When I first came, I resisted quite a bit, it was all part of the game. But then it wasn't real, the idea of spending maybe six years here hadn't yet hit me. And then later on it hit me."

Until he went before the Parole Board, Mark, like many prisoners, could almost ignore the reality of his incarceration. He could see his first six months as an intellectual endeavor or a tactical exercise. He remained remote from his own experience, yet was a spectator and then a student of the suffering of others. He could partition himself between the anthropologist and the inmate, the one identity fully occupying his awareness, the other completely unconscious. Since Mark had been eligible for parole after six months and because his behavior had been good, he believed that he might actually be released then, and the persistence of this belief helped to deflect the harsh realities of his incarceration. Mark had been unwilling to compromise his beliefs but, like many resisters, he felt that he was still carrying out a kind of contract with the government: so much time in prison in return for his beliefs. The refusal of parole imposed a certainty, a finality on his imprisonment; it hit him with the profound shock that it was for real. He would not be released after the minimum amount of time no matter how good his behavior. No matter how scrupulous his anthropology, he was now a prisoner. "It seemed that resisting was over after I went to the Board for the first time. I had six months in when I went to the Board. I talked for twenty minutes to the parole judge, and then when I got my denial three weeks later, I really did hard time. A couple of weeks in there were the worst. A horribly hard time. Really, really bad. I didn't think about much of anything. I just sat. Stupefied. Tremendous, tremendous depression. I did a lot of sleeping. No dreaming, just sleeping."

After having lived inside, few resisters would directly advise a prospective resister to choose prison. Many felt it would be arrogant to influence what should be a personal and private decision. They also feared that they might become a party to another's subsequent brutalization; they were reluctant to become accessories to the correctional process. When we discussed this, Mark's fluent conversation stumbled to a stammer:

"Now that I'm here, I have the feeling that other guys do, that I couldn't say to a person, 'Yeah, go to prison, refuse, just tell them to shove the whole thing up their ass.' When I was at school and knew that I was going to refuse, I said, 'Yeah, that's the best thing to do, the most moral thing, blah blah.' I, I can never do that again. I can never be so glib as uh, as, say, 'Come here for two years.' And I think why, even though, even though I feel it's the right, the right policy, every time I'd say to a person (I've thought, I've thought of this many times, in my cell, about what, what I will say when I answer people), every time I say, 'Yeah, go to prison,' I see *myself* going to prison, I see myself *also* going, and saying, 'No, no, I don't want to go there again,' and uh, it's just, it's me right along with him, I can't divorce it, I can't set up a hypothetical situation.

"Well, that's it, I don't see myself going for the first time, I see myself going *again* and I can't separate it. I've thought about this many times and tried to separate it, but it's, I don't know why, I just, I can't get it off my mind. The first time is so long ago that it's, I just can't do it. I remember, and yet I know, intellectually, but I can't, I can't bring back the emotional feeling. It's uh, it's a type of thing like dead. It *is* dead. I've sort of become dead in here. I'm wondering, when I get out, how I'm going to be; I know I'm going to be, be a little odd for a while and uh, and uh, you know, take time to, to readjust."

Readjustment might well be difficult for Mark. The sentences just quoted were spoken in a desperate tone which expressed Mark's own perception of the disintegration of his ability to abstract and to feel deeply. In common with many other long-term prisoners, Mark had suffered significant impairment of thinking. He was unable to conceptualize another man's going to prison hypothetically; he could see it only as repeating his own arrival at Lompoc. This mental repetition was not experienced as a recapitulation of his incarceration but as a *subsequent* return to prison. Furthermore, the mental picture he was describing was devoid of emotional color. ("I can't bring back the emotional feeling.") His "petrifaction" had so disrupted his capacity for reflection and symbolization that he was unable to maintain continuity with his memories, thoughts, or feelings.

Or with his future. Although his release date was approaching, Mark was unable to joyfully anticipate leaving. He could drily contemplate the prospect of his departure, but it aroused scant excitement. In becoming "inured" to prison he had also become inured to his own capacity for enthusiasm. He had become detached from his inner, instinctual sources of vitality by the progressive numbness and rigidity of incarceration. The place didn't irritate him as much, didn't "get under his skin," because it had penetrated far more deeply. It had become a part of him and he a part of it. He knew now that there would be no escape from the effects of his sentence, that to leave the prison was not to leave the prison behind:

"I used to think about getting out, about getting released, and the idea just elated me. It was like 'Wow!' It was just like when you were a kid and you're out with your grandparents and you order a sundae and them being the grandparents, they order you the biggest one, whether you can eat it or not. It was just, just fantastically great. Whereas now I haven't thought about me walking out that gate for a long time. I mean I've thought of being released, but not with that sense of, I don't know, euphoria. If they had released me a long time ago, I'd have been overwhelmed, I'd have been so happy. Now, I want to be released, and I'll be very glad, but I won't walk out three feet above the ground. Back then I wasn't yet used to this place. Getting away from it would have been, you know, so tremendous. But now I'm used to it, I don't have to run from it quite as much.

"I'm still appalled occasionally at what I see here, but it's not the thing that I want to run away from as much as I did, say, even last summer. It isn't as awful as it was two summers ago, when it was just, it was terrible, because I hadn't become used to it. I saw things all the time that bothered me. Now I'm, I'm inured, I think is the word, inured to it all, so this place doesn't get under my skin so much. Going out will not be as big a relief. I think the difference when I leave now, it won't be so much an *escape* from here to go out there as it would have been eighteen months ago. Then there'd have been the double benefit of not just going out there, which is good enough, but also escaping from here, I mean from this place."

10

Nick Manos, 27

Eighteen Months

AFFABLE, dark, and tentative, Nick Manos was imprisoned at Lompoc for almost the same period as that in which the
group met. Blessed and cursed with the ability to appreciate many
sides of issues and people (including himself), he was often plagued
with indecision and uncertainty. Other resisters sometimes had difficulty in understanding Nick's attempts to "understand" the prison
staff; they felt that there was something unreasonable about his
being so reasonable; the more he talked about trying to get in touch
with guards and case workers, the less they felt in touch with him.
Because Nick could see two things at once in a world where it was
better to see only one, his position was complex and dangerous.
His compromises were often seen by others as appeasement, his
hope as naïveté. Through his eighteen months in prison, his smiling
geniality wore down to sighing discontent.

Nick was an only child, a Protestant of Portuguese descent who
grew up in a Pacific coast town which was predominantly Italian
and Roman Catholic. He was raised on a small ranch, hunting and
going to school while his parents worked. His early memories were
of loneliness, discipline, and hunting:

"I can remember going to a preschool kindergarten and the
yard they had with lots of toys. Even with all the kids there, some-

how or other I felt lonely. I can remember going in and laying on the cots where we took naps and feeling lonely.

"My father got to a point where he wouldn't spank me; I can remember only one spanking from him. He had a tremendous temper; I think that's one of the reasons he wouldn't discipline me. The only time he could was when he was really mad, and he didn't want to discipline me then because he was afraid he'd hurt me. I can remember one time, I guess I had been a little smart-alecky, and he was whaling me across the legs with a willow switch; I can remember rolling around trying to get out from under that switch. He cooled off and I got a little smarter, really, about the whole thing.

"My mother did most of the spanking. She had a rubber hose that was administered with enough force to teach me a healthy respect for it. Usually I was punished only after a long discussion and numerous warnings. There was a point where she'd say, 'Now this is it, if you go beyond here, that's it.' I learned pretty well what the limits were. If I didn't remember, she always kept her word, she always meant what she said.

"I spent a great deal of time hunting, mostly by myself. I had a couple of friends later on who I went hunting with. I got a BB gun when I was eight and a .22 when I was ten. Guns were always available (my parents hunted, too) and I was taught how to handle them. They didn't let me use the pistol and never taught me how to, and of course I was curious because they never let me use it. When I was 12 I had my tonsils out, and when I was convalescing I got up and got the pistol and started fiddling with it. I aimed it out the back window, pulled the trigger, and there was a big roar and a hole through the window. It could've been very dangerous. I looked at the gun, put it back into the holster, and went back to bed. My mother came in later and said only, 'Well, *you* know what you did.' That was worse punishment than being hit."

Both of Nick's parents worked long and hard to support them-selves and to give him the education they had not enjoyed. His father was a skilled mechanic but he sometimes stalked off jobs in a huff, to return later or to get another. His mother worked steadily in a local factory. "I've seen her come home from work with the skin worn off her fingers, bleeding from building packing boxes. I know a little about the pain of working to struggle up. She soaked her hands in alum to toughen them so she could work. You can't do the work with gloves on and the wood they make the boxes from is very rough and just wears the skin off your hands. She'd catch her fingers on things and they'd be bleeding, they hurt."

When Nick went to college, he moved for the first time in a wider, more congenial group; he began to recognize his own growth and to enjoy it. "I'd never felt any particular desire to be part of the usual groups I'd seen before I went to college. I did have a distinct sense of community there, it was the most fulfilling, productive period of my life. I worked harder then and did more than any other time. I sort of lost that when I went out and went to work. Instead of doing things, I was just buying things."

Nick also met his wife at college; she was to have a great effect in changing the emphasis of his life, not least in relation to the draft:

"She played a very intimate role in bringing me to the frame of mind that made it possible for me to refuse. By being a very sensitive person and increasing *my* sensitivity. It wasn't so much in terms of violence and pacifism, but more in terms of what life is, from an, oh, an artistic point of view. She was a distinct pull in combating the deadness of the work I was doing, even though I couldn't really define or explain what I was feeling about it. It wasn't giving me any satisfaction. I was making money and that was it. Her drive to live, to experience, made me realize the difference. I didn't actually tell her I was going to refuse, but she knew I was thinking about it; when I went to the induction center I told her I might be home quickly, but I really didn't finally decide until I got there.

"Refusing out there was like going to The Hole in here, like stepping off into the void. My mother understood it immediately, but my father couldn't quite understand. He went along with it, basically because he figured the war was a lot of bullshit, but I don't think I got it across to him that that wasn't all there was to it. War in itself is just painfully stupid. Maybe he did understand, I don't know, about seeing a picture of shot-up babies; I can't even express it or understand it completely myself. There's no way I can picture my life or my freedom depending on doing such things. I see children being killed innocently *because adults can't control themselves* and it infuriates me. All I can do is say that I'm not going to do things that way. If you have to build your life on the bones of dead babies, then your life isn't worth shit. That's exactly how I feel about it. If I have to die for that, then that's how it'll have to be."

Early in his stay at Lompoc, Nick was assigned to the pot-and-pan room. While working there, he saw one inmate threaten another, smaller man. When the first man swung, Nick went over to defend the smaller man and was knocked flat for his efforts. The guard sent all three of them to The Hole for fighting and Nick learned the first rule of the inmate code: "Do Your Own Time."

"You learn quickly not to involve yourself with anything here. One value of the group of resisters was the chance to realize that the others were going through many of the same problems you were facing, although it also showed there were various solutions, all the way from complete withdrawal to blending with the surroundings. I don't think anyone here agrees with the officials, but nonetheless you wear the tan clothes and you're part of the woodwork. I've tried occasionally to step out, but it's like batting your head against the wall, all you do is mess up your head.

"I don't think I could go as far as to spend all my time in The Hole or be as bitter as some people; I've tried to keep some positive attitude to the people that work here. I try to tell myself that behind the gray façade of most of the guards there's still a little bit of human being somewhere, try to clear away the gray and find that little bit, set up some sort of relationship. It isn't easy. I think I've done really well with my boss, to the point where he admits in front of the whole work crew that the war stinks and we ought to get out. I couldn't ask him to treat me any better.

"But he's only one; it's hard to tell about the others. The atmosphere of prison remains around you. There's the continuous roar, and when it slows down you become aware of the lights. The two or three times when all the lights have gone out have been just marvelous, ten of the prettiest seconds I've seen here. Just dark and quiet. The worst thing, though, of being here is being completely helpless, unable to control your own life. That's the most frustrating thing of doing time: no control. So against that you really have to build up your self-control, against all the threats and the lack of initiative. I think I might cry on the bus when I get out of here, cry all the way to San Francisco. When I get there, I'll *really* start crying, just out of the intensity."

It was not only the immediate relief of leaving prison and returning home which would lead Nick to cry on the bus; it was also his sudden freedom to have feelings at all, to release emotions so intense that they had been dammed up for his entire prison stay. But he also doubted that he would be able to let go so quickly or that a few hours on the road would be sufficient to express eighteen months of anguish. Nick had exercised his concern, his individuality, and his humanity in going to the aid of the fighting inmate, and he had been severely punished for it. Faced with the pressures of dehumanization, Nick's unconscious response was that of reciprocal dehumanization and inner compartmentalization: strong feelings of every sort were walled off from his awareness and without his awareness. At the same time that Nick was losing touch with his inner life, he was less aware of the degree to which he was outwardly becoming "part of the institution." In working hard and well at his job, he salvaged some pride in workmanship and made a friendship of sorts with his boss, but he did not question the fact that he was working for the prison. In learning to look out for himself above all else by assuming the categorical moral insensitivities necessary for survival according to the inmate code, he not only accepted that code as his new moral guide, he internalized it. In assuming the protective noncoloration of the tan uniform and in becoming "part of the woodwork," he hoped to remain anonymous and indistinct, yet he remained unaware that his outward blurring into anonymity simultaneously eroded his inner mental reservations and his sense of specific individuality:

"I view the problem of the bad vibrations here as part of the problem of life. On the outside the similar response would be to become a hermit, which I've considered but which I think is avoiding life. You have to face the bad vibrations in life. My wife and I had thought about going off to the hills somewhere, but being a hermit with your wife is hardly being a hermit, really. From the practical side, we'd be very ill equipped to do that; still the sense of emotional peace, the lack of conflict, is temptingly pleasant.

"I don't think I understood, at 18, the obligation I had agreed to by being registered for the draft. I had never meant to accept the concept of killing a person. I should have understood it then and made a decision, but since I didn't, I felt I had to come here. Out of a sense of patriotism, would you believe it? I felt I *owed* this country that much. The essential foundation is so good, if they would only follow it. I feel I have that obligation and I'm satisfying it. Unpleasant perhaps, but I have it anyway. I considered Canada, but it didn't take. The idea of running, for one thing, didn't appeal to me. I didn't feel at the time that I was being unduly harassed, but if they try to reclassify me, I would feel terribly unduly harassed. I could go across the border then with a good deal of relief. Good riddance. I feel I've made myself reasonably clear by coming here. It would still make me very unhappy to leave the country, but I wouldn't view it as though I were reneging.

"One thing I learned from being here, from getting hit and from just day to day, is to look out for myself. Taking care of Number One in here can be a very ticklish business. There are times I remember being distinctly selfish, particularly as an only child, but I never put a great concern on looking out for Number One. I wasn't wisely or competently altruistic, not from a solid enough concept of self. I think this is one thing prison has done to me: by forcing me back into myself, in self-defense almost, I had to strengthen the foundation. How much I've succeeded remains to be seen when I get out there. I've reached the point of wondering what the effects of this place really are. Have I increased my self-knowledge or have I had to deceive myself?"

11

Ralph Lombardi, 26

Youth Corrections Act: Six Months to Six Years

MORE a strategist than an anthropologist, Ralph Lombardi tried to outwit the prison as well as to study it. The study was necessary for distance; the strategy, for survival. His struggle was as constant as it was frustrating. When the attitude of student or spectator no longer kept him at a comfortable distance, and when gamesmanship didn't work, there was still his wit, which liberated and elevated, lightened and purged many groups. Scoffing at first, it angrily progressed to caustic to acid to virulent. His dark eyes would gleam and his wide smile curl as he laughed blackly at the stupidity and absurdity of the situation.

Ralph's wit was not so much a succession of jokes or funny remarks as it was the most striking manifestation of a more pervasive humorous inner attitude. The attitude did not imply that he took incarceration lightly; rather, it expressed his refusal to be defeated by the provocations of prison life, his resistance to the overwhelming environmental compulsion to suffer. In emphasizing his invincibility through humor, he was even wringing some healthy pleasure from the arid life of prison and sharing it with the rest of us. Though his humorous outlook and benevolent attitude toward himself were profoundly deformed by his rising anger and the inescapable psychic numbing of prolonged incarceration, those literally saving graces were never entirely lost. In struggling to maintain his humorous posture, Ralph compellingly confirmed an observation of Freud's: "Humor is not resigned, it is rebellious."

As Ralph refused to be taken in by evil and hypocrisy, he took into himself as little of the prison as possible. He swallowed neither the lies nor the food. He ate as little of "that sloppy gruel" as he could and still survive. But as Ralph stayed hungry, his humor became more biting; as his cheeks grew more hollow, so did his laughter. Ralph's feelings about his imprisonment, like those of other inmates, could be summarized as "You've got my body, but you haven't got *me*." That core of being that he recognized as his self had to be protected from psychological attack by every aspect of the prison, even its food. He tried to maneuver his way, to remain one up in a very one down situation.

Ralph put himself through two years of the university in his home town by alternating semesters of work and school. When his military reserve unit demanded more time from him, he felt that it hadn't the right to make such a request. He angrily resigned and refused the inevitable draft notice. Expecting to be sentenced to the Federal prison near his home, he was amazed to find himself transported a thousand miles to Lompoc. He was even more surprised by the psychological distance from his former life:

"I expected physically to be taken care of, more or less, my needs for food and shelter, that kind of thing. I thought it would be kind of boring. I'm not even satisfied with the *physical* thing, and that's only secondary. I think the way they psychologically abuse you is outrageous. Their whole approach is strictly authoritarian. There isn't any such thing as the human factor. They're depressing because they come on with their thinking, subject you to it, and there's nothing you can do about it. *Reasoning* with them is futile. That's further insubordination. I didn't give any thought to this whatsoever before coming here. The bad aspects of outside are certainly present here, without any of the good aspects, if there's any good at all here.

"This may be unusual for a resister to say, but I think I would have been an above-average soldier. That's how I feel about the whole soldiering thing, forgetting the psychological aspect or the morality, forgetting the conscience. I don't know exactly why—confidence in my abilities, previous success, other accomplishments generally. I think I would have held up under extreme pressure. I would've been cool and calm. I would've survived things that perhaps others wouldn't have survived, or I would've survived them much easier. I feel I have above-average intelligence and I figure this would've carried over into the service, despite basic training, and because I've succeeded in other types of situations I think I would succeed there too, forgetting the moral aspects. I'd be more determined than the usual soldier, less likely to panic, more stable, more like an automaton maybe, forgetting the moral aspect."

Did good soldier equal good prisoner? "As far as just holding out, yeah, I think so. I'm not sure whether other people serving twenty-four months have been happier. I'm more sensitive to the stupidity in prison, the poor thinking. I'm really enraged by things, perhaps easier than other people, and therefore more unhappy about them." But it *was* the moral and conscientious issues that led Ralph to refuse any further contact with the military. The notion of acting in any other way than refusing the draft had hardly crossed his mind. The idea of going to Canada "seemed unthinkable then and in some ways still does."

"I guess still having respect for the government was the main thing that kept me from going. It seemed that Selective Service and their arbitrary action was the bad thing, whereas everything else was something with which you could work or live. I'd only go to Canada if the whole situation seemed unbearable. I thought I was behaving then as a good American, refusing the service. Now I have reservations, because the longer I've been locked up the more things I find wrong. Perhaps if I'd been more enlightened and saw the situation as more or less hopeless here in America, I would've gone away. It approaches that now, although I don't think it has really got to that exact point yet. I think it would get to that point if they started messing with me or harassing me right away, once I got out."

Ralph's initial refusal, like that of many resisters, was both personal and focal. It was his own response to the issue of the draft and was limited to that issue. But the longer he spent immersed in and dependent upon an oppressive, hostile, and depriving government institution, and the less contact he had with any other kind of life, the more he felt that the prison and the government were becoming less similar and more identical. At this point he was still able to distinguish between the two, to see the prison as only one agency of the government (although a more representative agency than he had previously thought), and still to have hope for the country as a whole. But he also felt that if he were as harassed after his release as he had been in prison, if life outside became as persecutory as that inside, then prison and government would have become the same. He would leave the country.

"Being in prison has to do with that insofar as it gives you a glimpse of the system. I've thought quite a bit here, which I probably wouldn't have done as extensively were I free, and now I'm more receptive to criticism of the U.S. They really ought to take the 'Department of Justice' off the letterhead because really it's not right. They haven't done anything, there've been too many examples where they haven't lived up to that ideal, so many that you become disgusted with them. I'm more receptive to critical thinking about the government, whereas before I would've just kind of sloughed it off as a question of the guy's motives. The guys who made the charges, that is.

"There's also, well, the psychiatric problems that arise in prison. They seem to be taken care of by the group, so it does have a therapeutic value for me. Its humanitarian end is the primary concern. Any other benefit, like getting together or meeting other resisters, is secondary. There *is* a sense of oneness. When you're alone in the inmate population, it's only your human feelings against the rest of the prison. With the group you don't always feel that you're some kind of screwball, someone that has weird ideas nobody else remotely appreciates. You find people in the group thinking along similar lines, upholding your ideas, reaffirming them. You don't feel the whole situation is lost. You're in sort of an area in which to be human, be yourself. Being around people in the compound who are not so receptive is just futile, so frustrating, so pointless.

"Hacks I really think are sick, just so sick. They embody totally what others have only minutely. They're vicious, and they promote that type of feeling in other people, which even makes the situation worse. They're the ones who have the power and the authority and they're vicious. At least in the resister group you can find human beings. I could cite cases of parole violators that are really hopeless wretches and they're made so because of what this place has done to them. They've locked them up, they've deprived them of the period in which they should be growing up, they've forced down them vocational training which is totally worthless when they get to the streets. They get to depend on the prison system so that they're unable to depend on themselves when they're released.

"Everything here is seen as a disciplinary problem; it's a problem because you're *bad*. It's that attitude that frustrates any kind of life. It's a kind of psychological Auschwitz. It ruins you. It causes you to think along their lines, that everything *is* a disciplinary problem. It causes you to think that your *overall* personality is bad because of one thing you've done.

"Instead of responding to the particular aspects which they call the disciplinary problem, they attack your *whole* personality. You're a bad *person,* you've got to be locked up for five years. You begin to think of yourself in those very terms, and that's bad, unless you plan to go from here to some kind of Nazi army where that kind of discipline would fit right in. As far as going out and leading a regular sort of life, realizing as much of your potential as possible, this place does nothing for you. In fact it screws you up for that. They get you thinking along the wrong lines. It's degrading. If they treat you like an animal long enough, all your experience in prison reinforces that idea.

"When I see all that happening to me, I kind of back off and assume the anthropologist position. I try to be aware by realizing where these people are coming from and not reacting to it personally. Kind of withdrawing or saying to myself, 'You know these people are wrong, this is full of shit, they don't know what they're talking about. They're automatons. They mustn't be taken seriously.' By discrediting it in my mind I prevent myself from the poison they try to inject in my veins."

Ralph was acutely sensitive to the dependency and inactivation which threatened him, warped others, and was a major source of recidivism among departing prisoners who could not cope outside the institution. He also quickly grasped the prison practice of recognizing a partial, and always negative, aspect of an inmate's personality or behavior and ascribing it to that person *in toto*. What was most heartening about Ralph was the resolution and intensity he brought to bear on his effort to diminish the prison staff and thus their influence upon him. What was less heartening was that in this self-defense he unconsciously identified with the prison staff in using the same tactics: viewing them as "automatons" in much the same way as they saw prisoners as numbers; feeling that they "embody totally what others have only minutely" in a manner similar to the staff's idea that prisoners were "nothing but" their criminal act and that their overall personality was entirely bad because of it. If the staff saw all resisters as suffering from "martyr complexes" or as "baby rapers," Ralph returned the compliment by seeing all officials as "sick, just so sick."

Ralph was indeed a virtuoso in the art and craft of prison survival, but by taking the staff's psychological maneuvers for his own he could not escape the reciprocal nature of dehumanization. The most effective way for him to defend himself against a decrease in his own individuality was to accept a diminution in his perception of the humanity of others. But that diminution had its benefits as well. The hatred of the staff which was openly communicated and unconsciously projected ("the poison they try to inject in my veins") aroused his own hatred and fear. By reducing and discrediting the staff in his mind, he could moderate the intensity of their effects upon him, project back onto them to the point where he could tolerate his own pain, and from there on use his wits and the rule book to stay on top of things:

"I try, by realizing where they come from, to possibly manipulate them to my advantage. In any kind of personal contact with them I try to dispel the idea that I'm an animal, try to do something concrete that seemingly rids them of that thought, make an extra-special effort not to conform to the stereotypes they have waiting for me. I know that the rules are all they're concerned with. If there was some church where they could worship rules, they'd be attending frequently. So I address all my arguments to the rules wherever it's possible, try to learn the things that safeguard me or offer minute protection. But my main strategy is just to avoid them. I don't expect them to be humane, so I don't deal with them. Only if I'm forced into it.

"One day I was assigned to the farm without knowing it. It just came out on the change sheet [the daily mimeographed announcement of job and housing changes]—they didn't ask me to go there and I hadn't asked to go. I knew I couldn't work there because of the dust and my trouble with my contact lenses. I went over to the officer, Mr. X, the first day out there and he says, 'What do *you* want? What's *your* problem?' I told him about the lenses, and he told me I couldn't leave. Then he tried to woo me onto the farm with, 'What kind of food do you like? How about some walnuts?' I told him I liked Chinese food and I wanted to see a doctor. He still saw it as a disciplinary matter rather than a medical one, and he told me either I'd go to work or I'd have to sit naked in the sun in a chair, some kind of disciplinary thing. I told him I had a right to see a doctor and he told me what I needed was a good ass-kicking.

"Finally I made a deal with him that on my lunch break I could see a doctor, but he told me he wasn't going to write out a hospital pass, I'd have to get one from the guard at the rear sally port. When I got there and asked for it, they told me X had talked to them and they weren't going to give me a pass either. I came down here anyway and saw the doctor. He gave me time off for convalescence and a note saying I shouldn't work in dust with my contacts.

"I had to go back out to the farm and get my shirt, and when I showed X the convalescence slip he said, 'How'd you get this? How'd you get to see a doctor?' He was really hysterical by then. When I got back to my cell, I found he had written a shot [disciplinary report] for refusing to work, malingering, and defiance.

When I went to the Adjustment Committee [disciplinary board] a few days later, it was presided over by Mr. X!"

Ralph had thought of not cooperating in prison, but he was intimidated by the elasticity of his Youth Act sentence and the prospect of staff retribution for even passive noncooperation:

"I agree with that whole line of thinking, of not cooperating, up to the point where they're threatening me with two years in The Hole over and above two years in prison. I really am ashamed that I, I'm uh, cowering to their force, too. By not going to The Hole. The reason is that I would just be, you know, detained here for four years instead of two. In a lot of ways, I even question whether I would be locked up beyond two years even if I were in The Hole, because I think their main objective is simply two years. Whether I spent two years in The Hole or out in the prison population would be of no consequence. Then again, given their whole disposition towards inmates, they may think a minimum of two years is a requirement, and if I go to The Hole they might feel that it's their *duty* to extend that for however long necessary, or to the end of the sentence. I don't feel easy cowering to their force. There are all kinds of rationalizations I can use, like saying I've got things to do outside that are more important than maintaining my dignity, physically, here. Psychically, I try to immunize myself from any harm they can do and furthermore not even take them really seriously. This is psychically a good way of avoiding The Hole, the whole prison experience, and the indignities, but you do put up a kind of physical show of obedience to get out in the two-year period. In some ways that's a minor concession compared to the more important things: psychologically submitting, accepting their premises."

Ralph was deeply troubled by the degree to which he was cooperating, even though he regarded it as a form of role-playing to maintain distance. He was clearly and painfully aware that his explanations were rationalizations for having compromised. But he was less aware of the inner compartmentalization of his life into two presumably separate and unrelated areas, the psychic and the physical. This partition of outer behavior from inner life, of external cooperation from internal resistance, was a common adaptation to prison ("You've got my body, but you haven't got *me*"). Although this unconscious partitioning diminished Ralph and narrowed his perspective, it also protected him from the full impact of his imprisonment so long as he could believe that there was a free self surviving within an incarcerated body. Like Mark Henley, who believed that he was an anthropologist without being an inmate, Ralph felt that he could physically comply without being psychologically affected. As long as Nick Manos worked hard and well at a job whose performance gave him a sense of skill and pride, and which was comparable to his work prior to prison, he could feel continuous with his life outside and less aware of the changes he had undergone.

Mark took the prison as an object of study, Nick as a vocational exercise; Ralph took it as an object of strategy. What is most important is that by taking it as an object, by conducting their imprisonment as a research project, a work experience, or a duel (in Ralph's case a duel with the prison's own psychological weapons), all three were able to provide a focus and make a contest out of a situation which otherwise could have been overwhelming; they were actively imposing a measure of clarity, form, and dignity upon an experience that could have been even more ambiguous, amorphous, and degrading. Whether as student, worker, or strategist, all three were bringing to the center of their lives what had been peripheral outside of prison, making one aspect of their previous selves an entirety, concentrating upon a narrower identity in order to survive the erosion of a wider one.

12

Ben Post, 20

Eighteen Months

Bᴇɴ Post described himself as a farm worker on the questionnaire every inmate fills out when he comes to Lompoc. Although he had the stocky build, the open face, and the direct manner of the 4-H Club member he once had been, he was different from most farm workers—and indeed from most prisoners. At the turn of the century, his forebears had been influential public figures. As liberal publicly as they were privately, they endowed their state with schools and research institutes, their descendants with a fortune and a tradition of public service, even a sense of *noblesse oblige.* Ben's grandfather had multiplied his own inheritance and took a benevolent if somewhat ducal interest in his family. If some relatives in the third and fourth generations were more interested in the *noblesse* than the *oblige,* that was not the case with Ben's immediate family.

The Posts expected each other to be exemplary and to act rightly. The importance of living in accord with one's beliefs was not lost on Ben. His father resolutely made for himself a life that was close to his own values. When he left the Marines after Korea, he did not return to the wealthy suburb where he had grown up but instead moved to another state, settled his family on a farm near a small town, and started teaching school. It was there that Ben grew up with his older and younger brothers and still younger sister.

"My grandparents' way of life is a lot different from ours. But the conflict in our family is at that level; the bigger generation gap is between my grandparents and my parents. My parents are much closer to us kids than they are to my grandparents; it's almost as if we were all brothers and sisters and my grandparents the parents. There was always a pretty close correspondence with them and we usually went to see them once or twice a year. We'd go and live with them a while in the splendor and the luxury.

"My father is patient and quiet, and he understood why I wanted to come here. My grandfather would just refuse to think about it and say, 'It's wrong; I admire your courage, but it's wrong.' He has his mind made up on a lot of things. You can't talk to him about things because he's already got his mind made up. He's very concerned about people doing what's right. He gets really upset and mad and gets very explicit and says, 'No, no, that's not the way it is, it's *this* way.' My coming here was a hard thing for my grandfather because I think I probably was the closest of all his grandchildren to him. My parents actually were pretty proud of what I was doing, once they had thought about it themselves. I made the decision so far ahead of time that when I actually refused there had been lots of time for the idea to slowly develop. It was all pretty well understood by the time anything happened. It was a year and a half from the time I decided that I was going to refuse until I did.

"The rest of Dad's family never could understand it. They're society; they worry about going to the right schools and all that. That's why my father broke away from it; he just got up and left as soon as he could. He'd rather do what he felt like doing, rather than be a money-maker only, and a socialite. My grandfather would keep sending money, kind of forcing us to take it, maybe only to keep the dependency thing going, I don't know; my father never really liked it, but none of us wanted to break off completely.

"We really didn't live any differently from anybody else around our farm. Only slightly, maybe. We had a bigger place than most, but there are better places than ours around there. But, like furniture: in our house a lot of it was inherited antiques, things like that, and when people came to the house they could see these things. Although the house wasn't any different from any of the other houses around, there was a touch of something different. It wasn't things just bought out of the store. We used to go down to my grandparents' a lot, and travel more than other people did. I was really self-conscious about that when I was a kid.

"I think when I was in seventh grade I used to daydream and stuff; I pictured myself getting hurt or suffering for somebody else, that sort of thing. I think my need for that came from the security, the better standing I had in my community than other people. You know, being from a wealthier background; that because of that I'm going to have to suffer for other people who've gotten gypped, or who'd gotten a bad break or something; that I had a debt to pay to somebody. My mother's always been socially concerned, but I went a lot further. I think I developed it on my own, sort of, in the way I felt committed. The thing is, I feel I don't belong to any group; it makes it hard for me to relate to other people in this country.

"When I was at [boarding school] I never got attached to very many people, only a few people. Oh, a lot of people were friends, and I knew everybody and I got along with them, but only a few people I really got close to. I had some trouble breaking the barriers. It's kind of like armor. I probably had as much armor as they did, I don't know, maybe a different kind of armor. I have to get to know a person informally by being around them a lot before I get close to them. I'm not inclined just to talk about the weather, that sort of thing, and I'm not inclined to build a relationship with somebody over something superficial. It's got to be something more, otherwise I don't get close to them at all. Maybe that's why I'm not close to that many people, because it takes something more than just talking."

Ben's reserve and even diffidence complicated his transition from a small boarding school to a large but highly selective university.

Like many men at Lompoc, he was even more reluctant to return to any kind of "structured" institution:

"I certainly don't want to go back to school. It's too institutionalized. I mean, if I want to study I can study on my own. I don't want to go through all that institutional hassle, particularly after being *here*. And like being at college. There were all sorts of things wrong there. It wasn't only just the crowds, the excitement, and everyone being stirred up at demonstrations. It was also that I wasn't able to get *attached* to anything there. And there were things that weren't at college, like the farm, and putting off the thought of the draft. Going to college is what everybody wanted me to do. It's what you're supposed to do. I sort of had to break away from that because I hadn't wanted to go to college in the first place and I went. I never really changed my mind, I just went. I got accepted, and I said, 'Maybe I'll go and maybe I'm not going to. I just can't turn down an opportunity just like that.' Then by the time the fall came I decided I'd go again, partly because the summer before I had worked at summer school and I got hepped again on education from that.

"Then I got to college and it was a completely different sort of thing, very different from high school and from what happened at summer school. It was very institutional, and there were large crowds. It was regimented. Not like in a hospital or in this place, but the teachers are doing their jobs, and they go to class, and you sit there for an hour, and you take notes, and then you leave, and you don't see those people again till the next day. There's no human contact, but I didn't make any effort to make any. I didn't make an effort while I was at college to get to know anyone. Partly because of inertia on my part; I think I felt like I wasn't going to be there very long.

"I spent almost the next year on the farm, mostly living in a cabin by myself and thinking. I think the idea of an ordeal was something which I sort of wanted, to put myself in that isolated position was something I needed. Just to break the security thing at home by trying to dislocate myself and at the same time trying to get relocated again. It's a funny thing (my brother notices it too), when we're at the farm we're much more in a security thing. When you get on the farm and you just start staying there, you become very 'oh well, nothing to do really,' and you forget about everything else that's outside.

"You're in a little world right there and it's very easy just to get stuck in it. It's a spot of inertia where nothing happens, especially if you're there by yourself. No motivation. No need to worry about anything. There's plenty of work to be done, but if you don't do it today it makes no difference. You can do it tomorrow. 'That fence that needs fixing—well, none of the animals are getting out today, I can fix it tomorrow.' It doesn't take more than half an hour to feed the animals and maybe do a few things around the farm."

Ben thought himself a ponderer, someone slow to action. Indeed, he often seemed the opposite of hasty. He considered facets of problems that would occur to few others, and he acted only after careful, even painful, rumination.

"I was just sitting there hoeing my field and after a while I began to feel that I wasn't doing anything in terms of the bigger world. This thing with the draft was coming up and my brother had already gotten his notice. He was involved with the resistance. I began to think about the alternatives, and the only alternative I could see was going to prison. I never really considered going to Canada. I just didn't want to run away from the problem and it wasn't in me to go away. The important thing was confrontation. To face the issue head on and decide it.

"Making that choice made a big difference in my life because, I don't know, everything became a lot better. I mean I enjoyed life a lot more. It made it pretty direct, deciding what I'm going to do and making choices. I was really concerned with making the decision and didn't think very much about what would come after that. I tried not to think of what prison was going to be like. The limitedness of it. That's why I didn't refuse to work when I first came here, because I hadn't thought about it; I thought very little about prison before I came here. I said, 'I'll find out about that when I get there,

I'm not gonna let *that* influence my decision of what I'm going to do when I'm outside. I'll learn to live with that when I get there.' What the consequences were was what I shouldn't be worrying about. That's why the first lawyer I went to thought I was crazy: because I wasn't worrying about the consequences of my action, whether I got five years or no time at all. He thought I'd have to be crazy to think more about the moral aspects than what would happen to me personally. He even thought that would be a good defense. He said, 'I'll plead you psychotic.'

"You know, I'm only living when I'm doing something. Otherwise I'm just existing. But when I'm doing something, I'm *being*. It's exerting your being to have control of what you're doing. To have a life, you have to make a choice about how you're going to behave. There really was no other alternative for me, but still I *chose* to do it. I think at the same time there was also the desire to stand up and face the government in my position of coming here and refusing the draft. And I think it was also the security thing again.

"There are things I've got to do, a lot of questions I want to find answers to before I get tied down. At times I used to feel that I wanted to get married—young—and settle down on the farm; but other times I feel I don't ever want to get married, and I want to just keep searching and be free and help other people. A one-man priesthood-type thing, almost. Buddha ran away from his family, and I sort of had a fear that that's what I'd end up doing. The same with Tolstoy; that was the hang-up through his whole life, his marriage, and he didn't run away until the month before he died. I think it's partly the same as the security thing I look for; and then I throw myself in an insecure position because of the desire to escape security. The security isn't what I want. You aren't living fully, maybe, if you're too secure. One day follows the next and you're not really thinking, you're just vegetating. In a way, it's like prison. If you get into the prison routine, you're really secure."

After pondering for several months, Ben felt he couldn't conscientiously cooperate with the prison by working on its farm or complying with its imposed routine. Accepting prison routine was accepting what he considered to be unjust authority; it also meant that it was "wrecking his character"—in no small part because it meant sinking into an intolerably dependent life imposed from without, a vegetative existence far more threatening than that which had enveloped him at home. Ben felt obliged to exercise his initiative against the inertia of prison life just as he had refused to remain embedded at home; he felt compelled to protest, in good conscience, the iniquity of imprisonment as he had protested the iniquity of the war and the draft. He had to exert himself again to unify his beliefs and his acts. He had to claim his independence from the prison's encouragement of passivity and from his inner temptation to accept it, from the institution's demands that he comply with the unconscionable and from his own reluctance to force confrontations. Thus, his refusal of work paralleled his refusal of induction.

In refusing to work and in refusing induction, Ben had delayed until he was sure it was right in his own mind and, more important to him, that his resistance would not do violence to another. After making both decisions, he had felt a sense of triumph, that he was "tremendously free" and liberated from the inner tensions of those decisions, even though their consequences would mean the certain loss of physical freedom and the likelihood of psychological restriction. In contemplating both prison and The Hole, Ben was not deterred by the physical consequences, but the psychic effects were more intimidating. In the end, however, he preferred those effects—though he refused to imagine their magnitude—to the less acceptable effects of compromise. He quietly refused to work and was sent to The Hole. He stayed there for the rest of his sentence.

"If I thought refusing the draft was wrong, if I thought I should be here, or if I thought that being in prison was doing some good for some people, then I might cooperate and try and help it. So I waited to see if it was really doing something, whether it was rehabilitative or not. I didn't want to interfere with it if it was. After the first four months, I tried to see what the prison thing was, and I decided that it wasn't doing any good for anybody. I was really having to sell out by submitting to the authority that was being placed upon me. First, being a slave and working for them; second, because it was wrecking my character. To cooperate with that kind of thing is to sacrifice my character, that's the way I feel.

"This whole place is an iceberg, and I think that it's really got me cold. That's just what it is, it freezes all the warm and friendly feelings you want to have. It's really hard to have them; it's icy, and you're sitting on it, and you can't get away from it. And it's so big; you might melt a little spot in it, but you can't get out of it, it's just a big iceberg. It's so big you can't melt the whole thing. It's colder than you're hot. "

In speaking of the prison as an iceberg and of its chilling effects upon him, Ben was describing the same experience of psychological arrest and social isolation that other prisoners called "turning to stone," what I have referred to as petrifaction. In recognizing that the iceberg was "colder than you're hot," he was aware that this process was not entirely resistible. In his choice of metaphor, Ben was also inadvertently pointing out that the prison's gravest threats, like those of an iceberg, were mostly below the surface. Although the overt behavior of many employees and prisoners was threatening to Ben, their unconsciously communicated hostility, their unwitting projections, their "bad vibrations," were far more destructive—not least because they evoked his own destructiveness.

Ben was hardly immune from the guilt-inducing and tension-arousing effects of this environment, but in undergoing the unconscious partitioning necessary to defend against those effects he was also losing touch with his own capacity for warmth and compassion. Although the promptings of conscience were primary in Ben's decision to go to The Hole, he also hoped, in its relative isolation, to be free of the "bad vibrations," to resist the arousal of what was most reprehensible in him, and to regain in that narrower and (to him) freer space his vitality and his concern for others. Going to The Hole, then, was not only an act of conscience and an exertion of initiative; it was also an attempt to repair the wreckage of his character, to restrain what was worst in him and to remain in close relation with what was best in him:

"The people here are awfully carnal! I think that's what upsets me most about them. It's not necessarily the physical aspect but the bad vibrations that you receive. I get very tired of receiving bad vibrations all the time. You're aware of them and they affect your behavior. Their being upset about things makes you upset about things. Their feelings tend to put pressure on your feelings and your conscience. You become self-conscious about what you're going to think, even. Just their way of *thinking* puts pressure on you to start living within their mode, their way of acting. It's only a slight manner which you change, but with their effect on you, it changes you. I get upset about things that have changed in me, like no longer being concerned about other people. It really bothers me.

"I've felt tremendously free since I've gone to The Hole. When I was in the outs [the rest of the prison outside The Hole], man, I was walking down the corridors and having men harass me all the time, 'Do this and do that.' I was doing this and doing that and I really felt that I was doing myself wrong. I couldn't react like I really wanted to react. I wasn't acting as I thought I should be acting. It would force me into a sort of regression. *I wouldn't stand up for anything I really believed in!* If someone started talking about something and I might disagree, it wasn't that I wouldn't say that I disagreed, but that I didn't have the words. I couldn't *think* of any.

"I get impatient sometimes, I get thinking, and I get upset about the way things are. I get impatient about the people around me, the hacks and the people who are possessive and petty and greedy, and that I'm likely to show them similar things back at them. You know, a similar type of upset emotions, being upset about their behavior, which is in a way the subtlest form of violence, just re-acting back with the same reactions they had to you. They get upset over the tiniest things and you get upset over them getting upset.

"It's just like violence. When you react violently to someone's violence, then you're only aiding the cause of violence. It's the same with being upset. If you get upset with someone else's being upset, it's just propagating the upsetness. A feeling of hate, or a feeling of disgust or something. It's only, well, you've got to have patience. That you've got to learn. That's what I find when I'm here in jail, you have to be able to control instincts. It's an instinct to get upset, and you've got to understand it and learn to control it. Even with eating habits. When I see food, I think my instinct would think in terms of 'Ah, there's food. Now, maybe not tomorrow.' As if I was an animal or something up in the woods, and I made a kill, and there it was, 'Eat now, for I might not get a kill for a few days.' I have to learn to control my appetites. It's like having to learn patience all over again."

Ben's experience of the pettiness, greed, and violence, of the "bad vibrations" of prison life, was revealing to him his own previously unrealized capacity for similar feelings. He struggled to contain these eruptions as well as those of strong and all but irresistible instinctual urges. Little of this inner struggle was apparent outwardly. As Ben wrestled with these severe assaults on his character, he resolved not to yield. He was determined not to lose his decency. He remained pleasantly implacable; he was amazingly, perhaps maddeningly, polite, answering the grunts of the guards with a courteous "please" or "thank you." Incapable of sarcasm or pretense, he simply refused to act in a way other than that which had been previously natural. He refused to satisfy his keepers by responding with newly found and clearly felt anger. When pressured, he demurred with genial resolve; when threatened, he answered with gentle courage. Ben's natural grace would have been extraordinary anywhere; inside Lompoc, it seemed extraterrestrial:

"Actually, I don't like confrontations; basically, I try to escape them. But something else is forcing me to put myself in a situation where they happen. A dual force, one trying to run away from what the other is, to put myself where I have to face them. But where I don't see any alternative, I have to follow my conscience. Some of the other resisters here think, 'Well, if the sacrifice is too great then it's not worth the doing.' They draw the line and say, 'This is as far as I'll go in making sacrifices.' I think I'm used to drawing the line a little further. I think maybe they're basically willing to sell their character for relative freedom. They aren't willing to sell their lives into the military or anything like that, but they're willing to sell their character into the system by cooperating, by being good prisoners. The problem is, if you're always taking the stand at the personal level, can you ever get beyond that level to helping other people? If you're always making the stand where it first concerns you or you lose your freedom, then the point may come where you can't stand up for someone else who has less freedom."

Ben drew his line at the point where physical violation meant the violation of his integrity. In refusing to be stripped and searched, he would not allow himself to be assaulted or invaded. He would not concede to the prison staff their assumptions that he was as base as every other inmate, that he was interchangeable with any other prisoner, that his dignity could be assaulted as readily as his body, that his identity had become government property as well as his person, and above all that he was unworthy of trust. The pressure of these assumptions was so strong, however, that Ben could not resist them by thought alone; he could counter them, and his own inner acceptance of them, only by direct action which contradicted them. If refusing to be strip-searched meant that he could have no more visits, he would go without seeing those he loved rather than allow himself to be debased or permit himself and his family to be impugned as potential smugglers. He agreed that he was a prisoner but he would never agree that he was a criminal.

In refusing to place his body or his beliefs in the hands of another, Ben was refusing to be searched in the same spirit in which he had refused to be drafted or to be put to work to support the prison. What is more, in drawing that line he was drawing the boundary of his honor: he would not submit to official rape any more than he would commit official violence; he would not cooperate in the prison's destruction of his integrity any more than he would comply with its work program. There, in the lowest depths of The Hole, in the dark and the cold and the wet, he was insisting on what he had come so far to uphold, what was most precious to him, what *was* him: the active assertion of his inviolable sense of worth.

It is doubtful if Ben fully realized at the time what a challenge he was presenting to the guards or that to draw lines is often to tempt others to cross them. The guards were used to processing prisoners as an inanimate, undifferentiated, and usually compliant mass; they could not tolerate his individuality or the strength of character it expressed, let alone insubordination. In an environment which demanded anonymity, Ben was standing out; in a situation which required a prone position, he was standing up.

"I decided I'm not going to cooperate with being frisked. I'd been thinking about it for a while. After the last group I went back up to The Hole. They frisked me at the hospital door when I left; you know, a hand frisk. I got up to The Hole and the hack said, 'Take all your clothes off for a strip frisk.' And I said, 'What? I haven't got anything on me!' When I came up there before they'd never done that, so I said, 'Look, I haven't got anything on me; there's no reason you should think that I have, I've been frisked at the door down there. Just trust me, can't you trust me?' 'No.' He opens the door to the hall and says, 'Hey, you guys, come on in here,' so fifteen, twenty guards came in there and he says, 'Well, are you going to strip down?' They were all around me, they had my back against the wall and they were all around me. So the guy says, 'Take off your shirt.' I didn't say anything to that, so he comes up and unbuttons it and pulls it off. 'Well, take off your pants.' The same thing. So they just lay me out straight, horizontal—and rip! they tore the pants off in three or four pieces.

"There were about twenty of them, I think. Everyone got a handful and in no time at all I was stark naked. I was in mid-air; they just sort of grab you on the throat, and the other guys grabbed my shoes; they grabbed all around me. It happened so fast it was unbelievable. Actually, I didn't want to put them in a situation where they had to exert such brute force, and then all of a sudden it happened and I was overwhelmed.

"Then they threw me in the strip cell there with nothing, absolutely nothing, so I spent twenty-one hours there with absolutely nothing. No mattress, no blanket. Then about three hours later, the guy I think I mentioned when I first went up to The Hole, this guy in the cell next to me who was pressuring me, who said, 'I'm going to get you when you go out, I think you're wonderful, lovely' . . . well, this guy heard that I was thrown in the strip cell, so he decided he wanted to go to the strip cell, too. He asked one of the other guys what you have to do to get torn down and stripped, and the guy says, 'Throw your tray out there and flood your cell.' And well, the guy was fed up because he never got out in the compound because he was a known rapist. Males. So that night I guess he flooded his cell, and the hacks came in and took a swing at him and clobbered his head and they dragged him down the stairs and threw him in the strip cell. There was only one other guy down there before, so there were three of us down there. He was stark naked too, but the other guy had blankets and stuff. [There were several strip cells in Segregation; in this instance each man was in a separate cell. No rape took place.]

"I won't put up with any frisking at all. If they say, 'Raise your hands,' I won't raise my hands; if they say, 'Strip down,' I won't strip down. It's just basically assuming that you're dishonest and also it's a sign of subservience to them, of recognizing their authority. Basically *I'll* decide about my behavior as a prisoner. I want to act in here just as I would out in society. There's no difference in my behavior just because they happen to have steel bars in front of me. One standard of behavior.

"This place is only a miniature form or a concentrated form of totalitarian society. All the bad points and all the hassles you can get into outside, it's just like this, except this is a condensed form. They're in very close contact here, but that is no reason to have a double standard. Just because they have you confined physically doesn't give you any cause to suddenly take a second standard and say, 'OK, I'll make a compromise.' "

Though Ben's firm resolve was sometimes clouded by depression, there was usually a shining gaiety about him that was heartening to us and infuriating to guards. His sense of purpose and his calm ebullience stemmed from his close identification with his home and family and with the moral sense which arose from them. It would be a long while before he would see his home or his family again, but the thought of returning to them kept him strong. Ben's release date was far in the future, but he was already aware of the grave changes he had undergone in prison and of the abrupt shock a quick return home would present. It was as much his concern for his family as his own need to work through his prison experience that led Ben to think of interposing time and distance between prison and home:

"I've just gotta walk home when I get out of here! A sort of displaying that things are slow. I mean, going a thousand miles should take a thousand days; however long it takes to walk it, not how fast you can do it. Going in the direction of home, but at a slow pace. Things like that take patience. Maybe in the time it takes to walk home I'll be closer to what I was when I left it. Just to be thrown all of a sudden into a different situation, I don't think I can do it. It takes time to think about what has happened to you. It shouldn't be something that is overnight from one place to the next. The thing is, if I wanted to give up walking home I could always hitchhike. It would still take a few days to get there. Even walking home there's a security wrapped around it, you know. If you want to be loved, you can always get home just like that."

13

Wayne Foote, 21

Two Years

Only briefly stunned by the weight of prison, Wayne Foote was soon trying to improve things inside. He noticed that the men trying to get their high-school diplomas through the education program had no place to study. The cell blocks were always noisy and there was no quiet place to read. He tried to arrange for the use of the empty dining room as an evening study hall; he was rebuffed. He wanted to start a tutoring agency to use the skills of the college-educated inmates to help the men who wanted them; he was refused. He urged that prisoners be paid for studying instead of for sewing pockets on pants; he was ignored. He slowed down.

Wayne was raised by his widowed mother in a small town in the Northwest. His father, a minister, had been a conscientious objector in World War II (as his own father had been in 1917); he died when Wayne was 5. With his lanky frame, thoughtful manner, deliberate speech, thinning hair, and pipe, Wayne appeared much older than his 21 years. He seemed to belong in a woolen plaid shirt, jeans, and moccasins and not in the brown and tan farm worker outfit he wore in prison. He looked and talked very much like the scoutmaster, forest ranger, or basketball coach he might have become. In high school he had been president of the student body, a good athlete, liked by everyone; in his own words, "an

All-American Boy." When the All-American Boy went to an All-American small college, he began to ask some All-American questions, particularly after he met an All-American Girl. He began to think long and hard about the direction his life was taking, and what he saw was a dead end, an All-American cliché:

"I don't like things all decided for me two years before I do 'em. That's kind of what I was confronted with during my sophomore year in college; I was going with a girl and we were going to get married. She very much wanted a conventional person, and I kind of saw a situation where I'd be getting a job in two years and settling down and supporting her . . . and I stopped and I went and I sat back and took a look at the thing. There's so many of these girls running around the campus, like they're inside a balloon, and you pop the balloon, and all of a sudden there's a world around them. The kind that says to you, 'Don't think so much, just take life easy, it's really nice, just float through it.' That kind of situation. She was always telling me I thought too much or worried too much about things.

"She helped me in one way, though; I was able to get mad for once. The first time I got angry with her I thought God was going to strike me down, I felt so guilty. I felt like in some ways I had been socially successful, particularly with this girl, but in order to do that I had lost sight of what *I* was. I was concerned that everyone like me and that I was nice and friendly, but I felt like I had a lot of surface friendships with a thousand different people. I realized at the very moment I was being nice to someone that I didn't feel that way, that sometimes I hated them.

"I think it was the church, the fundamentalist upbringing, the things I'd been taught, that put a box around what I was. I'd been taught to keep in my feelings, be nice, be kind, and to love everyone in a certain kind of way, and so on, but I knew sometimes the feelings were artificial, superficial. A lot of times I didn't feel like that. I'd been taught that anger was bad and to express a whole lot of feeling about *anything* was kind of bad. Kind of a stoic from the wrong end. Instead of starting from the inside I started from the outside. I was trying to control myself, my feelings, what I would say, in order to come out a certain kind of can of beans. Except I didn't quite like the can of beans that was there. I realized I had to get my anger out. If I left it inside, all it did was eat up in there, and it got worse, and I came out with grotesque feelings.

"I think part of it had to do with going to a church-related school; the philosophy there was quite a bit narrower than even *my* view of the world, much more ordered and much more sterile. Static. I looked at myself and I saw that a lot needed to be changed there, at least a lot that needed to come outside. That's a part of what I meant about keeping a guard up. I feel like sometimes I'd just like to say, 'This is how I feel, exactly how I feel.' I'd like to let down everything, just kind of vomit it up to another person. That's kind of how I feel. With most people there's always something left unsaid, part of it in reserve.

"My feelings are much less intense now, especially compared with what they were in the first couple of years. Some of those times I felt like nuclear wars inside, like I couldn't see. There were times I'd walk around the campus just kind of oblivious of everybody else, like I had blinders on or something because things were so intense. I was just trying to forget what was going on in my head and my feelings. It used to be a storm in the ocean and now it's kind of a ripple.

"There were two or three sides of me fighting. One was a fundamental good guy and the other one was how I really was feeling. One was saying, 'You can't express that feeling, you can't, you've gotta control it ("maintain" is the term in here, you know, "maintain"?). The other was, 'Tell all of them to go to hell, just feel, and go out and do it.' And one was saying about the draft— I went through some nuclear wars over the draft with myself. One would say, 'You know, you've got to be the good guy, still you've got to be a right guy, stay in the system; you've got to look at all the people who admire you for being that, and think of the people you'll alienate or disappoint.' The other one was saying, 'How do you really feel about it, and what do you know you should do? Are you going to do it?' When I made the decision to turn in my card, I really felt like I would be pretty much alienated from everybody, and I felt like I was risking that I was going to be isolated, and I was kind of scared.

"I was amazed, because some of the people I'd expected to really attack didn't, you know, and their initial response would be 'Oh my God!,' and then they'd say, 'Can I talk to you about it? Come over tomorrow at two, or Tuesday.' So I'd go and talk to them for a while and I'd explain to them the best I could and they came out saying, 'Well I guess you've got to do this thing,' and I was really amazed. I was expecting to feel mad, bitter against them, and I was all psyched up to feel that, and here I didn't have to.

"I was so busy at school I had no time for myself. People would want to see me. It got to the point where I was making appointments with them just to talk. I was thinking of taking off the whole semester and going up to the woods just to get away for a while. I finally got away for two weeks. I wondered if I could live with myself, by myself, for an extended length of time, keep occupied, would I get bored, if I'd feel alone, if things would start closing in on me. None of that happened. I don't remember getting bored. I kept pretty busy and I didn't feel alone at all. In fact, I felt less alone with myself than I did in the midst of everything at school.

"My family, though, was something else. My brother and I talked a lot about it. We had some, uh, long discussions about the situation and he ended up saying that he thought I was, uh, a traitor to the country. But I was still his brother. We talked lots till three in the morning, how he understood my past emotional background growing up, the effect of living with just Mother for many years, without a father, and this and that, and then he said, 'Ever since I've known you, from a little kid, whenever you started out to do anything, you always went whole hog with it.' So he says, 'You're doing it with this.' So I said, 'OK, let me do it.' "

In attempting to account for Wayne's "misguided" conscientious objection, his brother, like many amateur and professional psychologists, seized on Wayne's upbringing without his father. That loss imposed its special pain and Wayne did not deny it, but there were other dimensions to his fatherlessness which might not be so obvious. It should be noted that Wayne found many surrogate fathers in his teachers, his minister, and in that same older brother; furthermore, it should be emphasized how good a father his mother was able to be. Indeed, it was not clear just how absent Reverend Foote really was for Wayne. He spoke of him as an immediate, personal, and living "Dad" rather than as a distant, abstract, and long-dead "my father," and he spoke of him frequently and idealistically. If Reverend Foote was not alive in fact, he was very much alive in Wayne's psyche. His personality and ideals had influenced his entire family and were still discussed almost daily. Wayne's acceptance of those ideals as his own, his inner childhood identification with his father and his idealization of him, persisted all the more intensely into adulthood because it had not been modified by the evidence of daily personal contact. What was most obviously true of Wayne as a third-generation conscientious objector who had grown up in the way he had was also true of many other resisters: it would have been far more of a "rebellion" for him to have cooperated with the draft.

"My brother couldn't quite understand why I didn't feel like I was risking a whole lot, risking a twenty-thousand-a-year job. I said, 'Maybe I won't be monetarily successful, but I don't really care to be at the moment, I don't really think in the future it's going to isolate me from everybody, or really keep me that far down, even if I *want* to be monetarily successful.' I remember many times talking to him when I was all excited about something, anything, and he'd always caution me, 'You've got to look at both sides. You have to be open about situations.' And after a certain amount of time it seemed like one side of his thinking closed up. And I was saying to *him* now, 'Look at both sides.'

"As it got closer and closer, he tried harder and harder to talk me out of it, and he thought even the day before the arraignment that I could still go down to the draft board and cancel the whole thing. We finally got to where we didn't talk about it at all, especially after the arraignment. He felt I was crucifying myself, especially since I wouldn't have a lawyer, especially since I had long hair and a beard, and especially since I wouldn't accept alternative service. The night before I went to the arraignment to plead guilty to refusing induction, I was staying at the place where I had the least support. That was my brother's house.

"Mother went through a whole lot of changes. She wanted me to fill out a conscientious objector form, and after I turned in my draft card she and my sister came up and we went for a long ride in the car. The whole thing was really a high emotional response on both parts, mine and hers. We ended up all three of us crying. I had to get out and just walk up the road. I felt they were just taking me apart. They thought I was going about it in the wrong way. They agreed there were problems, but they thought I should work through the system. To them I was *choosing* to go to this place, this place they'd heard so many terrible things about. They wanted me to avoid it at all costs. They were afraid of what the prison might do to me, such as I might come out a bitter, dirty old man, and I don't know what else.

"Mom had been going through some real hard things. I had had the beard and all since the March before that. At home I was a successful son, the All-American Boy, success in the community, and when I came home with the hair and beard it really upset her. She said, 'What will people think?,' and I kept telling her that that's what I'd been concerned about too long, what other people thought rather than what I thought. Then there was this next thing of me going to prison and coming out an ex-con with a felony record, plus being a draft resister, some kind of a radical or something, with all those images of the radical people causing violence on the campus, especially in a community that's really conservative, where the editor of the paper is a John Birch Society member, there weren't too many people she could talk to. Some friends told her I was really letting the country down and one of them used to call her up every night.

"Others came to my support and to hers, too. She's amazed at how many people, some she's never heard of, call her up and write her letters and support me, and her. All the time I was telling her, 'Mom, sooner or later I have to go to prison.' And she'd keep putting it off. I could tell she was putting off facing it. Once she wanted to hide it and she wanted to hide me. Then she began to change. By the time of the trial she said, 'I couldn't understand what you were going through before, but now I really do.' She was no longer trying to persuade me; she was saying, 'You've got to make up your own mind.' Now she's really coming through; like, they had this party and this other gal got up and said, 'I'd like to announce that my son's just gone to college,' and Mom got up and said she'd like to announce that her son had just been through court for refusing induction and was in prison down in Lompoc, California. She finally came down to where she faced the situation, and it wasn't so bad. I guess.

"Canada did occur to me once, but not for too long. It's a situation you can't run from. You can run and hide, go into exile for a while, but you really haven't left the problem, and sooner or later it's going to come around to face you. I was interested, not in getting away from the draft, but in changing the situation, so if I was going to do anything to change it, it didn't make sense to run to some place and have less effect. I just figured the situation with the draft is not an isolated situation, not an isolated decision. That kind of decision is going to have to be made, I don't know how many more times, the rest of my life. It's an attempt to affirm myself and to affirm other people, an attempt to break down barriers between me and another person.

"Prison had some appeal for being kind of a rest, maybe, from all the emotional activity that was going on. It had some kind of appeal to be able to read and write because of the solitude. I really looked forward to the time to read. I've read, but not that much more than I did outside. I don't find myself with any more time. In fact, the same thing's happening again, you know, helping this guy with history and helping this other guy write his letters, talking to people, going out into the yard and playing basketball. I don't have any more time than I had before. If anything, it's more strenuous than it was before. I'm not getting any rest. It's harder to 'maintain' in here, harder to take care of myself. It's the opposite of rest. I'm going to need a rest when I get out. Some of these activities that were so tiring before are going to be resting by comparison.

"Some people suggested that in the back of the situation I really was coming here to get away from the confrontation, the confrontation with the institutions out there and the people I had to talk to. If anything, the confrontation is more intense in here, the strain to talk to the authorities is more intense. It's much less two-way, it makes it harder in a sense. The barriers are thicker. At least on the outside there are little things to grab hold of, so you could say you're making some progress; there's some hope, one more little thing has happened. There's less of those little things, maybe there's none, that you can grab ahold of here. It's harder.

"It's the same thing with the inmates. The barriers are there. This friend of mine wrote that his wife's going to have a baby. I got really excited, but there's nobody to get excited with. I sat up in my cell and laughed and cried to myself. Just like air going out, going nowhere. Just petered out. You get afraid to let out your feelings. You have to tell a person how much you like them by riding them, or joking offhandedly, or making a caustic remark. Sometimes I get tired of having to turn things around in order to tell someone I care about them and what happens to them.

"That's what I miss most about a woman; with them, it's easier to drop off and say, 'I'm weak,' and *be* weak, and not have to be the kind of pseudo-masculine tough guy that's demanded here, the tough guy, the strong guy. The guy who doesn't feel, who's going to bash in his partner's head at any minute and doesn't even feel *that*, doesn't really have the capacity to love anybody, to have positive feelings. The typical guy here is the weight driver, the muscle-bound freak. The ironical thing is a lot of the muscle-bound freaks are homosexual. To me the concept of a man involves the part of me that's able to love a woman.

"Even if you say they don't have any valid right to keep you here, you're still here, you're still confronted with the environment. There's two things you can do: you could say, 'OK, I'll spend my time reading and writing and ignore the rest of it and do my time,' or 'I can do something about what's here.' There was the question whether I was going to *prepare* for the rest of my life and never *do* anything, or do something at each stage that I developed. The situation is the same thing here. For a time I felt there was no use doing anything here, no use attempting to change anything that's here, so you stand still and do your time.

"I felt the barriers between myself and other people long before I came, but I feel I can see them a lot clearer since I've been here. I feel like some of the fog's gone away. You hear a lot about bigotry against blacks. That kind of attitude is not just an isolated incident with black people. It's a situation that happens all the time with everyone. We're bigoted against the hacks just as they're bigoted against convicts or against dopers or resisters or against hippies outside. It hits everybody.

"If anything, this place has doubled my determination to go out and do something. So if it's supposed to be a deterrent, it's failed. If anything, it's helped me in seeing the problems a little better, a little clearer. Instead of dissuading me or making me want to take off to the hills and hibernate for the rest of my life, it's made me realize how important the struggle is and how much it's got to be the rest of my life. And somehow that doesn't seem so tiring any more.

"Once upon a time I'd think about that and I'd just get tired, I'd just want to go to sleep. I'd think, 'Man, you gotta be up against the gun the rest of your life, when are you going to rest?' The demands of other people, the demands of myself, of what I want to do in terms of changing myself. I'm still not content to stay as much Milquetoast as I still am, but somehow it's not such a thing that has to be done overnight any more. Once upon a time, I'd really get frustrated because only a little thing would happen just every so often and I'd feel like there was a whole bunch of things still needing to be done inside me. Now I kind of feel like I've got the rest of my life and that's what I'm going to be doing.

It's going to be an ever-changing, ongoing process and *I'm* going to be doing it, and I kind of like that.

"Anything I'm going to do, it's got to be connected with some action some place. When I was up in the woods that was fine for that time, but I realized that I got tired of that, in the sense that I knew I had to get back and do something with it. Likewise when I'm in activities I want to get back, to get another kind of perspective, so it's got to be a marriage of things. The choice that I had with the draft on the outside and the choice of doing something in here is the same. Part of using time in here by doing something is good preparation for what to do on the outside. It's a way of seeing what the limits of an institution are, whether it's so cemented that it won't move, or won't change. How you can go about changing something structurally, how you go about making some changes, what kind of action is necessary. You could just sit idle here; I feel if I wait any longer maybe I'll be so dead I can't do anything."

14

Calvin Jones, 23

Three Years

THERE was an undeniable looseness about Calvin Jones. He flopped into chairs and sprawled as he sat, but his posture was the opposite of the way he carried himself. His slight build and young face belied a tough determination and old, shrewd knowledge. His earnest, cool manner barely obscured a scanning intelligence that missed little. Alone and untutored, he had quietly refused induction after his own research and instincts told him he had no choice. Like many black inmates, he found prison marginally easier to take than did white prisoners. He had talked about prisons with friends who had been in them, and he found that life inside was close in many respects to black life outside. He was quicker to see the correspondences and was a better interpreter of those similarities to those of us who had to deny our prison experiences and our prejudices longer. He approached his own conflicts over race and violence with the same candor and courage he brought to ours.

The Joneses had left their native South after their marriage and settled first in the Midwest. Calvin was born there, as were his older brother and sister. When he was six months old they moved west, and three more sisters were born in California. Of the six, Calvin was someone special:

"My parents think quite a lot of my intelligence; they set me up as an example to my brother and sister. I guess they, the two older kids, found it hard to accept the fact that I was kind of smart. I never tried to use it to my advantage or anything; I always tried to help them because I figured if I had it, I could transfer some of it to them. I helped my younger sisters too, when I was at home, when I had the time. The last couple of years I've been here and I haven't been able to do anything. I was committed pretty much to the family, the immediate family.

"My mother works in a factory. She's worked ever since I can remember. Most of the kids lean towards her because she seems like she's stronger than my father. She's the kind of person who'll deny herself, give everything to her family and kids; she's benevolent, I guess. She likes discipline, but if you'll help yourself, she'll help you. Mostly she'd help me in my school work and things. She provided the courage to go ahead and study; she just placed emphasis on going to school and making something out of your life instead of running around on the streets and acting crazy. She'd say, 'There are better things in life; stick with your books, the rewards are there.' She gave me the courage to feel I could do the work, inspiration. She inspired me.

"I could see, just in my own family, a person without an education, compounded with the thing that you're black, you can't do any work, you're dead. My father didn't have any education in school. He's been to night school—well, he's gone to night school; he was going to night school when *I* was in school, and I guess he's gone up to about the ninth grade. My mother, when she was in Mississippi, she went all the way through and she's trying to get her teacher's credentials. I'd say she has about first or second year in junior college.

"My father works for an aircraft company. He's the type of dude who just goes to work, comes home, and wants everybody to lay down to his will. He's king and we're his servants. He has no understanding at all towards his kids. I've seen a change in him in the past couple of years now, but he and my brother never got along to begin with. I still don't think they get along very well, but now that a lot of blackness is coming out and you're finding out a lot about yourselves, he looks like he might be coming over. He's trying to re-establish some type of rapport with the family, especially with the kids, trying to get back in.

"My older brother, he was in the service; he was in the Navy four years and he had quite a lot of trouble with different types of jobs they wouldn't give black people. The officers were very prejudiced and he got shipped to three or four different ships while he was in the Navy. I look up to him pretty much and I think he has a whole lot on the ball, and he told me a lot of different things that I later found out to be really true. The way the truth gets distorted in papers and things, stuff that's usually held away from black people. The way the white people are, what to expect from them, what not to expect, don't let them take advantage of you. You really have to set your format down, let them know where you stand before you get anything together.

"When I was around 11 or 12 years old I used to watch Army pictures on TV, and it always struck me kind of strange that there were black people in the service but they were never on TV. My mother had a bunch of Negro history books, and there were black soldiers in the history books. I knew that black people had made some kind of major contribution to the country and in the service, but they just weren't represented. I just didn't get involved when I was younger, but when the war crisis came up I got more interested in it. My brother had been in Vietnam. He wrote and said there was something going on there and it wasn't right. I started investigating and digging back in the library in different files and books to find out just what was happening and looking at the Selective Service laws. It all seemed like garbage to me. Garbage in the sense that it's first instituted and then they let the laws go on and on, you know, without ever changing to meet the times."

Although his brother's personal experience and his own intellectual curiosity prompted some interest in the draft, it wasn't until after the Watts riot in 1965 that Calvin began to think about it more carefully and in relation to himself:

"The riot didn't have much of an impact on me until it was all over and you could see, well, see that black people came closer together. Before the riots, you had white gang fights and blacks against blacks, but after the riot, more blacks against whites. More friendliness and more togetherness on the part of the blacks toward each other.

"I was in the big riot area when they had the curfew, but I didn't participate in it at all; I just couldn't get out into the main stream of things. My parents and transportation and all. They wouldn't let us out of the house, and my brother had the car because he was working out in Glendale, and my father's car was in the shop. There was just no way to get to where it was happening. And if you were smart, you weren't going to run out into the streets by yourself with no protection. It was five or six miles in two directions to get there and it really wasn't worth it. Besides, my parents thought we'd get hurt. They just told us to stay inside. My first impression was, 'What are those crazy people doing?' I guess I didn't really understand what those people *were* doing, but I knew after the first couple of days they really meant business and it was time for me to start looking into it and see what was happening.

"After the riot, all of a sudden they were drafting black men out of the community areas in which the riot was really heavy and where there was a lot of looting. Most of the people I knew hadn't even finished high school and here they were drafted. They didn't even have jobs, they were just walking the street and things, and they're usually young, and all of a sudden the government needed their services for something. Every time something comes up when they need someone, the blacks are the first ones called. They wanted to get the black youth off the streets and out of the communities so they could avoid another riot. The older people had jobs and they could handle them more like puppets. There wouldn't be any problem in the military because they'd break them and ship them over somewhere else and fight some other battle, while the true battle was right here at home where they need people.

"From what I've read and seen, in every major war they barely let the black people in. You look at the veterans, the black vets. You can see that the blacks have more trouble collecting their benefits than the whites and they go through a lot more changes afterwards. I just felt that if you don't care enough about me to help me in my own community, then nothing from nothing leaves nothing. 'If I can't get help from you then you can't get my help. You've used my father and my grandfather to meet your ends, but when it comes time for me to get mine or even try to, then it's no go. I can't get any at all.' As far as constructive things for black people, there's nothing out there.

"Around about my first year in college it was starting to come out that the government had made promises to the Vietnamese people about helping them out when they needed help and the government also made certain promises to the black people, which they haven't kept. I was starting to say, 'Well, you know, they haven't fulfilled *our* promises yet. Besides, I don't see why we should be responsible for anybody else's decisions when we didn't really have any power to decide for ourselves whether or not we wanted to go over and fight.' We're just delivering our bodies, helping them out, and not getting anything in return.

"I have three or four buddies who went into the service. They were drafted. Most black kids, you know, most of their brothers and fathers have been in the service, their families would consider it a great dishonor if they didn't go in. They don't want to break off relations with their family, and they think by going to jail they'd cause some type of split in the family. I'm different in that respect; because of six kids in the family I've had my own way most of the time—I'm sort of the kingpin.

"I have strong family relationships too, but my parents always told me that you have to live your own life the way you see fit, and whatever you decide to do we're going to be behind you. I thought it was about time to test it and see what they really meant. My family passed the test. I didn't *have* to test my family, but I knew one thing—I had to *do* something. I didn't know what it was, but I had to do something to try to straighten my people out. Not just my family but the black people as a whole.

"They have a strange sense of guilt; they feel that since they've been in this country so long they owe the country something, and the country doesn't owe them anything. I guess their values have been torn down so much that somebody's got to build them back up. They need some backbone, that's all I can say; they just need some kind of backbone to actually show them. Most of them are tied up in their religious behavior; they've been wiped out with their religion and they can see nothing else.

"My brother had a few friends who'd been in state prisons and when I was thinking about coming to jail I figured, 'Well, I know just about enough of what happens in the Army, I may as well find out something about jail.' So I asked them some questions about the food and the way you were treated in institutions and just what type of situations you ran into. They gave me the answers and also what they *really* thought about it. A lot of things. A lot about the police brutality. I thought something about Canada, but it just didn't seem right. I didn't know too much about Sweden. All I knew, it was a neutral country, but I didn't know how they'd accept black people there, and generally there wasn't much information about exiling yourself. White kids can go anywhere, but not blacks.

"So I thought more and more about going to jail. I even sort of got ready for it. I'd just go to school and come back home, conditioning myself for this sort of place by not going anywhere. Sleeping on the floor to get used to the hard mattresses in the cells. I didn't eat very much for dinner and maybe I'd eat every other day. I just stopped doing everything. I didn't answer the phone. People would call and I'd be the only one there and I wouldn't answer. I was getting ready for the jail; you don't have phones in jail. It helped out a lot, yeah.

"I was ready to do the time but I was not ready to face the environment. All the putrid smells. Different people you run into. I thought I was ready for everything, but I didn't think it was going to take six hours to get booked in and all those people cramped up in one room. There's no way in the world you can get air in there, and you're just slammed up into one room just a little bigger than this one; no windows, no doors, no fans, but there's plenty of toilets and there are all these odors all in one place. All of a sudden they serve you some dry baloney and you can't drink any of the water, and the next thing you know you're taking off your clothes and spreading your buttocks and they're looking under your balls and spray you just like an animal. 'Lift up your arms and open your mouth,' and they spray."

Although he had been supported in his decision by his family and his immediate friends, Calvin was more than a little apprehensive about how he would be received by other black inmates, and he also felt more than a little superior to them because he was not a criminal. But he found almost no opposition and much sympathy among black inmates, most of whom felt they were resisting white society in one form or another. Indeed, Calvin encountered far less opposition from black prisoners than the white resisters found among the white prison population:

"The way I carried myself when I first came in, I considered myself something special, a special convict from the rest of them. A resister, a draft dodger or whatever, and the others were ordinary criminals. But I just came right in, it was real smooth. I expected maybe some violent repercussions, but it seems like most Brothers were in sympathy with me, and if they tried to attack me it was in a sly manner. They wouldn't come straight out with it in front of an officer, or white guys, or in front of three or four hundred Brothers. They'd come out with it more privately. I was prepared if they were going to try to expose me in front of a bunch of white guys or hacks. I could just throw the situation up, that they're much more embedded in the system than I am, out there stealing and going on for themselves. Perpetuating the system by robbing banks and buying Cadillacs. The money keeps going back into the same place, just revolving around. With me, I'm going to stop doing it completely. I'm not even going to participate any more. When I know something is wrong, I'm not going to keep buying it, I'm just going to *stop* buying it.

"My case worker must have read the file of letters I wrote to the draft board. They were waiting on me when I first came in, and

I got attacked by a couple of them, my case worker and another officer. 'Just look at this! Just who do you think you are? Here's your great opportunity to serve your country and you turned it down. What are they teaching you guys at school?' My case worker couldn't understand why I should be worried about black people in the South. 'Well,' he said, 'you shouldn't be worried about things that are happening in the South or in other parts of the U.S. because *you* live in California.' I explained to him that once you put on your uniform you represent the whole country, not just California, and if I'm going to put on the uniform to represent the whole nation, the thing's got to be right all over the place. It doesn't make any sense for me to go ahead and defend something when black people can't enjoy the benefits of those things. I couldn't see any reason for me going into the service, voluntarily or involuntarily. I guess that shut him up for the time being because he never asked me anything about it; he just kept cool and calm. It sounded as though he was implying that black people didn't have the right to resist. It was something a white guy could do, but a black guy couldn't even have a feeling of conscience for that sort of thing.

"It gives me a sense of self-satisfaction to do what I said I was going to do. I didn't go against my convictions. I guess I just feel good. I don't think I have any hang-ups now about whether I should have gone into the Army or not, or whether I should have gone to jail. I knew what the Army was like but I didn't know what jail was like. I'm not planning on coming back. I don't think it's worth coming back a second time. I just feel that if a person has to come back a second time for something like this, I don't think the country's worth saving.

"If you're going to come back a second time, you're going to keep coming back after that, and you're still going to have the same opinions and you're going to feel the same way no matter how much time you do, and it just doesn't show me anything. How a person would allow himself to be brought back two or three times on the same thing—you make a stand once and you get shot down, that's cool. But if you make a stand a second time and you get shot down for the same thing, that doesn't show me any progress at all. *You* see what they can do to you in here, Doc, the different crazy mental changes they take you through.

"I feel I stood up for what I believed in, but I don't expect anything from them, and I know I'm not going to get anything from them. Coming back from the service, expecting to get a better job, you know; you're not qualified to get a better job, you haven't learned anything at all. All you've learned is how to kill somebody, and you can't use it over here. If you do, you go right to jail. You've got a lot of ex-soldiers in here, and what happens? The only thing they knew was the gun, and they went out there and robbed a bank or shot somebody or something. Hijacked a car or something. They don't teach nothing there but to kill, and then they throw you back out in society.

"I had to find out what it really was like to kill, so I went out to the slaughterhouse and worked there. It was a little bloody, but you get used to that. It was interesting just looking at the different parts of the body and things. The heart, the liver, and things that I'd never seen in real life except in a textbook. It was interesting to see a cattle heart in your hand and the muscle still moving, contracting; and tongues, and kidneys, and things.

"The animal is helpless, and that had a lot to do with it. You're almighty king now, you've got him all bound up. You might say you just changed places. With things that happen, the way the white man has treated the black man, you just put the animal in the white man's place and you're on top now, so it's a way of getting even. I recognized lots of them in here in the animals I killed. There might be a slight resemblance to someone on the farm and this, that and the other, and you know for a while it reminded me of a lot of people. Pigs looking like so-and-so. 'They've got to die!'

"It sort of brought back pictures of the Nazi camps, the way they used to kill the Jews and put them in the oven and burn them up. You don't know how the people felt, but you can place yourself in the position of the Man. The executioner. He didn't really have to do it but still he was responsible because he was doing it and he wasn't objecting to it. It might have been because he was afraid to object, and he'd go along with the thing because he didn't want to be placed in the same position himself. He just went along and did what he was told. After a while, some of the guys in the slaughterhouse got to where they felt 'I want to kill!' but that wasn't me. We went around a cycle of killing one week and the next week you'd be on something else. When my week was over, I was glad it was over and then it was no more for me. I could do without it, put it that way. It was something that I wasn't looking forward to doing.

"It seemed like once you had one down, then there was another one, you had to hurry and get him and quick, there's another one, quick, and it seemed like maybe you might get used to that. Get used to seeing the blood and seeing something—you know, life—just stop. Something might snap upstairs, and you might want to make everything stop. Just go on a spree, wipe out everybody. Then what?"

15

The Necessity of Conviction

W<small>HAT</small> follows is a sketch of the men of this group. Not
an attempt to delineate a "typical resister," or to characterize
every man, it is a restatement, highly condensed and impressionistic, of themes openly stated and implicit that arose in individual
conversation and in the group. These themes seemed directly rele-
vant to the evolution of the resisters' characters, to their choice of
draft resistance and of prison, to the manner in which they met
the particular challenges of prison life, and to the meaning with
which they endowed it.

What distinguishes the resisters is the necessity of their convictions: their principles were as vital to them as was the incarceration that confirmed them. They came to prison, not under the
inner lash of masochism or in "rebellion against authority," but
with the slowly realized and quietly accepted belief that they
could act in no other way and still be themselves. In exercising
judgment and then submitting to it, they were neither willful nor
perverse, but willing and persistent in pursuit of personal and
specific life goals. They saw themselves primarily as distinctive
men of principle acting responsibly. To maintain that specific
identity through the continuity of ethical thought and action was
the task before them. But their decisions and their acts were not
only statements of ethical concern; they were also the milestones

of a developmental passage from late adolescence to adulthood. The consolidation of a lifelong attitude of ethical concern with an act of moral courage was both the capstone of their youth and the cornerstone of their manhood: they could not act for others until they had acted for themselves, they could not accept a definite life pattern as adults until they had committed themselves to acting for their beliefs and for their belief in themselves.

Opposed to violence and educated to responsibility, the resisters could not support an unconscionable war led by men they considered irresponsible. They were, however, bound by their upbringing to recognize the necessity of law and to accept the consequences of its administration. One resister, the son of a philosophy professor, expressed his feelings this way: "In relation to that draft law, I guess I have to be a criminal. I don't think I've done anything criminal, though. When I made my statement in court, I said that obviously I had broken the law and, just as obviously, I hadn't done anything wrong. The basis for my defense was that for a person to be found guilty, he should have done something wrong; because I'd broken the law didn't necessarily mean that I'd done something wrong. They didn't go for it, though."

If a sense of obligation to the community and themselves brought the resisters to court, they could not deny that sense of obligation by going into exile. To "split the country" would have been to provoke an intolerable split between conscience and self. To go abroad would have meant not only a painful and possibly permanent separation from their families and the love and values shared within them but also an impossible alienation from themselves.

Nonetheless, a few resisters experimented unsuccessfully with exile before they went to court; others shared the sentiments of one of those who had gone to Canada and returned:

"I needed some time to think before the trial, and I wanted to be alone anyhow. It wasn't very far to go and I had been there before on vacation. After the first day or two, nothing seemed to be right. I had been away from home before, and I knew it wasn't homesickness I was feeling; I was bothered all the time by the thought that I shouldn't *be* there, that it would be wrong to stay. Even the people I knew there, the places I had visited before, seemed strange, like they didn't really exist or they were unfamiliar in a strange way. There were times when I doubted that they were even really there, or that I was there. I *had* to come home. It wasn't only the idea of evading something, or going against my family and my beliefs; it was that other feeling—of strangeness— that made me decide. As soon as I crossed the border coming back, I felt better, more alive, felt that I was doing the right thing for sure. Put it this way: if that's what going into exile does to you, I'd rather be in jail in America."

What this man experienced, in addition to his clear feeling of guilt, was a more pervasive and indefinable impairment of reality testing, what is known clinically as derealization. Though very different in circumstance, this episode was not greatly different in its pattern of inner elaboration from Freud's "disturbance of memory" when he visited the Acropolis. At the age of 48, Freud rather unexpectedly visited Athens, and while standing on the Acropolis he had an experience of derealization which he later summarized as expressing a momentary feeling of "What I see here is not real." Freud later traced this feeling to the action of the superego, the mental agency of conscience, and to an unconscious sense of guilt for having "gone beyond" his father in traveling to Athens and in social, intellectual, and professional attainment.

Similarly, the derealization experienced by the resister quoted above had much to do with his having "gone beyond" the borders of his nation as well as the limits of his conscience and his identification with his father. Both he and his family had thought it preferable to go to prison rather than to Canada. Once he was in exile, however experimentally, the intensity of the inner realities of conviction and belief, of family ties and inner coherence, overcame his capacity to judge external reality.

What is more, to this resister his episode of derealization was as much an inner realization, a direction-giving experience, as it was what he called "a mental symptom." That it was a symptom is undeniable, but in its manifestation of the inner predominance of the laws of conscience, family, and nation—of duty, honor, country —that symptom was also a sign: of patriotism at its most profound.

The prospect of prison and the stigma of a felony conviction were less intimidating to many resisters than was the inner shame of having compromised a basic belief, of having forfeited their self-esteem, of not having met their own high standards. Some of their parents openly stated their preference for prison over exile. The anxiety and opposition of others stemmed from their fear of injury or corruption in prison, or of the limitations a felony conviction would impose. Again and again, however, I was to hear, from parents who visited or wrote, how proud they were of their sons.

As young adults, many resisters were not merely acting on the beliefs they had learned from their parents and had integrated with their own developing personalities; they were also looking toward future generations. Many said that they had come to prison, at least in part, for the sake of their children, even for those children yet unborn. One man, only half flippantly, said, "It's the only answer to the question 'What did you do in the war, Daddy?' " It certainly was that for him, but it was also the kind of commitment to personal, ethical, and generational continuity embodied in Camus's observation that "real generosity to the future lies in giving all to the present."

But generosity to the future does not occur without a significant gift from the past. That gift was what Freud called a "precious acquisition," a sense of self-respect and pride, a close cohesion of conscience and self which was the core of many resisters' identities. Most resisters grew up in families which emphasized the importance of certain essential values and of living closely to them. They were taught to see things through, not to accept half measures, and to face the consequences of their acts. Family conflict was usually settled by discussion and compromise. The normal aggression of childhood was not condoned but firmly contained, and punishment was generally carried out by withdrawal of privilege or by moral suasion. They were encouraged to cooperate actively rather than to comply passively.

Although the resisters' parents were concerned with principle, self-restraint, and right action, their interest was usually limited to their own personal lives. Few had a particular interest in political or social matters, in theory or in practice. The fathers tended to be quiet, sober men with the kinds of jobs which are more often practical than socially concerned; they were in small business, factory work, engineering, medicine. Matters of conscience, while necessary for daily living, were still intimate concerns, related to wider social applications in the abstract but not to personal activism. It was partly in this context of private self-delineation and fulfillment that many resisters approached their decision. Indeed, many felt that they were acting as their fathers would have had they been in the same situation. But if they were in some ways as private as their parents, the resisters were in other respects more aware of larger issues and of their need to be part of them. What was clear but compartmentalized in the parents was more intense and pervasive in the sons; the boundaries between private and public morality were far less distinct, even nonexistent.

However important the influence and example of their families may have been, the resisters made their own decisions to meet their own challenges. Many seemed quietly certain that their values and aims were not only shared but were also individual; in experiencing the demands of conscience as fully their own, they were able to feel and to say "I demand this of me" as well as "This is demanded of me." The decision to refuse was rarely made without deep conflict, but many looked back on that decision as inevitable, and one described in a calm, almost casual manner. Although there was an urgency to the conscientious concerns of many resisters, there was also a kind of earnest naturalness to them. When the decision was finally reached, most felt the relief that comes when an ambivalent situation is resolved. Some also described an increase in energy and clarity of vision, that sense of renewed vitality which characterizes the completion of an important developmental task.

Many resisters emerged from early childhood with a conscious sense of their own inherent value, often a sense of special distinctiveness as individuals within their families. Several resisters felt that they occupied a special position in their families—irrespective of the order of their birth—which required them to fulfill the dreams and hopes of the families, or to perpetuate their traditions, or to resolve their conflicts, and in one case to personify those conflicts. In later childhood and early adolescence, the feeling of distinctiveness became more noticeable. Intellectual and physical precocity, a concern for responsibility and fairness, and an unprepossessing (though sometimes very prepossessing) self-confidence attracted the trust and admiration of others, which led in turn to a certain social success and appointment or election to positions of leadership.

But this distinctiveness brought its own burden of unsought prominence and its consequence of relative isolation. Several resisters did not always share the high opinions of friends and teachers, and they were sometimes given to self-doubt. They took their successes in stride, but they hesitated to accept what might be premature eminence; they were reluctant to receive what might be undeserved honors; they frequently paused to consider whether they were being taken for more than they were.

The physical, social, and instinctual challenges of adolescence were more often met by the inner restraints of asceticism and intellectualization rather than by emotional swings or by flagrant behavior. Ordinary adolescent emotional conflicts often evoked new conscientious regulation and sometimes a stringent limitation of spontaneity. Mark Henley's childhood illness aroused in him both rage at his helplessness and fear of abandonment by those he loved and on whom he depended. His childhood experiences fostered the subsequent elaboration of a highly prized yet highly private sense of self, one that at the same time was easily threatened by intense emotion and by the fear that the loss of any "significant other" would not only be a desertion but also a loss of substance. When renewed and modified in adolescence, these powerful feelings found regulation in a carefully constructed attitude of social detachment and in ideological concerns which reached, in Mark's own words, religious intensity.

But if Mark seemed to fear abandonment, other resisters, in adolescence, seemed to fear abandon—and the momentary loss of control it implied—thus limiting their direct sexual and social experience because of the identity diffusion it entailed. The predominance of conscience that informed the moral judgment of many resisters also imposed an intensified self-restraint that limited their range of social contact and of sexual and aggressive expression. As they matured, many resisters allowed themselves deeper involvements; others retained a certain reluctance to "lose themselves," a reticence to combine either sexually or socially.

In late adolescence, many resisters alternated between social withdrawal and involvement. The withdrawals took many forms— to a cabin in the woods, to a simplified life in the country, to cross-country hitchhiking, and often to an exclusively psychological withdrawal, an interior journey with no change in physical surroundings. Most of these episodes were marked by heightened concern for deeply personal issues, an internal questioning and defining of themselves and their direction in relation to specific matters: what to do about a girl, about school, about a job, about the draft, about life. This questioning was sometimes ruminative but it was usually reflective; it was rarely autistically preoccupied.

These periods were more often retreats to a time of self-examination and thinking through than they were evasions of a difficult decision or situation, and most of them ended with a sense of renewal and a return to closer and more coherent social involvement. Those involvements were varied; they included deep relationships with others, intense study, what one man called "really heavy career development," and serious exploration of the counterculture. However diverse their pursuits, all of the resisters devoted serious thought and intelligent consideration to the moral issues of the war and the draft. With sustained concentration and anguish, each man slowly worked out his own "position" and decided that prison was his destiny, for it was there that withdrawal and involvement converged.

Every resister was concerned with aggression, that which he saw around him and that which he felt within him. Several had been alarmed by campus demonstrations and some openly feared the daily violence in prison. They lost few opportunities to remind themselves, as well as those who impugned their courage, of the daily physical risk in the cell block or on the yard. Although one man had gone through a period of adolescent vandalism, most resisters were not in communication with their own abilities to express or regulate their aggression, and some, dreading their unknown capacity for violence, magnified it. In fact, several said that although they were opposed in principle to bearing arms, they feared that once given license to kill they would not, in spite of themselves, be able to restrain their impulses. It was not so much that they feared the aggression directed at them in battle as it was that which battle would arouse in them. Indeed, it could be said that some resisters were far more threatened by the prospect of being overwhelmed by their own aggression in combat than by the likelihood of death or injury in battle. To the extent that their refusal of conscription and their choice of prison was an exercise in such excessive self-restraint, it appears that some resisters went to Lompoc to put themselves not so much in a safe place as in a cage.

Nick Manos was particularly impressed with the need for containment of aggression. He appreciated both the intensity of his father's anger and his hesitation to act in anger lest he lose control. His mother, who did the actual punishing, acted only after Nick had breached the many verbal and physical limits on his own aggression and hers. One can begin to understand his particular sensitivity to pictures of injured children; he saw himself in those children, and in refusing to base his freedom on injuring more, he was saying, in effect, "I will not do unto others as has been done unto me."

The prospect of violence evoked in many resisters a mixture of fear and fascination. Calvin Jones had been attracted and aroused by the Watts rebellion, but his own judgment had coincided with his parents' warnings to stay away. Like many other prisoners, he confronted more of his aggression in prison and he was able to test further his capacity to experience it through his work in the slaughterhouse. But he quit that job when he felt his imagination getting out of control. Similarly, Ben Post's intolerance for the "bad vibrations" of prison life was not limited to his sensitivity to the viciousness of other prisoners and of the guards. His own mounting anger, however justifiable, became intolerable to him. The "bad vibrations" from within reinforced his resolve to go to The Hole, the better to resist them.

If in refusing conscription the resisters refused to be the agents of official violence, they found themselves, in Lompoc, to be the objects of it. That they did not anticipate such a position did not entirely quiet the accusations of masochism directed at them from all sides. Perhaps the most vocal of these critics were the prison employees who, without fail, characterized the resisters—collectively and without knowing them—as suffering from "martyr complexes." (When I asked prison employees why a martyr would come to a rehabilitative institution, they had no reply.) I must say that when I began to meet with the resisters I felt obliged at least to keep the possibility in mind that there may have been an element of *unconscious* masochism in their choice of prison. Clearly, I was not concerned with the masochistic perversion in which sexual gratification is derived from physical or mental pain. Rather, I was listening for elements of what has come to be known as moral masochism, a condition in which a need for punishment leads to unconsciously self-inflicted suffering.

After having spent two years with the resisters, I could discern in their lives no evidence of pleasure in pain, no pattern of repetitive self-damage, no tendency to complain that such misfortunes as they had encountered were the machinations of a malevolent fate. It could not be said of any resister, as Freud said of the true masochist, that he "always turns his cheek whenever he has a chance of receiving a blow." It has often been pointed out that moral masochism stems from the need to suffer at the hands of internalized parental figures in the superego, and though it is true that the resisters went to prison at the urging of their consciences, it is also clear that those internalized parental figures within their superegos benevolently favored the decision—as did the parents themselves in the real world.

For most resisters, to go to prison was a clear choice among considered alternatives rather than a blind leap in search of adult punishment for infantile wishes. The resisters felt that going to prison was in their own interests, not against them; that they went *through* prison with a sense of purpose rather than *to* prison for gratification. Theirs was no "victory through defeat"; their time in prison was a route to affirmation, not the affirmation itself. To have assented to their own diminution for the sake of their later growth was not masochism but recognition of reality at its most mature.

Neither dour, humorless, nor rigid, many resisters did insist upon personal value in their relationships, substance in their attitudes, and meaning in their acts. They were self-controlled and self-observant, self-sufficient and, not least, self-mocking. Though they could be firm, they could be flexible; they often took things seriously, but not always themselves. They sought as they matured to strike a balance between distance and intimacy, to retain their inner sense of value and distinctiveness and to achieve a greater sense of unity—distinctiveness as men primarily concerned with moral questions and ethical action, unity as integrated men in touch with their selves and with others.

As they reached out, however, they also felt the limitations of inner restraint lest their reach be met by the excessive grasp of others, lest their private selves be exposed or diminished. It was common to hear resisters speak of their sense of isolation, and it was moving to hear of their efforts to overcome it. Ben Post had his "armor" but he often felt trapped by it as well as defended; Mark Henley was protected from abandonment by his detachment but he knew that he was lonely; Wayne Foote spoke of being surrounded by barriers but he was restless and eager to break them. Sensitive to the urgency of their sexual and aggressive energies, the resisters moved slowly toward involvement, sometimes fearful of inundation by their own impulses, often reluctant to hurt another in a relationship not genuinely mutual.

As they moved from the narrower world of home and family to the wider social universe of college, work, marriage, and parenthood, the resisters sought to integrate their inner growth with increasing external demands for a more fixed commitment and a possibly narrower identity. In this respect, adult life presented the same threat of engulfment by an inhuman, apparently monolithic system as did conscription. They would compromise in many ways, but they would not yield the faculties of reflection and discretion, nor would they give up their continuing sense of identity based on their perception of themselves as distinctive men acting responsibly. Having been raised to cooperate but not to conform, they would not now adopt a false self based on compliance, or values that could not reconcile with their own. They made many personal and social accommodations, but they would not compromise to the point of killing other men or their own idea of themselves. They were flexible men of principle but not men of flexible principle.

Confronted with the demands of school, marriage, and career —in addition to the draft—which they felt would impose premature closure on their growth or the loss of inner vitality, they found themselves in conflict. Wayne Foote's description of his "nuclear wars over the draft" is more than coincidental. Not only does he allude to the obliterating physical force of this era, but he also refers to the war within himself over his nucleus, the inner self which had to control those potentially obliterating forces which also nourished it. For Wayne, as for others, it was necessary to exercise both judgment and action, to exert that part of the self which had to be free, to defend that core of self without which life would be worthless.

To the degree that resisters were certain of themselves, they could make an active commitment; to the degree that they were often solitary, they could choose the isolation of prison; they could "precipitate out" of a wider social order to crystallize their identity, and they could do it with a certain specific gravity. To the degree that they were sure of their distinctiveness, they could act to preserve their autonomy by temporarily yielding it. To the degree that they saw themselves as responsible men perpetuating their personal, familial, and universal values, they could stand alone for principle. To the degree that they were confident of the persistence of their inner core of identity, they could approach a situation which was fraught with risk.

Wayne Foote had rehearsed for prison by withdrawing to the woods; Calvin Jones, by fasting and sleeping on the floor. Ben Post did not contemplate the possible risks of prison lest his apprehension undermine his purpose. Mark Henley and Calvin Jones had interrogated friends about prison life and had asked the usual questions about physical brutality and homosexuality. But none of the resisters was sufficiently prepared—and it is doubtful that they could have been—for the psychological effects of imprisonment. In taking action consonant with their inner world, they acted to confirm themselves as men who went to prison for principle, but not as convicts. They came to Lompoc to affirm and unify themselves, but in search of consolidation they would face petrifaction; in seeking wholeness they would confront totality.

PART THREE

The Group

16

The Consequences of Rehabilitation

Whether it was called treatment, correction, or rehabilitation, what was practiced at Lompoc was punishment and confinement. Whatever the announced policy, the effect of incarceration is the erosion of each prisoner's identity; he feels neither sameness nor continuity but stasis and disjunction. Moreover, each prisoner is pressured toward an arid mental life, concreteness of thought, social discontinuity and a psychopathic pattern of human relations; toward the acceptance of the debased identity, not of prisoner but of convict. This process is carried out gradually rather than by direct attack, by requiring a sequence of minor adjustments rather than by open assault. Within a closed environment, it is accomplished through physical intimidation, social control, and psychological coercion. With arrogant self-righteousness, guards and officials perceive their charges as simply delinquent, as nothing but what they appear to be, as no more than their criminal behavior. One aspect of a prisoner is ascribed to him completely; a partial quality of his character is made to define him totally. If they hear it enough and feel it enough, many prisoners actually come to believe it: "They cause you to think that your *overall* personality is bad because of one thing you did."

Such an experience resonates deeply through the psyches of prisoners, arousing dormant emotional conflict and painful inner tension. This situation not only evokes conflict, it exploits it. It is castrating, to be sure; shaming, without doubt; depriving, obviously. All too often, the prisoner's response to both his immediate pain and the enforced recapitulation of his infantile fears is to feel nothing.

Resisters were immersed equally with other prisoners in the time-bound yet timeless world of imprisonment. In the following pages, they recount their prison experiences and their responses to them, both heartening and disturbing. The group transcripts which follow fall into two major sections. In the first, the resisters discuss those aspects of prison life which are more or less common to every inmate. More than a catalogue of influences, these episodes sketch as well the pressures upon every inmate, no matter what his background, to accept the debased identity of convict. The resisters speak of their experiences in court, their appearances before the parole judge, their confrontation with violence, and their entrapment in riot. They bear witness to the force and the survival value of the inmate code by their acceptance of it and of the degree to which it influenced their own values. They refer to the difficulties of sexual deprivation and the subtler dangers of homosexual threat. They describe the suspicion, if not quite the paranoia, which prison life promotes and which is necessary for physical, not to mention psychological, survival.

With the arrival in the prison of a man who was clearly a draft dodger and not a resister, an issue which had only been briefly discussed was forced upon the group: the definition of cowardice. Prior to this event, there had been occasional remarks in the group about resistance being a form of "creative cowardice" and less frequent reiterations that "conscience makes cowards of us all," but it is with this event that the emphasis of this book shifts to matters more specific to the resisters, to their relationship with me, and to the tensions within the group itself. The pressures of incarceration were bound to produce such tensions, and these were evident in the changes in thought and feeling in each resister as well as in their behavior toward one another. These tensions were heightened by the successive arrivals within the group of several genuine resisters with sentences widely at variance with those the group had considered reasonable and proper.

By this point in their incarceration, the older group members were in no mood to recognize, much less to tolerate, distinctiveness and diversity. Still less were they ready to confront their own sense of victimization by the prison authorities, the degree of their self-victimization, or the extent to which the presence of the short-term resisters aroused their hatred and envy and "violated" their sense of their own worth. That there suddenly appeared to be glaring differentials in sentences led to the suspicion that there might indeed be grades of conscience and degrees of conscientious objection— and thus to a struggle, which probably could have been enacted nowhere else, to restore the group to its own definition of equilibrium, to exact its own form of justice, and to impose its own sense of equity.

Throughout all this, however, there was another struggle, one which was more basic than those of conscience and coercion, wholeness and totality, consolidation and petrifaction, strength and power. It was a struggle which was certainly beyond psychologizing and almost beyond belief. The struggle to retain the identity of man of principle and to reject the identity of convict was only part of it. It was the struggle to confront, define, redefine, but never to yield that configuration of identity, value, and conviction which had brought each man to prison. It was the struggle for their sacred honor.

In addition to the six men presented in Part II, the resisters quoted below appear in the group transcripts which follow; they do not comprise the entire group of resisters at Lompoc, but they do complete the number of those whose words are reported in this account.

Jay Bowman, 21; Three Years, two and a half suspended:
> "I've been losing faith in some institutions; it was time to see if I still had faith in myself."

Carl Bronson, 22; Three Years, two and a half suspended:
"I do believe in facing things, you know."
Joe Cox, 21; Three Years, two and a half suspended:
"It's wrong to kill."
Ned Farley, 24; Three Years, two and a half suspended:
"I won't cooperate in my own destruction."
Steve Martin, 22; Two Years:
"Real cowardice is not acting on your beliefs."
Dan Parker, 23; Two Years:
"Coming here was more a practical thing for me; in relation to that law, I guess I have to be a criminal."

17

"Everybody Has a Bum Rap"

For every resister, his trial was a last chance and a last hope for a responsible hearing. None felt that he got one. Two of the seventeen had gone out and hired a lawyer to defend them. A few others had been represented by court-appointed public defenders with whom they felt no rapport and from whom they got no sympathy. Many others, including some who could have hired their own counsel, preferred to present their own cases directly to the judge because they were unwilling to negotiate through an intermediary who might force them to compromise their stands in order to avert conviction. They felt that attorneys' stratagems and procedural maneuvers would only delay the case and obscure the issues. They felt that their beliefs should be as clear and as obvious to the court as they were to themselves, and that to present them personally to the judge was the more convincing and less compromising approach. To haggle over precedent or procedure through counsel seemed far less important than to approach the judge directly, in order to stand in as close relation to him as they stood in close relation to the ideals, sanctions, and prohibitions of their own consciences.

Indeed, many of the resisters did not want to get off. For some, the trial came as a welcome relief after a period of intense anxiety and suspense; for others, the idea of imprisonment was not unattractive. For most, their simple integrity was more important than a sophisticated defense. They had not evaded the draft, they had refused it; they would not evade the consequences, they would accept them.

There were few judges who were not affected in some way by this direct and simple attitude. Judges probably vary as much as, say, draft resisters, but within the experience of this group, two judicial attitudes seem to have predominated. One of them I observed when I was in court to appear as a witness in a subsequent case on the docket and a Selective Service violator was brought in for sentencing. (This particular man did not come to Lompoc.) After pronouncing sentence, the judge delivered a tirade against the defendant's appearance and that of his friends in court, and he impugned his veracity, his masculinity, and his patriotism. A milder attack than that would have provoked a fist fight outside the courtroom and would have guaranteed a knifing inside Lompoc.

Several men in the group endured such attacks from this and other judges, but many more faced a subtler judicial and human response: indecision. Like other prisoners, the resisters constantly rehashed the details of their trials, in part to moderate the anxiety generated by the experience as well as to contain the tension evoked by incarceration. Even in the retelling of all those trials, it was possible to sense the reluctance, even anguish, some judges must have felt at having to sentence to prison men who were "not usual jail material." They tried last-minute compromises and little chats in chambers; they looked beyond the defendants themselves for scapegoats or for outside influences; they even called in psychiatrists or sent resisters to them for evaluation, unwilling to credit the sanity of men whose lives, before their refusal of induction, had been unremarkable.

When reading the files of the resisters in this group, I came across some of the psychiatric examinations which had been requested by the courts. There was never any question regarding their ability to understand the nature of their offense, of the charges against them, or of their ability to assist counsel in their own defense, and therefore no reservation regarding their competency to stand trial. Several psychiatrists found no evidence of psychiatric disorder and said so. Others, however, found no evidence of psychiatric disorder but evidently felt that because a law had been broken a diagnosis was mandatory. This attitude was best expressed in the statement of one psychiatrist who concluded his examination of one resister with the following opinion: "This man is the product of a stable family, has a good scholastic and employment record, and appears normal in every way. But he has broken the law and apparently feels no remorse. For these reasons he must be diagnosed as: Sociopathic Personality Disturbance, No. 000-x60."

But the resisters would accept neither hasty compromises nor gratuitous diagnoses, and the judges evidently could not bring themselves to impose suspended sentences. The resisters saw the regretful and self-pitying sighs that accompanied the judges' pronouncements of sentences as sheer hypocrisy, doubly painful for their own disappointed expectations of judicial candor. The indecision of some judges seems to have been resolved by a philosophy of "when in doubt, punish." Other judges, however, manifested their uncertainty by imposing curiously split sentences: six months in prison and the remainder of the time (from two to four years) on suspended sentence. The catch was that if these men refused a second induction notice after their incarceration, they would be returned to prison for the remainder of their sentence. This well-intentioned compromise was to have drastic consequences for the resisters themselves, but no one except perhaps a very wise old con could have anticipated them.

MARK   The judge thought I was a little loose because I came from a nice family, had been to college, had gotten good grades, had no more than the usual adolescent problems, why should I *do* this? Obviously it didn't fit into his scheme of things. I didn't have a beard, I didn't have long hair, he just couldn't fit it into a pattern, "There had to be something wrong with this man." So he sent me up here for observation to find out whether or not my cap was loose. [Mark had been interviewed by my predecessor at Lompoc.] He talked to me in his chambers, partly for my parents and partly for me. They were seeing the public prosecutor and the public defender and him before I even knew about it. They were worried about me going to prison. It was all tied in with the fact that they charged me with refusal to take the physical rather than failure to report for induction. If I would just take the physical, I'd be declared 4-F, all charges would be dismissed, and I'd be guaranteed not to be redrafted. The judge and the prosecutor had it set up with Selective Service. It was an on-the-sly thing, it was set up in a roundabout way. You're not supposed to do this, naturally. The prosecutor and the judge had it set up with my parents and they were to try and pressure me into doing this. So if I would go down and take the physical, the DA would ask to have the indictment quashed and I'd be guaranteed a 4-F. The family doctor was also in on it, I forgot to mention him; the judge would throw it out, and that would be it.

LM Who presented the scheme to you?

MARK My parents and the public defender.

LM What was your response when you first heard it?

MARK No! Absolutely not! I mean, I wouldn't have refused in the first place if I thought that compromising was a moral way to act. I dismissed my lawyer. He wanted me to plead not guilty. Basically what he wanted to do was show that I was duped: "Young innocent lad duped by 'Commonists' and 'Arnachists'.' " I said, "The hell you are, you have no right to do that." I pleaded guilty without help of counsel, because I felt I *was* guilty, you know. Guilty as hell.

RALPH It gave you a greater insight into the way the system works, don't you think?

MARK I got that anyway. But since I went that far, the judge didn't want me to have a felony on my record, so he gave me the Youth Act. I guess he figured I wasn't completely mad, he just thought I was misguided, and going through all the problems of the young twenties, and rebellious, and this kind of thing. You know, as I matured I would grow out of this stage, invest in the stock market and all, and he wouldn't want to handicap me with a felony on my record. So he gave me this tremendously lenient sentence. Six years.

LM   Did anyone else do that, plead without a lawyer?

CALVIN   I had a body, a body if you wanted one to stand next to.

LM   Did he tell you about different sentences and that sort of thing?

CALVIN   No, he was an ex-Navy man.

MARK   I don't think the judge really wanted to send me here and yet he couldn't bring himself to give me probation. He felt it was too serious a thing to do, too much of a moral . . .

RALPH   . . . Defeat for them.

NICK   I don't think it's that. What they're afraid of is their own personal dignity. They're afraid someone's gonna come up to them and point the finger at them and say, "You aren't doing your job." They're gonna say, "You're too lenient." These are the words my judge used; he said, "If I don't do this, then I'm gonna have to look at people who say to me, 'Look what you did,' " and this is what they're afraid of, the personal confrontation they'll get. I don't think they give that much about the system.

WAYNE   Judge Davidson keeps sitting up there and saying, "I know what it's like down there. I'll send you down there for some reality for a while. Get out of your ivory tower, it'll do you some good."

RALPH   This *is* the government in reality.

BEN   As soon as you see "reality" you hate it all the more.

LM   Why is the judge discussed so much in here?

RALPH   He's a representative of the establishment.

WAYNE   The physical manifestations of everything shitty that happens, and his hypocritical thinking is representative of the population.

STEVE   It's just trying to figure out exactly how much rope you have. How much you can trust him to protect you when you're trying to change something. You're trying to stand up for something.

WAYNE   You go in there with this idea about justice that's always talked about in the courts and law system. Then you run into a judge who's arbitrary, who's also ignorant of quite a few things, especially this place. Who's also representing the things you're trying to change and keeping you from doing it. Especially when you get in here. They say so many things about how this is for everybody's welfare and for rehabilitation and all that. And when you get in here you realize how really unaware he is of what this place is. He's also the one that says, "I have found you guilty and I have decided that you must, that it's *best* for you to spend such-and-such a time in a correctional institution," and it's kind of the ultimate of that one-man arbitrary authority saying, "I know what's best for your life."

NICK   Did you ever hear him actually say such a thing?

WAYNE   What?

NICK   That it was *better* for you?

WAYNE   Yeah, Davidson says it all the time.

BEN   Oh, wait a second. He says it as if he doesn't want to do it at the same time.

WAYNE   But Davidson says, "I'm really your friend, I really have your best interests at heart."

BEN   They try to get away from claiming responsibility for what they're doing.

DAN   Davidson's a pseudo liberal, man. He really is. You know the way he jokes around in the courtroom and tries to have kind of a happy atmosphere, and then screws the guy at the end every single time. He wants to play the grandfather role and doesn't want the liberal-intellectual end of the community to get down on him. But in the end he nails you. I could see being sent to jail by someone who says, "I believe you did the wrong thing and you're going to jail," but not by someone who says, "Man, I'm sorry."

BEN That's what he does, too. He does it every time. Originally I thought the courts were something fair, that they were actually going to listen to you. Before I went to court, the court was the only thing in the government I had any hope in. This was the thing that would keep control over the executive branch. I went up there, man, and they're the *pawns* of the executive branch. He said he was sending me here as a deterrent; to keep other people from doing what I was doing. On the induction bus on the way to take the physical, none of them except for one guy, only one guy, really wanted to go in. Everyone else was saying, "Man, one more physical, I hope I fail it."

NICK My judge didn't give me that impression at all. He was quite clear that he was putting me in prison to punish me and that it wasn't going to do any good at all.

RALPH That sounds ridiculous. Why's he doing it if he doesn't think it's going to do any good?

BEN My judge thought the draft was right; he thought maybe the war in Vietnam wasn't too good a deal, and, well, he'd give me a year and a half. "Don't think it's going to do you any good, but I've got to do it."

NICK You'll find that the judge will do exactly what the hacks will do here. If you put the finger on them, they cease to be; they suddenly separate themselves as a human being from their job, their function.

WAYNE Judge Hamm did a really weird thing. At the trial he told me he would like me to reconsider the conscientious objector form. I'd already broken the law, refused induction, and refused to sign the CO form. The prosecuting attorney got up and started citing off how it was illegal because I'd already broken the law and it was after the fact, and at that point the judge said, "I think I'm aware of the law." At that point he was willing to go outside the law, to do something different than just pass sentence, because he said at the same time, "If it looks like I'm trying to get off the hook, I am, because I don't want to send you to prison." But then when we got to the sentencing part, then he says that it's not his job to interpret the law, it's his job to uphold the law, he has to give me two years.

RALPH   He's washing his hands of justice entirely.

NICK   Yeah, that's one thing that mine tried to plead. He didn't make the law, he merely determined whether or not it was followed. If it wasn't followed, he did his thing.

BEN   Just following precedents.

NICK   I think, given the judicial system that we have, they're correct. Their job was not to interpret the law, their job was to determine whether or not it was followed. It's the Supreme Court's responsibility to determine it.

LM   I can see why you're all, uh, put off by your experience in court, but I think the amount of time you spend on it in here has more to do with your life in prison. If you question the validity of the judge's sentencing, his ability to judge the situation, and yet that same invalid judge has sentenced you to prison, then being in prison, your time in prison, is . . .

BEN   . . . Invalid!

LM   And therefore, perhaps, easier to put up with.

STEVE   Why is it easier?

LM   Because you're here "unjustly." It may be easier to get through the two and a half or six years if you clearly keep in your own mind the idea that you're here because an invalid judge sent you here.

RALPH   But it's full of injustice, and injustice in fact is what prompted the whole situation.

LM   If you're completely in the clutches of the government in prison, it puts you in a defenseless position. If you're here defenseless, in the hands of a hypocritical and invalid system, then perhaps you feel less defenseless. If you're here as the result of an insensitive or invalid judge, then perhaps the psychological oppression of being here is less weighty.

STEVE   Yeah, the psychological oppression *is* less weighty. It's probably a lot healthier but it isn't any easier.

LM   What I'm saying is that concentration on the judge's insensitivity or invalidity is a means of dealing with the situation in the prison psychologically.

WAYNE   That's why there are so many bum raps around the prison.

RALPH   Oh, everybody has a bum rap.

18

Parole

For all prisoners, and in this the resisters were no exception, one thought was uppermost: getting out. Commutations, reductions of sentence, and, for that matter, successful escapes were rare indeed; the overwhelming majority of the prisoners left Lompoc either through the expiration of their sentence or on parole. Many prisoners were relieved to know that with a fixed sentence they could not be held beyond a mandatory release date, even if they lost the benefit of time off for good behavior. Still, the hope of parole led many prisoners with fixed sentences to appear before the Parole Board despite the anxiety and uncertainty which were built into this process. If defeated by the Kafkaesque character of a parole hearing, a prisoner with a fixed sentence could always "relax" and pull his time until it ran out. It was a different situation for prisoners with an indeterminate sentence under the Youth Corrections Act. Unless they chose to wait out the full extent of their term—four years with "good time" or six years without it—Youth Act prisoners had to make several appearances before the Parole Board until they met its unfathomable criteria. Although the Youth Act was intended to be flexible and individualized, its application was rigid and categorical.

Parole decisions are initialed by a member of the Board of Parole, a presidential appointee, who visits the prison every two months. Having reached a decision, he consults another Board member in Washington. If he agrees, the matter is settled one way or the other; if he disagrees, a third Board member is called in to resolve the conflict. It is difficult to comprehend the basis for these decisions. The case worker presents his recommendation, which is based largely on the guards' evaluation of the inmate's behavior, and the judge interviews the prisoner for a maximum of fifteen minutes. The prisoner is not permitted to see his record and cannot effectively dispute or challenge the evaluations presented. He is not permitted to be represented at the parole hearing by an attorney. Even if the parole decision has been made on the spot and confirmed by telephone, this tense interview is followed by an even more tense (and punitive, in this era of rapid communication) period of waiting, sometimes a month long, for a formal announcement of the decision.

It was not surprising that many prisoners viewed the Parole Board practices, and especially their administration of the Youth Corrections Act, as a form of government extortion. It raises false hopes of parole at the time of minimum eligibility, yet few if any men are paroled after six months. Indeed, it is rare for any prisoner, no matter what his crime, his sentence, or his mental state, to be paroled as soon as he is eligible. Prisoners are led to believe that good behavior will hasten their parole, but in fact it is determined far more by the nature of their offense: bank robbers at Lompoc were not paroled before marijuana smugglers even if they were similar in background, sentence, and prison behavior. The Parole Board relies, for the most part, on gross evaluation of behavior by unskilled, limited, and scarcely unbiased employees. Although there does seem to be some arbitrary formula based on the nature of the offense and the amount of time served for it (ignoring "individualized" extenuating or incriminating factors), parole decisions seem to be determined as well by the values of the parole judge and, to a lesser extent, by the impression made by the prisoner.

When I asked a prison official about parole policy, I was told that there were no fixed standards and that the Parole Board had only a "system of practices" governing their decisions. These practices were evidently never written down because, despite their frequent references to such a document, the prison officials could never produce one. One prison official told me that for resisters the Parole Board required that a minimum of two years be served "for parity with military duty." For resisters, like all other prisoners, parole was determined categorically: it depended primarily upon the nature of their offense and not on "individualized" aspects of their personal histories or their imprisonment. In view of this attitude at their parole hearing, the best behavior in the world could not shorten their term, while bad behavior, if they were sentenced under the Youth Act, could bring an intolerably long one. It was a bitter joke among the resisters, all of whom could be reclassified and redrafted, that a better way to avoid the draft was to be sentenced for smuggling marijuana—*that* usually meant parole within sixteen months and, because of felon status, no further draft notice.

Most of the resisters in this group did not receive parole. They were released at the end of their sentence, less the usual discount of 30 per cent for "good time." Most of these men were scheduled by the prison officials for parole hearings anyway, and they went to them in hope and fear, unaware that the Parole Board would routinely deny parole to anyone who had not served two years. For the men with the Youth Act, a parole hearing was more important than it was to men with fixed sentences, since their elastic, indefinite sentence could keep them in custody for years longer than the fixed period faced by men with "straight numbers." For men with the Youth Act, such as Ralph Lombardi, the institutional pressure to conform and to tell the parole judge what he wanted to hear was as great as the inmate pressure to be a quiet, code-bound prisoner.

Like other inmates, Ralph was not eager to spend any extra time in prison, and he made many more compromises with the rules, the code, and himself than he liked to admit. But even the appeal of parole was not sufficient for him to cooperate in his own debasement to the extent that the prison required or that the parole judge seemed to want to hear. He would not recant, he would not deny his contempt for the prison or the anger and pain it aroused in him, and he would not let the judge forget, as his case worker had, the enduring responsibility and probity on which his pride depended.

NICK   How did your hearing go, Ralph?

RALPH   So-so. I don't know, I'll know next week. He doesn't provide anybody with any false hopes. He gives everybody the impression that you might as well find something in the institution that interests you because you've got more time to do.

LM   What'd you tell him when he asked about your confinement?

RALPH   I told him my situation hadn't changed any. That my conscience remains the same. Seventeen months of prison doesn't alter that. It's essentially a matter of right and wrong. He asked me what kind of problems I have in the institution. I told him how the place is run authoritarianly. I told him this was a very, very depressive environment. I told him I didn't think much of it. He told me he didn't think much of my work reports. I told *him;* I said, "I don't really think how well I sweep a floor or how well I perform janitorial work relates to anything in the real world." Then he tried to blow this up to where I had no respect for the rules. And I said, "No, I think if I sweep a floor an *x* amount of hours, it's not significant. I don't expect to make a living out of it when I get out." But, uh, I don't know, I'll know next week.

NICK   All he has to do is share with you his thoughts.

RALPH   When he asked about the problems I had here, I felt like just turning around in my chair and pointing to my case worker and saying, "This cock sucker hasn't told me the truth since I've been here." That's the type of attitude I had towards the whole thing.

LM   But you didn't turn to the case worker?

RALPH   No, no. Instead I went into this thing about the authoritarian environment crushing individuality. How the staff here seems more concerned with the particular wording of a rule than in the feelings of human beings. He didn't seem to relate to that, or he tried not to. He flinched. Whenever this guy thought he was providing hope, like saying, "Well, when you get out" . . . if this sounded too hopeful, then he would add something like, "whenever that might be, blah, blah, blah." The thing sounded like I'm getting a [parole] date, but he wants me to think that I'm *not* getting a date just for the sadistic pleasure of it. I was in there quite a while, much longer than the average. The procedure is that they talk about you, then call you in, then get rid of you and talk about you when you leave. Well, it seemed that the period they were talking about me was stretched out over a half hour or so, which is about twice as long as the normal conference.

19

Violence

VIOLENCE was always present at Lompoc. It was a means of resolving conflict, was usually private, and was carried out man-to-man or in small groups, occasionally escalating into mass riots. It was allowed to go on without intervention from the staff, and it threatened the lives and safety of everyone. For every prisoner, his own focused anger or more diffuse rage at his humiliation and helplessness required massive inner control by extensive exclusion from consciousness and by extreme insensitivity to external events. The necessity of such broad and deep psychological processes brought with them a flattened emotional life, narrowed awareness, a contracted range of consciousness, impaired judgment, and the erosion of more balanced and flexible ways of experiencing and of linking inner and outer realities.

These extreme defenses were maintained with the very intensity and urgency of the drives they contained, and the energy so bound and binding left inner life as impoverished as outer. What could not be contained was usually attributed to others, so that they were seen as intensely threatening figures: first for their manifest behavior, then doubly so for what had been ascribed to them.

Many prisoners could sense their own disintegration, and the approach of psychic death was often indirectly expressed through their mounting fears of annihilation by uncontrollable forces from within and without. Some external dangers were as potentially over-whelming as internal ones, but at least those outer threats could be recognized and named and the fear of them could be openly expressed. Winter rains swelled the Santa Ynez River to a raging torrent every year. There were nuclear warheads on the missiles in the ground all around the prison. The seismic time bomb which is the San Andreas Fault was not far away. The immediacy of these realistic dangers fused with the urgency of inner fears to produce in many prisoners outspoken apprehension of flooding by the Santa Ynez as well as inundation by their own impulses; of nuclear catas-trophe as well as psychic and physical obliteration by aggression and assault; of earthquake as well as splitting, upheaval, and chaotic destruction of their personalities.

There was another threat, however, which was so immediate and so pervasive that it was hardly discussed and was only partially symbolized by the imagery of cataclysmic destruction by natural disaster. It was as general as the anger which simmered in every prisoner and as specific as a razor slash. It was the fear of riot. Since small-scale violence was a daily practice at Lompoc, the potential for riot was always present. Riots break out for many reasons, but those which erupted at Lompoc while I was there were rooted in the intense conflicts of homosexual practice and—more importantly—commerce, and in the ubiquitous racial tension. Not to be ignored was the less specific but no less oppressive deathly monotony which made the chaos of riot seem a welcome change in the direction of activity if not of life.

Though the riot described in these pages grew out of homosexual conflict, it was abetted by the intense racial hatred of many inmates and guards. Even when the fighting stopped, the racism did not. After this riot, which was not controlled until it had culminated in the all-out race war everyone seemed to want, a number of injured prisoners were brought to the hospital for treatment. White and black, fractured and bleeding, they lay on stretchers or sat on benches in the hospital corridor waiting for medical attention. Some of the guards then began a series of racial catcalls which were soon taken up by the white prisoners and which threatened to revive the fighting on the spot. When the doctor on duty asked a prison executive to replace the guards, he was refused with the excuse that they, and only they, were necessary to enforce security.

MARK   They were running guys into C Unit, and I guess other units too. Even if you didn't live there it was just, "Get in, get in, go on in, any house, any house." Racking 'em shut.

LM   Did it take you by surprise?

CALVIN It was expected. Could've been stopped, though. Could've been stopped last Thursday night when it started. Started during the night up in E Unit. They knew it probably would happen.

LM   By "they" you mean the guards?

CALVIN The hacks knew, yeah. Any time something like that happens in an institution where it involves two races, there's bound to be some kind of repercussions afterwards, no matter who was in the right.

LM   What happened in E Unit?

CALVIN From the way I piece things together, it involved a homosexual and a Hawaiian dude to begin with. Then a Brother stepped in and then they jumped on another Brother.

LM   A black homosexual with the Hawaiian?

CALVIN No, it was a white homosexual with this Hawaiian dude. The white guy fired on him [hit him], knocked him over into the Brother's bunk. The Brother jumped up, fired on the homosexual. The homosexual went back and told its Daddy. Daddy came back and another Brother went to help the first Brother out and they went to it there and they had a little ruckus for about half an hour. This is about 10:30. There was a bunch of police running down to E Unit. So they took maybe two or three guys to The Hole. The next day there were rumors that it was going to happen, and then, that Friday in the yard, it just exploded.

LM   What happened in the yard?

CALVIN   The way I hear it, some Brothers came out into the field because the white dudes called them out, friends of the people up in E Unit. They coaxed it on. So the Brothers, they just fired away out there; it was between the gate and the rec shack.

LM   You mean the white guys had dared the blacks to come out and fight?

CALVIN   Yeah.

MARK   There were more whites than blacks, and so in this way what they were saying was, "It's OK, we're together now. You jumped us before, you outnumbered us. Now here we are *en masse*." They came out more or less all the same time, and so you had I don't know how many black guys and how many white guys. But the black guys came out as one and said, "OK, if you want to get it on, you know, we're all here ready now. How brave are you?" And it got going. No kiddin' around.

CALVIN   Reminded me of the '65 riot we had in Watts. Just people running everywhere. Shouts, sirens, whistles, police standing by, people jumping over fences.

MARK   I heard the siren go off and all of a sudden everything just fell into place. Wheeeeee. And at the same time the telephone rang for the hack. I never saw anyone go so manic in my life. "All right, let's go, let's go, let's go, fellows." My God, the guy slipped three or four times running up and down the stairs to get to the rack end so he could shut the doors.

CALVIN   Yeah, it was a madhouse.

MARK   It was.

LM   Were you scared?

MARK   Was I scared? No, the door was locked. Are you kidding? I'm invincible when my door's locked.

CALVIN   I was relaxed up until the point where the Man came out of the tower with the rifles. It just reminded me of '65 and I know how crazy those police get when they have guns in their hands. This tower over there, he fired at least three shots. And this maniac over here, he hadn't been working in the institution no more than six months. The young police, he called up to the tower, to the second tower, and asked him could he shoot inmates off the rec shack. He says, "I can hit 'em, I can hit 'em, can I shoot? Do I have permission to shoot?" When I heard that, I wasn't going nowhere.

LM   How did you hear it?

CALVIN   He was *yelling* it. He was on the phone, he reached back, and he had the phone in one hand, the rifle in the other hand, talking to I guess it was the other tower. They told him not to shoot. The way it went down with me, he didn't care who was black or who was white, he was going to down every inmate he saw. He was a marksman, he didn't care who it was. Then the gallant police came out in their helmets and night sticks.

MARK   Well, that's the thing. They were ready. They knew.

CALVIN   They knew, they knew, man, they knew it in advance.

MARK   Because [two employees] were over talking to some blacks in E Unit Friday afternoon saying they knew it was going to come down. They could have stopped it either of two ways. One, close the yard and not even open it for a night or two; or open it and set out all the extra police they called in later from off duty.

CALVIN   Like I said before, it could have been stopped that night. It all started in E Unit and they should have just sealed it off from the rest of the institution.

20

Value Reversal

I_F going to prison was an integrative task for most resisters, staying in prison was an adaptive challenge. Under the control of a regime as absurd as it was vicious, each prisoner to some extent found himself neglecting or ignoring moral valuations even if they had a considerable integrative force. The price of adaptation was frequently reintegration and action in a diminished, if more appropriate, way.

As his incarceration progressed, Mark Henley became progressively "callous"—insensitive to his own feelings, to the outside world, and to the promptings of his own conscience. Although he came to prison out of his sense of responsibility and though he detested the irresponsibility of others, Mark was not alone in his realization that the facts of prison life were directly opposed to the facts of his own life as he had previously known it. Hard work and delay of gratification seemed pointless; impulsive action and theft appeared to be far more logical. Mark had been a model prisoner in many ways: he accepted the rules, however idiotic; he got himself into the routine; and he learned to numb himself, not only to the pain but to all that he had been.

Mark was such a model prisoner that he not only accepted the tenets of the inmate code, he also came to feel that the best defense against the petrifaction of imprisonment was to act psychopathically. He began to steal. But there was more to Mark's stealing than his appropriation of things which, in any reasonable situation, would have been his for the asking; there was more to his thievery than an adaptive value reversal required by incarceration. In stealing, Mark was doing precisely what had been most intensely forbidden in childhood and what was most reprehensible to his moral sense. In becoming a thief, Mark was only one of many who discovered, with a shock, his negative identity: "That which he has been warned not to become, which he can become only with a divided heart, but which he nevertheless finds himself compelled to become, protesting his wholeheartedness." As in all of us it had been there all along, that shadow self, to be evoked when summoned by the conjunction of inner need and outer demand.

MARK How have I changed in three years? I don't know; I do, too. Less aggressive, more docile, yes, I am. I think that's a function of this place. I very seldom get worked up any more, really feel something personal.

LM You don't feel or you don't get worked up?

MARK Both. I know I don't feel it and I don't get worked up. Even what I do feel I don't feel as intensely.

LM How do you feel that's a result of this place?

MARK Getting yourself into a routine, losing contact with what goes on outside of prison. Usually to get worked up about something, you have to follow it. I just don't follow things any more. I'll go weeks without reading the *Guardian*. I'm not interested. I imagine I'll get more interested as I leave. I'd really get outraged when I first came here at the injustice, the idiocy. Like the silverware in the chow hall, even something as small as that. I remember getting into a hack's face some time last year. I got very insulting about the fact there was no silverware one day. Lately there's been no silverware constantly and I take it in stride. Nothing really gets to me any more. I'd be belligerent to hacks and tell 'em precisely what I thought when I first was locked up; now it's so petty, it's so useless.

LM   That does tie in with some of the things we were talking about, particularly your change in feeling last week, your noticing how the institution had changed and how you had changed. What you say now also has to do with that, since one of the interests of this group is how do people change in jail, particularly people who are "not usual jail material."

MARK   If conditions go to the Right, a good number of us *are* going to be regular jail material. There'll be a number of us in jail quite often for any and every type of activity. Besides, living here *makes* you jail material. Since being here I've come to think, in lots of ways, when I go to a big department store and if I need an appliance or something and it's sitting *there* and I'm standing *here*, and my pockets are open, it's mine. Before I came here I don't think I could've thought that. It's open and it's there, and they're not going to miss it, it's yours.

LM   Is that because you see things being frequently stolen here?

MARK   It's that plus everyone plays games here. To get something, you'll steal from the institution. Even a pad of paper to write letters on, if you don't like the plain type, you like lines. That's theft, really; you're not supposed to have it. It seeps in from this place. Here I'm a thief; on the streets I'm not, or at least I wasn't.

LM   You never thought of stealing before?

MARK   No! The first and last time I ever stole anything was in second grade when a friend and I went down to the A&P and stole a bag of M&Ms and a Hershey chocolate bar and I felt so guilty about it I couldn't eat it.

CALVIN A convict talking like that!

MARK   I can remember it so vividly, I can still remember where it was—one of my most vivid memories of childhood, even. Stealing that.

LM   Do you have an idea why it's so vivid?

MARK   Yeah, because it was the first time I'd *ever* done anything

like that. It violated my middle-class Puritan upbringing.
Thou shalt not steal! By God! But it's really different in
here, stealing. You have no other way to get it. *Hard
work* isn't going to get it for you. There's no way you
can buy it, yet it's not something which most people
should not have. So you learn to take it if you need it.
Even if you only *want* it.

RALPH   That's precisely my feeling: I'm entitled to it. I've got
half a dozen of these pens in my locker. I don't think I'd
have, on the streets, gone into a government office and
rummaged through the desks looking for something I
could use. If you try to work through these people, trying
to get something, you get so frustrated because the hacks
are just idiotic, or they're sadistic, and say no even if
there's no reason. So it doesn't work that way, you take
it into your own hands and you get it.

LM   It seems at least for this group that one effect of the
rehabilitation program of this institution is to make you
into thieves.

CALVIN That's what keeps the society goin'.

MARK   The main object is to get out of here and steal a car
and come back and take some VT [vocational training]
and learn something.

Although the code was adaptive to the stresses of prison life,
its more important effect was its reinforcement of the dehumanization carried out by the prison program. In their depreciation of
empathy and of ordinary human decency, the prison and the code
were carrying out the same process of dehumanization which
characterizes everyday life. For the resisters, to act "appropriately"
often meant to act in direct opposition to the very concerns which
had brought them to prison. The extent of one's response to these
pressures had as much to do with one's personal history as it did
with the immediate environment, but to some degree each prisoner
of conscience had to adopt the conscience of a prisoner.

NICK   I had an interesting experience a few days ago which you perhaps know about. Some inmate was smacked over the back of the head with something right outside I Block. I happened along right after it happened. My normal street reaction would have been to go over and assist the guy that was lying there with blood running out the back of his head, but of course the inmate code took over and I looked to see that he wasn't really bad off and the bleeding was not great and I kept on going.

LM You went over to him and looked?

NICK No. I was in the corridor within seven or eight feet of him, and I looked to see that he wasn't too bad off. There were hacks inside I Block and hacks at the other end of the hall, and I figured, "They're there, they can do their job," and I just went quietly on my way.

RALPH What gave you assurance that he was all right? He's laying there and his head's bleeding. I mean, could you actually perceive heartbeat?

NICK No.

LM Did you see him get hit?

NICK No, I didn't. I have a hunch, perhaps I know who did hit him or who was involved, but this is something you keep to yourself.

LM No, I'm not asking you who hit him, but you didn't actually see it?

NICK I never saw it, I have a hunch.

RALPH Yeah, but you didn't break stride?

NICK I saw another individual running around the corner. There were two or three other inmates in the area, but I noticed one in particular who picked up this fellow's cigarettes and matches and laid them on his chest and then walked off with a kind of smile that indicated, "He got his."

LM You didn't go over to him?

NICK I wouldn't become involved unless it was really necessary. As I say, there was no further activity going on, the guy was just lying there.

LM   Well, I think the interesting thing is, why do you feel that no further action is necessary?

NICK   As I say, there was a guard right inside I Block and he was lying right outside the door, there was a guard right at the end of the hall, and . . .

LM   Were they coming?

NICK   I can't remember. Well, anyway, there was an officer down at the end of the hall and another right in I Block, and obviously to become involved wouldn't have helped the individual any. It could have brought heat on me. In here, no thanks.

LM   What could you do on the streets?

NICK   Very little. If I saw someone with a cut artery, I could stop the bleeding.

LM   I mean if you saw the same guy in the same condition?

NICK   With a policeman not ten feet away?

LM   No, but if there wasn't a cop ten feet away.

NICK   It was no further than ten feet to the hack inside I Block.

LM   To the door, but he may not have seen him because the window in the door is fairly high.

NICK   Certainly in that situation, if they hadn't seen it I would call for their attention.

LM   Did you?

NICK   No.

LM   But they didn't come, either.

NICK   Well, as I say, I minded my own business because I knew that there was a hack there, and he is after all being paid to watch these things in a situation that is *not* a street situation.

LM   Right. But what I'm comparing it with is if the same guy were lying in the street.

NICK   Oh, I'd certainly call a cop for assistance.

LM   Right, OK. Is there something different about it happening in here?

NICK   I could very well become involved.

RALPH I'm not sure what I'd do, but I don't think I'd operate with the same detachment as you. Maybe I would, I don't know; I don't think I would.

JAY   Something happened to me on the yard, playing ball. I couldn't decide. I felt kind of guilty about it. You see, this guy hit a foul ball and it was coming down at this hack's head.

RALPH   We have a feeling you're going to say you warned him.

JAY   No, no. Actually, you see, it was this old guy out here, the one who works at the door [to the hospital]. Yeah, he's kind of a nice guy, or he seems to be. Well, I don't know if I would have warned him or not. I don't even know now because it missed him by about three feet. So maybe I did what was right, and kept cool, because if I'd hollered, "Look out," maybe he'd turn around and be hit. But I was pretty sure the reason I kept my hands in my pockets and kept walking was because I didn't care, you know, at first. I was kind of shocked.

CALVIN   Shocked?

JAY   Yeah, at my own actions, because it was the old guy. If it had been anybody else I wouldn't have cared. But it might have killed him or something.

NICK   There is another aspect to my reaction to that thing in the hall. I know that there were homosexuals involved. Again, the inmate code says you don't get involved in a situation, not even as a normal human being. The only reason you get involved in any situation is because you are personally involved.

RALPH   Already.

NICK   Already, right.

LM   And the homosexual aspect of this was what?

NICK   This would have been a very "No thank you" part of it.

LM   Because you would have been suspected of being homosexual?

NICK   Not only that. I don't think there are many people who would suspect me of being a homosexual in here. Not so much that, but from what I could see, the homosexual group, particularly the male counterparts, are among the most violent and brutal people in the joint and I don't particularly care to become involved with them. It's plain and simple. I don't need my head smacked in the back when I'm looking the other way.

LM   So it was first that you were concerned about getting in trouble with the officers, and second . . .

NICK   No, my first reaction was to go over and behave as I would in a normal street situation.

LM   But you checked that.

NICK   I'm not actually sure that I didn't take the first step. I caught myself as I realized that during the period I probably started to take that step I saw the other individual set the cigarettes and matches on top of his chest. In fact, at this point I hadn't actually seen any blood yet. I just saw that the guy was down and in fact I thought that someone was already helping him. And then the guy just walked off and the guy rolled over and the back of his head was full of blood. At which point the individual involved made it prohibitive to continue, to get involved, unless he was in very bad shape.

LM   He made it prohibitive because you knew he was a homosexual?

NICK   Right. At that point my impulse was to just walk on. I saw the other hack on the inside of I Block and I saw a hack down at the end of the hall, which is thirty feet away.

LM   Did you go up to either hack and tell them?

NICK   I didn't. I felt sure that they were able to see the guy.

LM   OK, the point that I'm struck by is that there were two areas of concern which you had. First, that you were concerned for yourself.

NICK   I'm cognizant of taking care of me, too.

LM   Right, but the point was that you were concerned first because you'd get into trouble from the hacks for being near the guy, and secondly because you'd get into trouble with homosexual studs.

NICK   As far as getting into trouble with the hacks, I don't care; that aspect wouldn't prevent me from becoming involved if I felt that I *needed* to become involved.

RALPH   But you don't feel you need to get involved?

NICK   I didn't in this case; well, again you have to look, make a judgment.

LM   But the problem here is retribution from the hacks *and* from the homosexual studs.

NICK   I was not particularly concerned about retribution from the hacks but from the homosexual studs, if I can accept that term. This is something that I would prefer not to get involved in, and I would say my sense of, you know, my feeling about that is very strong.

LM   It seems that one thing that's a product of a fair number of months in prison is loss of a sense of decency. I don't say this only personally to you or to single you out, Nick. I'm pointing out something that's general.

NICK   In general, yes, it's part of the maintenance of society on a very low level. It's unavoidable in a situation where you have twelve hundred people living in one building and under the circumstances you have here. You can't make any real changes in a situation like this.

RALPH   But do you think to any extent, because of the prejudice you have toward sissies, that conceivably you didn't see the situation as a human being in distress? It was rather some foul lower form of life that was in trouble? Do you think that had anything to do with it?

NICK   Not necessarily connected with sissies, but in itself. I reached a judgment. How much it was influenced by the fact that it was a homosexual is difficult to evaluate.

RALPH   Do you think a good reaction of a person who was, say, threatened subconsciously by homosexuals would be strong hatred for homosexuals? You know, a reactive sort of thing?

NICK   It's difficult to say, Ralph.

LM   Ralph was talking about your feelings about the guy as a homosexual. Perhaps you saw him as not worthy of rescue because, being a sissy, he was less human.

NICK   Well, I'm sure that I wouldn't have the same feeling toward a homosexual as I would for instance if it was *Ralph* laying there with blood coming out of the back of his head.

RALPH   I don't want to delve into that.

NICK   If it were Ralph I'd have gone over and given him a kick.

RALPH   That's an interaction at a very personal level as opposed to other situations where it's more remote.

NICK   That's the point. You consider homosexuality something just everyday. You're blasé; it's not a loss of decency to you, and it is to me.

LM   You're saying he's right, that you considered the guy, because he was a sissy, less worthy of aid than someone who was not a sissy.

NICK   Yes.

LM   That adds a third area of concern that kept you from intervening. It was the problem of the hacks, the problem of the studs, and your knowing the guy was a sissy.

NICK   Well, as a matter of fact I didn't see the guy's face and I had no positive identification that he was in fact a homosexual. Outside of the fact that it was definitely a homosexual (I think he's still a Daddy) who put the cigarettes on the guy's chest.

LM   So that's what made you feel that the guy was a sissy?

NICK   That and the fact that I could see he had a bonaroo shirt on.

LM   Well, I'll point out two things—one that Jay mentioned earlier, that he had the impulse to warn the hack who he thought might get hit with the softball. But then he, Jay, hasn't been here very long.

JAY   Well, he's the older guy who's sort of nice.

LM   That's what I mean. You saw him as a person who's fairly likable rather than some hack, period, or a hack stereotype, and the impulse to warn him was still there.

NICK   Yeah, it's interesting too that Ralph finds a homosexual worthy of care and attention but a dirty pig fascist cop is no longer human. It's an interesting prejudice or criterion for making a judgment. Hacks are not human, listen to Ralph; he'll tell you, "I think they are sub-human."

RALPH   They *are* subhuman, by valid criteria.

JAY   Do you think maybe you've got maybe a loss of ability to empathize with people? You can see a lot of people here and you never get close to them.

NICK   Society maintains itself here by maintaining impersonality, and this is part of the inmate code. Again this is what I'm trying to get at, that this is forced by the fact that you're living together in such tight circumstances. People that you normally wouldn't associate with, you're stuck with, or at least coming face to face with. Brushing arms in tight places because you're in a confined area.

LM   The way, then, to protect yourself from viciousness is to be uninvolved, is that it?

NICK   To a certain extent.

RALPH   I'd imagine you'd react favorably to a Selective Service case lying in the hall?

NICK   In at least five cases out of six I might.

21

Women

THERE were a few women working in the prison as secretaries, confined to the executive offices, the file room, and the hospital. Although every female employee was free to move unguarded among prisoners in the area where she worked, none was permitted to walk in the main corridor unless she was accompanied by a male escort within arm's reach. Unlike other prisons, Lompoc housed very few men guilty of rape; it is hardly ever a Federal offense. In fact, very few of the men imprisoned for other crimes had such an assault in their background. Nonetheless, the male staff was intensely anxious, much more so than the women, about the possibility of assault, and not least because they were aware of the sexual deprivation of the prisoners.

In response to their guilt and anxiety, as well as to their propensity for identifying all prisoners with one another or with a repudiated aspect of themselves, the staff acted as if they considered all inmates to be equally and constantly ready to commit assault. If this were actually likely, there should have been guards with the women all the time, since a rape would have been far more likely to occur in the relative privacy of the file room or the hospital than in a public passageway. The incongruous requirement for escorts only on the main street of the prison suggested that the obvious, if limited, risk of attack by prisoners was compounded by the inner fears of the staff; specifically, their unspoken assumptions that not only might the prisoners act like rapists but that the secretaries might act like prostitutes.

The close escorting was an embarrassment and an inconvenience to some women, who did not like being associated so publicly with either of its implications, but a few others seemed to relish it. The public chaperoning did reassure the prison staff and clearly tell the inmates to keep their distance as social inferiors and sexual cripples or deviates. Simultaneously, it emphasized the fear that those same prisoners might also be physically superior and sexually powerful. For prisoners, it was a situation that would have been comical had it not been so degrading; for female employees, an ordinary walk from their desks to the staff dining room could not be taken except in an atmosphere of titillation and sexual fear and envy. Despite the impediments to decent contact between prisoners and female staff, a few of the secretaries managed to be kind and dignified to the inmates who worked with them and who reciprocated with equal humanity. Other women, though, could be as seductive, hostile, or indifferent as any other prison employee.

The great majority of prisoners, however, encountered women only in the visiting room or in their dreams. The frustration of brief and infrequent visits was compounded by the constant supervision and harassment under which they took place. What would ordinarily be regarded as normal, casual expressions of affection were viewed by guards as perverted and forbidden, and any approved contact which appeared excessive was openly disrupted in painful and public humiliation. If it was difficult to express affection during a visit, it was also difficult to keep the intense hostility of daily prison life from tincturing a loving relationship. After enough time in prison, it was even less possible to bring one's loving instincts to bear upon one's anger. Ralph Lombardi was not the only prisoner who felt that his only freedom during a visit was to talk with his wife in the everyday obscenities of prison language, to feel as degraded in relation to her as he had been made to feel in relation to the prison staff of either sex.

As prisoners adapted—often against their will and without their knowledge—to the isolated stasis of life in prison, the visits of friends and family often became a greater burden than pleasure. They were at first a painful reminder of the discrepancies between life inside and outside, and later a reminder even of the existence of a life outside. In order to defend against this psychic pain, when visits became intrusions, many men actively discouraged their friends and family from coming to Lompoc. The disruption of personal contact was often accompanied by a more pervasive disruption of emotional connection. After ten months in custody, Nick Manos barely responded to his wife's presence, and he and other prisoners often had difficulty even thinking about their loved ones. As prisoners were psychologically mutilated into "partial men," they often could no longer tolerate the emotions associated with contact, in imagination or in reality, with the people they loved the most. Thus, both inner and outer ties were broken, an old identity erased, a newer, narrower one imposed.

RALPH   Working around a woman can have a kind of humanizing influence. This particularly applies to the women who are the newest. Take Mrs. X now, she's been here for years, and even ignoring her appearance, she's repulsive. She's as bad as a hack. She threw a person, an orderly of hers, in The Hole for refusing to get down on his hands and knees and scrub the floor before her guest. She sat in her soft chair smiling down at him, like a devil or a dyke or whatever.

CALVIN   She wanted him to look under her dress, huh?

RALPH   No, I think she just wanted him to comply with her wishes. As if she said, "Mop," or "Scrub the floor, you, get down there and scrub." Your fucking dignity is in a locker downstairs, that sort of thing. And I think most of the women who've been here the longest are less human, I guess, or less warm. And the opposite seems to be the case with the newest of the women. When they first arrive they're human beings, and you may want to associate with them for that reason.

CALVIN   There's so many changes a visit can put you through. I don't know really how to explain it, it's always that, well, she's here, you can't really do what you want to do, and it just creates a block.

NICK   What you mean is it's emasculating.

CALVIN   Partly, yes.

RALPH   In a way it seems that only partial men show up in visiting rooms for visits. You have *their* rules to contend with. *They* authorize one hug, one kiss at the meeting. Then you sit down. Those are the regulations. If you get a dog [of a guard] in there, they do sometimes enforce that. I was told to stop kissing my wife. I was called outside and interrogated: "Who is that woman? What are you doing in there? Let's knock off that stuff. Regulations don't allow for it."

LM   So you mean it's emasculating in the way you're humiliated by the hacks?

RALPH   Well, the hacks intrude into your visit and personify the emasculation. Even when the hacks stay out of it there are still their rules to contend with. You're so very limited as to what you can do in there.

NICK   It's a crowded room.

RALPH   There's no privacy, which also imposes limitations, assuming you have some pride.

NICK   There's also I think the aspect of being dressed the same as everyone else. Also, whether they intervene or not in any way, you're under their authority. That is emasculating as well. If you were in a normal situation and someone came up to you and said "Stop that kissing," most red-blooded men would be ready to jump up and sock the guy in the face, if not a good deal more, and that's out of the question. There's the chain that goes back through the door to the ball they don't show. It's still there.

RALPH   I mean it's obvious they have you physically. They have you coming in in brown clothes and white socks and battered shoes. You come in that door and *they* unlock it.

You sit down in the seat *they* point to. You kiss, hug once when *they* authorize it. When you sit down it's "Keep your hands to yourself." There's no rules against smiling. I think if you were unduly happy and smiling and laughing they would tell you to shut up. And then they can come over and just break it up any time they want to. This all bears out the fact that physically you're a prisoner. Your number will tell you anyway. I don't know what kind of options are available. They can't govern the words you use. You can sit down and look at her face and say, "fuck, shit, piss, cock"; they don't come in and break that up.

LM   So you're free to talk to your wife or girl friend in those terms.

RALPH   I guess the words you use is about the only freedom you have.

NICK   Except you can't psychologically respond to her presence.

RALPH   I said there's a repressive atmosphere, there's a psychological thing called *fear* that they intrude on your visit.

NICK   That is the most thoroughly emasculating thing. The fact that the response you would normally feel cannot be expressed. The first time you come out (I've had three visits from my wife); the first time, my response was almost normal. The second, my response was considerably diminished; the last time, my response was almost "Oh well, so I got another visit." And this is, even though —well, three visits in ten months. Obviously I'm not tired of seeing my wife.

LM   But the response was diminishing each time?

NICK   The atmosphere was such that you couldn't even begin to respond anywhere near normally. It makes me more disgusted. Other than that, it's hard to say; I don't even want to think about what it might mean.

22

Homosexuality

Heterosexual contact was curtailed and closely supervised by prison authorities, but there was little official interference with homosexuality. Though its practice was clearly forbidden in the rule book familiar to both guards and prisoners, it was unusual for prisoners to be disciplined for any but the most flagrant practice. Much of prison homosexuality, as on the outside, was undertaken with consent and with pleasure, but much more was forced, and it is doubtful that the relaxation of the homosexuality rules stemmed from any respect of the guards for the rights of consenting adults.

For all but the most willing of men, the prison's apparent goal of psychological destruction was clearly expressed and condensed in the physical intimidation, psychological coercion, and impersonal exploitation of prison homosexuality. To observe the practice may have gratified a few prison employees, but its prevalence was more important in its confirmation of the prisoners, in the staff's view, as deviant, subhuman, or debased. Moreover, the discharge of aggression through homosexual practice and intrigue appeared to be a valuable ally of the administrators in keeping the general peace by allowing low-level violence. The violence associated with homosexual practice and commerce was so intense and widespread that it often saved the guards the trouble, officially forbidden, of physical oppression. The murder, the stabbings, most of the fractures, many of the beatings, and at least one of the riots in my two years at Lompoc all arose from homosexual conflict. This covert reign of terror was clearly the complement of the official rule of force; if the administration of the institution could be characterized (as Gresham Sykes has done) as operating through the intimidation of an "invisible fist," the physical and psychological threat of sanctioned homosexuality closed that fist around the genitals of every prisoner.

A prisoner could often deflect the more common tentative approaches by the assumption of a "pseudo-masculine tough guy" pose. But the possibility of a surprise attack could never be excluded, and since the guards could not be relied upon for protection, that threat resonated with many prisoners' deep but not always unconscious fears of physical assault, of rape, of exposure to forcible entry from behind, of being killed by penetration and tearing. The open practice, as well as the recognition of one's own vulnerability, left many men in increasing confusion and doubt—through the reactivation of deep conflict—of their sexual identity. Those who resisted approaches were relieved, but they often felt guilty at having faked a tough-guy response. Those who gave in were often mortified at having yielded to, and worse, become (since the identity of "sissy" was imposed with a force equal to that of the initial physical contact) what to them was base and shameful.

The physical and psychological threats were complicated and distorted even more by cynical commerce. The active trade in "sissies" was an exploitation of another person for gain and a denial of mutual humanity not without parallel in other prison activities. The difficulty of visits and the limitations on them effectively disrupted deep and continuous ties to the outside world, but the assumption of homosexual relationships did not restore such ties, as compensations, within the prison. The majority of homosexual relationships were not those of personal, meaningful attachment but rather were transient, brutal, and masturbatory; they were often accompanied by grandiose fantasies of violence and destruction, and —most important—were characterized by the substitution of bodily for emotional contact.

No resister was raped, but some had to fight, and all were deeply affected by the prevalence and power of homosexual threat. Joe Cox was deeply troubled by the prospect of rape. Unable to tolerate close at hand and inescapable what had been, outside prison, bearable at a distance, Nick Manos reduced homosexuals to "things," a common enough psychological device in prison. Ralph Lombardi went to the other extreme of idealizing a mutual and consenting relationship he witnessed in order to tolerate the more prevalent opposite kind.

JOE   A guy in my unit keeps saying how they're pressuring people in A & O [Admission and Orientation Unit].

RALPH   Pressuring what people?

JOE   Well, I don't know what people, I just hope they're not.

BEN   About what?

JOE   Well, homosexuals and that sort of stuff.

RALPH   Oh, you mean an initiation?

JOE   I've had a sheltered life; if something like that happened when I first got here, it might have really messed me up. Whereas some of these people that have been around on the streets, and violence, it might not hurt them so much.

LM   How might it have messed you up?

JOE   Well, maybe it might have made me so paranoid that I wouldn't be able to talk to people or associate or something. Maybe I'd be so afraid of it happening. Maybe I would have worried about it destroying my manhood. When I was first in A & O, I was fairly scared of violence and getting beat up and things.

LM   How was it frightening for you?

JOE   Well, all these people around. I'm not used to that much contact anyway, having people that close. All these people around and the muscle men, all this stuff. When they chest-punch or whatever that was, I could see that that was playing around because they weren't hurting each other, that type of fighting. But, uh, I don't know. They still, it still showed the potential that they could hurt each other.

RALPH   Well, if that potential were, let's say, the threat, in some ways it's as damaging as the act itself.

JOE   It probably is, because not long before I came in here I had a friend that was in [a county] jail on a drug charge and he was raped in there. That really sort of bothers me. I worried about that for quite a while even before I came here.

LM   Worried about how you would resist it?

JOE   Yeah, what could you do against twenty people or whatever? If you didn't cooperate you'd probably get killed.

LM   And if the situation arose, how would you handle it?

JOE   I don't know. That's what I was worried about, what I would do. I suppose the only thing you could do is cooperate, really. That's what most people do here anyway, from what I've heard.

RALPH   Well, it's my own experience that it doesn't happen. You're not approached, but I would guess it's your physical masculinity. But given the situation that you *are* approached, irrespective, it's fighting really, that's the only way to go. It needn't be twenty against one. You have protective custody to go to.

LM   Certainly makes it public. From my experience here, not only with this group but with other people in this institution, it doesn't seem to me that only the slim, likely-looking prospects are approached. Different people in this group have been approached, not necessarily the slim people either. It doesn't mean that anybody's cooperated, but I think the problem is more general than that.

RALPH   I think I've come up with a more liberal attitude on homosexuality since imprisonment. Just being around it, you see some of these guys really do love each other. There's genuine affection between them. Mary and Dusty, they're together all the time; there doesn't seem to be any exploitation. They just mutually love each other's company, they're continuously together; and even when they're not together (they're in separate units), they go to the top of each unit, and they go to the window and communicate back and forth, looking into each other's eyes. The whole thing. Unlike some exploitation that might occur, where you might seize on some puny guy in A & O and force it. I've learned a liberal outlook on the whole thing, compared to on the streets where I had no contact with it at all.

MARK   You no longer consider it a perversion, then?

RALPH   No. The moral stigma has since been erased.

MARK   Why don't you get an old lady?

NICK   Or better yet, why don't you *become* one?

LM   What do you mean, better?

NICK   Just kidding. Maybe there is a significance in this problem of masculine self-image. If everyone is male, how does it affect their image of themselves if you ask Mary how she feels about it, or he? When I came here, I would've taken the opposite viewpoint. I had known at least one homosexual on the streets. Not well. In fact, I worked with this guy and he was all right to work with. He didn't bother me, and I figured, he didn't bother me, why bother him? However, after being in here, to be quite frank, when I go out in the yard and see a couple of these, these *things* cuddled up together out on the lawn, I really feel an urge to walk up and start pounding on them. This is something that's happened since I've been here; now this is probably a feeling in response to it, inasmuch as it threatens me.

RALPH   Yeah, yeah, I went through the same feeling. You come in with the conventional wisdom about homosexuality, and then after a couple months of witnessing homosexuality in varying degrees, my initial response was more hostile; perhaps I didn't reconcile myself to the whole thing or didn't properly adjust, perhaps I felt myself threatened. Suddenly questions were occurring about virility. Seeing that this was their standard, if it's mine also, what does that mean? Do I have to get myself a sissy? Then you get a more relaxed outlook after a couple of more months.

MARK   In my area in E-2 we all obliged and left and they brought up a sissy from E-1 and ran a train through. Ran 'em through one after the other.

LM   Is it generally not interfered with?

RALPH   Never saw it broken up.

LM   Even when the hacks are right there?

NICK   Not then either.

LM   What is there about seeing it that makes you want to break it up?

NICK   It strikes me as perversion, out and out. We're living in perverted circumstances; this is probably the only thing that I can justify for holding back from breaking it up. If I was looking at nineteen or twenty years in here, I might find homosexuality a lot more interesting.

MARK   It's relative. A lot of the Daddies have longer sentences; it *is* partially a function of the time, at least on the part of the aggressive ones.

NICK   I can no longer picture them as healthy males. I feel very strongly about it. I've noticed this taking place while I've been here. It's less and less tolerable to me. They have reduced themselves to being less than human.

RALPH   What about all human beings? Men and women need approval, affection, love. If you get those things from it, is it a male-female thing or is it a human-being thing? If you could see the time Mary puts in on her hair before she goes to the movies, you'd really know that she's out to get Dusty's approval. She goes down to the clothing exchange and searches through all kinds of clothes to find the ones to give the best effects to her buttocks. It seems to be a thing that's transcended, or whatever, the male-female thing.

MARK   The guy's very conscientious in regard to his lover.

LM   I think the key is where Ralph says "she" when he's describing. He's seeing him as a her. It doesn't upset him to describe someone who's obviously male as a woman.

NICK   I accepted prison terminology at first, but I've rejected it. If you start accepting something that is destructive, it's

	like justifying petty thievery. Pretty soon you'll justify stealing a car or whatever.
MARK	When I came here, "she" struck me as odd, the same way as the other terminology did. Then I started to use it automatically. It's the same idea as if you see this one homosexual and there are two or three other people standing around. To differentiate, you say "her" because then you focus on one person. It's an abbreviated communication.
RALPH	It's more efficient to swallow the vernacular.
LM	One point of conflict is using the word "she" to describe someone who is obviously male.
CALVIN	It's not facing reality.
RALPH	But is it in conflict with *his* reality? With the other person's reality? Mary isn't a turned-out punk. She came in here, or he came in here, as he or as she was. You're perceiving him as he does.
MARK	The "she" is performing a female function, sexual release, companionship, comforter. Builder of the male ego.
LM	I think it has to do with how tolerable to people the idea of sexual ambiguity is. Nick is saying that a man is a man, no matter what he does, or what social act he performs, what sexual act he performs; as long as he has male organs and looks like a man, he's a man. Where Ralph is saying if he's socially female, then he's female even when he has male sexual organs.
RALPH	I realize Mary has a penis, though at the same time I recognize that she enjoys the role of a female and she likes to be thought of as a female, and if you call her "he," you blow her trip. If you say, "Hey, man," *she* doesn't like that. You're not approving, necessarily, what's happening by using the word "she."
CALVIN	I look at it as an escape clause, a way of getting away from reality, just a substitute and not the real thing.
LM	It can be one way of escaping the reality of homosexuality.
MARK	It's one way of escaping the idea that you're deprived of

women in here, too. You're not deprived of women: there's one, look at her; there's another, there she is over there.

LM   You're very accurate. Calling someone who is acting female "she" does deny the lack of females here, in a kind of pretending way saying, "Oh yes, we have ordinary sex here." It also denies the fact that it's homosexual: it's a man and a woman.

MARK   Right.

NICK   Some Daddies even end up becoming Mamas.

CALVIN   Guys that mess around, they get turned out. If you flip, you'll flop; the episodes I've seen, they both flipped and flopped.

23

Spies

SUSPICION was necessary for mere survival in prison. One could never be sure of another prisoner: he might be "running a game" of exploiting drugs or sex or rumor to his own advantage; he might be an informer, a snitch; or he might plant a knife in one's cell or one's belly with no motive other than sheer perversity. One could be a little more certain of some guards who spoke of help in accents of hate: "We're here to help you, you piece of shit," was the way one inmate interpreted their attitude. Other employees were more confusing and disturbing because they concealed their dislike with managerial indifference or pseudo-rehabilitative jargon, obscuring both their contempt and the relative virtue of at least a clearly hostile relationship. Intermittent threat and ambiguous communication provoked in many prisoners the inner tensions of uncertainty and doubt, not only of others and their motives, but of their own perceptions, judgment, beliefs, and identity.

Constant supervision and exposure led to a heightened concern for privacy and to intensified fears that it would be invaded. To be guarded yet not protected led one to become more guarded toward oneself as well as toward others. In a persecutory and isolated environment, ideas of persecution became more natural, and the constant presence of outer watchers often led to the *omni*presence of inner watching. All too often, reflective self-observation hardened into stringent self-criticism, healthy self-awareness into morbid self-consciousness, reasonable self-reliance into anxious self-scrutiny. Inner and outer lives were harshly governed by a wary attitude of tense watchfulness.

No resister reached the degree of paranoia that was common among other prisoners and staff, but many became more and more suspicious as time went on. Trust and distrust, candor and suspicion often alternated in the group and they were explored in a deep relationship over time. But a balanced, flexible view was very rare, and an open reception was never accorded strangers. Although I earned a certain degree of trust by my actions in demonstrating verifiable confidentiality and reliability, that trust could sometimes be withdrawn, and suddenly. Resisters new to the group were often suspected, at least initially, because the others feared that the government would send an undercover agent to the prison disguised as a conscientious objector.

An arriving resister could eventually win the confidence of the others, but the sudden intrusion of a total stranger evoked only total distrust. On one occasion, the surprise arrival of an unknown and vaguely identified visitor aroused deep fears among the group. Those fears were stimulated in part by the resisters' painful experiences of investigation, prosecution, and trial, but the psychological changes undergone in prison and the specific sexual stress of the actual encounter intensified them.

One day Ralph and Calvin were called from their cells without warning to see "a visitor." Without introduction or preparation, they were escorted to an office in the administration building, where they were met by a young woman who introduced herself as a visiting sociologist gathering data for a paper on conscientious objectors in prison. The surprise of the interview aroused their sensitivity to questioning; the sudden proximity of a young woman evoked the tensions of sexual arousal and fear of seduction as well as the tensions and fears of interrogation. At the next group meeting, both men were convinced, as were the others, that the aims of the interview had not been academic.

MARK   This one was an FBI agent, from what Ralph said. He was running down inconsistencies in her story.

RALPH   She mentioned a few things that just don't jibe. For example, she told Calvin that she was interviewing COs in prison in the United States. She talked about going to Sandstone, which is in Minnesota. She told him she was up in Utah State, and there's nobody, no COs anyway, in that state joint. That was an inconsistency. She did know some sociology, for all that's worth.

LM   You tested her?

RALPH   Yeah, I talked about the concentric theory of city development, with which she seemed to be familiar. I really wasn't ready; some hack yanked me out of my cell, took me down there, pushed me in, and I guess stood outside the door to listen.

LM   Did she see everyone or just you?

RALPH   To my knowledge, Calvin and I were the only ones called out. She took your name when I mentioned you. If she doesn't see you, it proves she's an agent.

LM   How is her not seeing me a test for FBI-ship?

RALPH   If she was an agent, she wasn't going to risk her identity being uncovered by seeing too many sharp people, and definitely you are on a different level. For example, I couldn't converse that well with her, get her in different situations, where you could.

MARK   I guess part of it is that her credentials can't be examined by an inmate. The element of uncertainty is there. Even a vague knowledge of the FBI and their doings would trigger off a natural, logical chain of questions in me. Plus the fact that you were summoned, Ralph, right? They didn't say, "We have someone here with this name and this degree and she would like to talk with you"; it was more like "1234, put your clothes on and don't use any foul words, there's a woman here to see you. A civilized human being."

LM   She wasn't introduced to you as a visiting sociologist?

RALPH   They simply said, "There's a visitor downstairs." She introduced herself. She didn't bring any sheepskins or give any historical background about herself. If she had told me what she had told Calvin, I don't think I'd have even talked to her. Saying she came from some state prison in Utah seeing COs—I'd walk out and tell her there aren't any up there.

NICK   What did she look like?

RALPH   I didn't wear my contacts. There was only four or five feet separating us. She wasn't too bad-looking, very little make-up.

LM   Did she say how she'd gotten your name?

RALPH   The office was apparently the source. She also went through our jackets [files] afterwards. It sounds like someone was bending over backwards for her, and that's how various government organizations respond to each other.

LM   You mean if she were a bona fide Ph.D. she wouldn't have had such easy access?

RALPH   Right. But she was very good-looking, so that might explain why the hacks in particular were extending the red carpet.

MARK   Did you get her name?

RALPH   I heard her name but I don't remember it.

NICK   Well, it would be just like the FBI.

CALVIN   They're no fools, they do it right.

MARK   The one who interviewed me before my trial was a fool. A perfect fool.

RALPH   Fortunately there was nothing said that was incriminating.

NICK   Well, I would imagine she's also single.

RALPH   I didn't see a ring.

NICK   Well, you lock a man up and then bring in a fairly attractive, reasonably young woman and it's sort of disarming.

LM   Did her femininity affect you, as Nick suggested?

RALPH   Nick's suggestion was that she would be disarming. She may have been disarming, but there was nothing incriminating about it. Just a CO in prison. If indeed her objective was to be disarming, disarm you and then gather facts that justified the imprisonment, or detracted from the quality of your [parole] case in some way, then this might be her purpose.

LM The purpose might be to delay your getting parole?

RALPH Yes.

LM But your concern, as I hear it anyway, was more personal, rather than the fear that she woud impugn resistance generally.

MARK They want a lot of funny things: to see what draft resisters are like, whether they can deduce any evidence from us that it might be widespread. Are we red-diaper babies to begin with, or do we come from good middle-class homes? There's a definite danger if we come from stable backgrounds, whereas if we're all red-diaper babies or if we're from very bad home lives, the chances are we might be . . .

RALPH Only isolated instances.

MARK Yeah.

RALPH Assuming she were attached to some government body, that would seem to be her only justification. She couldn't really be here for any other purpose.

MARK It's a hell of a long way to ride around, all around the country, just for some little paper she's doing. That's pretty weak, that's pretty God-damned weak!

LM Weak justification for the trip, you mean?

MARK Yeah, yeah, right.

LM It's possible that she might be doing it for her thesis, particularly if it means a free trip to California.

RALPH Actually, she also wants to see all the COs.

MARK But she didn't. She only saw you. It wasn't worth her trouble. And going to Utah? Why the hell would she go there?

LM There may have been someone in a county jail there.

MARK How could *she* know? Even the *resistance* has a hard time keeping track. Why didn't you cross-examine her, for Christ's sake? I would have spent half my time asking *her* questions.

RALPH   I wasn't that suspicious. I was waiting for the thing to develop. See what was actually happening. Everything seemed innocuous.

MARK   That's the whole point.

LM   How long did she spend with you?

RALPH   About two and a half hours. She asked me about parts of my life, but her approach was really spotty. She left a lot of gaps. Most of her questions were about my background. She didn't get too much into my views. She had a few odd-ball questions at the end that I guess she was dying to get in, like if pacifists had problems here like at Sandstone [Minnesota] where there's no contingent of hippies to soften the population. Now that doesn't apply to background. I was talking somewhat facetiously about it. The tape recorder was spinning all the time.

LM   Did she appreciate the facetiousness of it?

RALPH   Sort of. She squirmed in her chair. A lot of thigh was being exposed.

LM   Did you have an erection?

RALPH   Did I have what?

MARK   An erection.

RALPH   No.

MARK   Did you not hear him or have you forgotten what it is?

RALPH   No. I was yanked out of my cell, I didn't have my contacts in or my hair combed, and I wasn't shaved. I wasn't on the prowl.

LM   An expanse of thigh might do that almost by reflex.

CALVIN   The way I look upon things, when it comes through the administration like that, it's got to be some kind of trick. I might as well go along and play the game so long as I have everything before my eyes, because *they* want to find out something from *me*. *I* don't want to know anything from *her*. The more she asks me questions about what she wants to know, the better I can evaluate her and see what she's really up to. I was suspicious all along; I just feel that anything can happen while I'm in here.

RALPH   They've got us in prison.

CALVIN   I'm here and it's just like in the zoo. Anybody comes through can throw a peanut at you and you can't respond.

RALPH   You may throw a peanut at them.

LM   What are you wary about?

CALVIN   The newspapers don't want to publish about black people going to jail for draft evasion. There *are* black people going to jail for draft evasion, and the way I see it, so long as the general public doesn't find out about how many black people are going to jail, this will keep black people *from* going to jail. Actually, they want to get more black people in the service.

LM   For what reason?

CALVIN   Get them fitted into the system. So long as people don't know what's happening on the other side, they're going to keep going to the side they know about. So long as black people know that there are black people going into the service, they're going to keep going there, because most of them, they don't want to step out and be first.

LM   What is it you feel that you have to be suspicious about?

CALVIN   They already know enough about me to make anything out they have to. Since I came in here without any organizations behind me, they may want to find out what *is* behind me. They don't know anything about what's going on in the ghetto, put it that way, and they want to find out in a hurry because they can tell that this is a top-notch problem.

LM   And what you feel suspicious about is people coming in here to see whether you belong to some organization or whether you're just a nut?

CALVIN   Yes, yes, yes. Right on the nose. They've got to have something to start with, a basic foundation. They've got to have some type of model to look at, to distinguish between the militant and the nonmilitant.

MARK   Are you sure they really care?

CALVIN   I'm sure they care. Black people *have* to be suspicious when they talk to white people.

LM   I'm a little surprised that you're as open as you are in here.

CALVIN   Well, I guess I just know most of the people in here. I keep a whole lot back, too. I might as well admit it. I like to talk but sometimes I get carried away, run off at the mouth. I watch what I say most of the time, though; at least I try to.

LM   What interests me is the feeling of guardedness, both right now with each other and your feeling of vulnerability after prison. We've talked a lot about the risk of being re-classified and having to decide whether to come to jail again or leave the country. But I'm also impressed with the general feeling of personal vulnerability, having your life interfered with by psychiatrists and sociologists, and other less "benign" people after jail.

MARK   Maybe it's because we've all been so much on the line publicly that we're more prone to reserve some things privately. Much more than the average person, who's never really put much forth publicly. In other words, we've exposed our whole physical being for public display and public handling in a place like this. We're all more jealous of some little part that we can keep to ourselves privately.

LM   While the government is literally handling your body?

MARK   Right. I think there are some things that we all want to keep to ourselves, which are really no one's business, even if it is the function of the group to make it its business. It's no one's business. It's, it's that simple. Like Calvin said, he's become much more guarded in here. I've become much more that way; I was willing to talk about anything when I first got here, and now I've become more guarded generally.

LM   Because of being in jail, or what?

MARK   I don't know, I really don't know; but, well, I'll know that when I get out. I've just become much more reserved, let everything be superficial. I'll let someone talk to me on really anything, but I won't give anything out except something superficial. I never even thought about it before, why I'm not willing to talk about anything really personal. That's the only thing I have to myself. Everything else is totally open. I can't go any place I'm not watched. There's no privacy other than the privacy I can make for myself by going into my cell, turning everything off.

LM   That does have some parallels with what we were talking about earlier; the decrease in spontaneity and in imagination, the concentration on prison routine and things to be done here rather than thinking about people outside or thinking about yourself outside.

NICK   I think that's part of learning to do time. It's a trick that you play with your mind to literally not notice that time is going by.

CALVIN Well, they really can't change us. They know that we see a deficiency in their system and it doesn't matter what they do unless they kill us. They're not going to change us and make us go into the service. We made our decision, and some of us might come back to jail and some of us might not. I'm just looking at it from my point of view, and nobody's going to change me, no matter what they do.

LM   You mean as far as your attitude towards the system is concerned?

CALVIN Towards the service, and towards the system, and its application towards black people. They're trying to push us in some direction. They're putting us in here with all the common criminals. They're making us live with just the trash, people that just don't make it as far as they're concerned. They're not going to kill us directly, they're going to kill us indirectly. *You* know, by making us psychotic or just having us one of the people who function within the system.

LM   How do you feel it's affected your interest in changing the system?

CALVIN I know what I want to say but it's hard to get it out. It slows you down somewhat, but I don't know, I'd just say it slows you down. You might be able to change it out there, but it's going to take a lot of work. Not only on your part but on everybody's part. You're just going to have to force people to do it. Force. *Make* them aware. If they don't want to be aware, you got to *make* 'em.

MARK   That's the way things are done around *here*.
CALVIN That's right.

24

"America Is Prison"

THE most destructive accomplishment of incarceration is its capacity to evoke and exploit those universal conflicts out of whose relative, stepwise resolution a growing character evolves. The pressures of prison life act as an entering wedge, widening those inherent and usually unconscious splits, the potential spaces persisting in the most coherent personality, into deep fissures, sometimes fragmenting a tenuously balanced character into its many components. The early effects of this process were often only dimly felt but later became deeply alarming.

As time went on, the pattern of thought of many prisoners began to change, and with that cognitive change the points of correspondence between their psychic state and their political attitudes increased. The total control of the prison administration and the totalization of the thought of many prisoners altered many inmates' opinions, not only of the prison but also of the government which administered it. Many wondered what kind of government other than a cynically despotic one could permit such treatment and then call it "treatment." As their attachment to those outside was loosened or broken, as their ties to those inside were usually transient and often brutal, as their inner worlds became more static and constricted, many prisoners felt themselves to be hardly human at all. As their physical world was compressed to a cell and an exercise yard and their view of the outside narrowed to that through a barred window, many inmates felt that the principles by which the government ran the prison were exactly those by which it ran the country; that prison was not a domestic exile to a different kind of life in a separate place but an immersion at the core of a concentrated and intensified version of what already flourished outside.

It is no distortion to see prison life as a totalitarian existence. Virtually all the elements of a police state prevail in prison: the borders are sealed, movement is controlled across those borders and within them, the population is under surveillance, there are paid informers, assembly is limited, speech is restricted, censorship is exercised, and—to differentiate prison life from existence under a merely authoritarian agency—the population is required to exhibit not only passive assent but to demonstrate active cooperation.

It is not necessary to attribute the equation of prison with government to the fact that some prisoners may have been ideologically minded or politically concerned prior to their incarceration. Indeed, it seems that the opposite was the case at Lompoc. The overwhelming majority of prisoners were incarcerated for the first time, and their previous contact with the government, and with political thought of any kind, was as limited as their contact with prison. For many inmates, the squalid gauntlet of their arrest, trial, transport, and incarceration was their first direct involvement with any government agency. Lacking any experience of benevolent government to contradict their first impression, and with the subsequent psychological changes compelled by incarceration, prisoners could indeed feel that the entire nation was as much a police state as was one part of it, the prison. By its penetration into the most private areas of their lives, the government became far more real and far more threatening to many prisoners than ever before. Restriction of freedom of movement was soon followed by the restriction of freedom of thought. Not only did many prisoners feel that their bodies were in custody; many felt that their thoughts had also become government property. Men experiencing such direct influence and control, already beginning to totalize partial aspects into entireties in other matters, could not escape the idea that the part of the government exercising total control, the prison, was identical and coextensive with the whole. Thus, the social control at Lompoc was not seen as a *partial* function of the state, but as its *essential* function.

The equation of prison and state was fostered by the significant disorder of thought which prison life promoted: the tendency for concreteness to predominate over abstraction; the profound disturbance in symbolic integration known as part-for-the-whole thinking, in which a single aspect of an object is taken to *be* that object. This pattern of thought was no figure of speech, no expression of synecdoche—by which a part represents the whole. The use of synecdoche depends upon the ability to express and to comprehend metaphor, and it was precisely that ability which was impaired. The prison was not seen, metaphorically, to *represent* the state; it was seen, concretely, to *be* the state. The resemblances between the prison and the government had always been manifest, but as similarities became identities, as parallels converged, as analogies became homologies, the recognition of the differences was impaired. Reciprocally, the state was not becoming *like* a prison, it was not functioning as if it were a prison, it already *was* a prison. The metaphor of America *as* prison congealed into the concrete fact, the certain conviction, that America *is* prison.

Whether or not an inmate thinks himself a political prisoner, the impairment of symbolic integration is a major step in his cognitive incarceration. Once imprisoned in a state of mind deficient in symbol and metaphor, the prisoner is deprived of the essential mental operation—abstraction—which is both the key to escape and the psychic freedom to which he would escape. Part-for-the-whole thinking characterized the thought of many prisoners, and this development was particularly notable when it occurred among the resisters, most of whom had been reluctant in their resistance and selective in their protest. Most had come to prison stating their opposition to little more than the war and the draft. Those issues and the men who personified them—President Nixon and General Hershey—had formerly been seen as no worse than limited aberrations, as "benign tumors" in the body politic. But after incarceration and immersion in a government agency "with the gloves off," those issues and their personifications were seen as far more threatening and dangerous, as "malignant tumors" in a body riddled with decay.

In obeying the laws of conscience rather than the Selective Service statutes, most resisters had not forfeited their respect for law in general; indeed, many had felt that coming to prison was the only lawful thing to do. Once inside, however, their minds had changed. With the heightened and narrowed perception, the constriction of thought, the loss of reflection, the impairment of abstraction, what they had once seen as a partially authoritarian government they now saw as an entirely totalitarian regime. All of them had rejected the idea of exile and had come to prison "out of a sense of patriotism," as Nick Manos had expressed it. But with their progressive inner equation of the prison regime with the Federal government, many resisters were less certain about the future of the country and of their future in it. They were all vulnerable to subsequent draft notices and prosecution, and though their view of America as a police state was momentarily fixed, some still hoped that it might be amended after their release from custody. But subsequent induction calls, surveillance, or harassment by the government would confirm that their perception from inside Lompoc had not been a temporary evaluation but a permanent state of affairs. Then they would leave; they would regret it, but they would leave.

Many resisters hoped that this would never be the case, but from inside the prison it seemed to be the most likely outcome. What was most striking to see among both resisters and other prisoners was the development of their view of the world as only a prison with a larger yard, their progressive difficulty in conceiving of a different existence, and worst of all, their inability to imagine freedom.

NICK   I think it's much easier to see here than on the outside just how authoritarian the society we're living in has become. Because, in here, it's right there, you're banging your head against it every day. On the outside the same authority is there but it's just not so . . . so close.

LM   You're certainly not confronted with it daily the way you are confronted by the hacks.

RALPH   I'm saying the government is really bullshit. It really is, Nick. It writes your history books, it regulates your education to the point where you have people that aren't happy with it.

NICK   This country did allow you enough freedom to develop the viewpoint that brought you here.

RALPH   And they regret it, so don't pat them on the back for it.

NICK   Freedom in this country is something that is allowed and not an inalienable right. Obviously, or we wouldn't be here. This is the way the system looks at it, not necessarily the way I agree with it.

RALPH   And I'm saying I reserve the right not to like it. You're saying I can't do it.

NICK   I don't like it either but I'm saying that it exists. And I can't see that it's suddenly just going to disappear.

BEN   The first place it's going to disappear is in you.

LM   You say that the government is bullshit, right?

RALPH   Yeah.

LM   Nick says that the government is bullshit and not bullshit. If he thought the government was totally bullshit he'd have left the country, rather than going to prison, then going back out and living, and paying taxes, or whatever.

NICK   Right.

LM   What I think Nick's saying is that he recognizes the government as a mixed force, with both good and bad in it, but that it is not a thing that can be denied out of hand just by calling it bullshit. It may be bullshit in many of its functions, but if it is bullshit then it's certainly powerful bullshit. It's not just a paper government. Whether their premises are justified or whether they're bullshit, they act on the premises as if they were justifiable. The government is exerting a certain force which he feels is mixed enough to live with and not so oppressive that he has to leave.

NICK I came here with that opinion and now I'm not so sure. I may have to leave.

RALPH Why should you have to leave? This is *your* fucking land.

NICK Living in an arbitrary environment, like this prison, you come to see other things which are arbitrary outside the prison. Let's say you're more sensitive to arbitrariness.

RALPH You [learn to] see authoritarian things everywhere. I think you go to prison because you still have some respect for the government. You don't get to the point where it's beyond redemption. You see the draft or the war or Nixon or Hershey as benign tumors. Now that you've been here in prison you feel less certain you can live in this country. You disagree with more positions the government takes than when you first came here, when you essentially only disagreed with their position on induction. But now the respect is gone.

NICK That's part of the "not doing it a second time" thing.

LM Any particular reason for that?

RALPH I feel like I've been to the bowels of the government. Basically they are repressive. They're sick. I don't think if I were drafted again it really means anything. I very well may piss on it and send it back. I sure as hell wouldn't answer any call, because I don't think I'm going to be prosecuted. They may go through the whole rigmarole trying to intimidate me, but I think at some point it will be stopped. Maybe the grand jury won't be asked for an indictment, or the prosecutor'll quash it, but I don't think it'll get that far. If they schedule me for a court date and I know it *has* gone that far, then I know it's good-by.

LM If Nixon and Hershey are benign tumors and don't represent the whole government . . .

RALPH That's what I thought before.

LM How is it that now the prison system is, let's say, a more malignant tumor, and how is it more representative or pervasive, more like the entire government?

RALPH I think the principles this place is run by are identical to the principles by which the government does everything.

WAYNE   It's the system rather than the people.

RALPH   Everything is. Well, they overuse force. Force is the way they accomplish the thing.

WAYNE   It's like now you get down to the skeleton of the thing. Like you said, you get down to the bowels and they stink. It's like all the façade is taken away.

RALPH   All the semblance of rights.

WAYNE   All the legitimate stuff. They say you can go through with legitimate grievances. Just try it.

STEVE   Also, there's the courtroom experience, and you know what that is. You begin to realize that it has nothing to do with human beings.

BEN   Before I went to court, the court was the only thing in the government that I had any hope in.

RALPH   That's the Department of Justice.

STEVE   This prison is really the whole key to what keeps it together. This is the repression that the government executes. This is their power.

LM   Do you mean the prison, then, is exercising the essential quality of the government, which is repression? Because the prison is carrying out the government's policy?

STEVE   Right.

LM   The thing that interests me is how prison is seen as being the whole government, where Nixon and Hershey were seen, as Ralph said before, as only partial representatives of the government. This group seems to now feel that the government is more like prison generally in all its aspects rather than that the prison is one arm of the government which is obviously repressive, just as the State Department is another kind of arm, and the postal system is another.

DAN   It's not like a caricature here. It's not that far apart. I think it's down here with the velvet gloves off, I think they're identical.

STEVE   In prison you cut out one whole arm of the government as not worthwhile. There was the military before, which we all got here for. We somehow understood how bad it was, OK? Now that we see how bad prison is, there's the whole court system. Well, what's left that's good? Maybe the post office? So I think you have in here a large per cent of what the government is. It's another chunk of the government which you throw away. You know now, you're more sensitive to just how bad they are, you're more sensitive to the double-talk.

WAYNE   And to expect them to treat us like human beings is unrealistic, too. It really seems to me that their system, their dehumanizing thing, is not only affecting us but it's turning back. They have lost their humanness too. It's turning back onto them. It seems a lot of times the guards and the parole officers are twice as paranoid as we are.

RALPH   They live in a mortal state of fear. They're afraid of The Hole. They're afraid of you when you're *not* afraid of The Hole.

WAYNE   You get in here and you see the guts of the things, and you begin to see how . . .

RALPH   It *is* what's out there.

WAYNE   Yeah, right. My case worker was trying to tell me how I'd left the outside and come to the inside. What you come into here is the *heart* of the outside. You begin to see the system working on the outside in the same way.

BEN   All the cushioning's squeezed out.

WAYNE   It's just twice as clear as it was out there, what's happening to you.

RALPH   The image you have of convicts on the outside is just grossly distorted. They're not animals. You may have a few people in here that come close to that. You find bank robbers are nice people. They have a sense of humor. They love their wife, common-law or otherwise, they're just like everybody else.

LM   What about prison guards?

RALPH   Oh, they're definitely not.

LM   They don't love their wives or have a sense of humor?

RALPH   They don't love their wives in any healthy way. Maybe in a symbiotic relationship or a parasitical one. It's sick.

WAYNE   It's having someone who's ignorant who treats you like much less than a person having the key, not allowing you to come in and out of the cell, or in and out of the door, and treating you like, well, the only thing I can describe it, as a little part in a machine that's supposed to fit there and that's about all. Someone told me when I came here, a friend, a bank robber; you know, I was feeling much better here the first week, it was much better than the county jail was. He says, "Just wait until the shit comes down." I thought he meant when I got out into the population and people'd try to do things to me. But that wasn't it, it was when you get the runaround about four times. When there's no logic left to anything they say, it's just an arbitrary rule. You keep running into the whole illogic of the place, and you keep running into never being treated like a human and then you begin to feel like the shit starts to come down. Here they say they have your best welfare at heart. I've heard Lieutenant Russell say that. You can't believe it. It was after I'd been here about a month, and they'll say, "We're really trying to help you," or "You know that you got the best education here." Things like that. When you know by their actions that they're just sittin' there lying to you. They say you can't look out for yourself under any circumstances. That's what's oppressive, the attitude of the people in here towards you as a person. What I didn't realize before was that their locking the door meant that kind of attitude.

BEN   I refused to think about it. People would come and tell me how bad prison was and I'd answer them, "Man, I don't care, I'll take whatever comes."

WAYNE   What they're saying to you once they put you in here is how much more attractive it is to hide than it was before.

RALPH   Your respect for authority disintegrates in here. There's suddenly nothing wrong with hiding. It's like running from the Gestapo. Why not?

WAYNE   I have a hard time even *thinking* about it myself. Except it seems to me if you take off and hide, you legitimize what they're doing to you.

NICK   And you're cringing under their authority.

CARL   If you're hiding you aren't doing anything for 'em.

RALPH   You're not playing the game at all.

LM   You're saying, "Your law has the power to make me hide."

STEVE   I think there's one real, real question. Because I tried that, just before I decided to refuse induction. I knew I was supposed to receive an induction notice and I just didn't give them an address to send the induction notice to. I was fairly open about it, I told them what I was doing.

CARL   You wrote them and said, "I'm hiding"?

STEVE   The question is, what do you do while you're hiding? What kind of a life do you live? I tried to hide in the United States, and finally it came down to the fact that I was really spending full time, you know, *hiding*. That was my major occupation.

BEN   Were you paranoid or something?

WAYNE   You don't have to be paranoid. They're really coming after you.

STEVE   I was living a relatively interesting life. I wasn't really scared about getting caught. But all my decisions ultimately revolved around the fact that I was hiding. And I really didn't have anything to do.

RALPH   Did they catch up with you or did you turn yourself in?

STEVE   Finally I just got tired and decided to refuse induction. I got tired of running and wrote them another letter.

NICK   "Here I am, come and get me."

LM   So it was something of a relief to refuse induction?

STEVE   Yes.

LM   Whether by going into exile or hiding, you're validating the effects of the law. It may be bullshit, but it's the kind of bullshit that makes you go into hiding.

STEVE   What it ultimately comes down to is if you go into exile you have to have more reasons than just wanting to evade the draft.

LM   You have to be able to tolerate what exile means.

NICK   I've been thinking about that. Kind of curious, since I'll be out there pretty quick. While I don't really expect there to be any further hassle, I know what I'll do if I get it. It's awfully hard to make a decision on it, whether I'd come back and serve another term or not; it's very debatable in my mind, very debatable.

STEVE   I really wanted to do something to change things in some way, and about the war and all that, but I really couldn't think straight when I was leading the kind of life I was leading. I figured that going to prison would be a good first step.

NICK   But the point you raise about exile is important. Is it more effective to go into exile or to come to prison?

STEVE   Depends on what exile means, and exile will vary depending on who you are and what your circumstances are. It's certainly cowardly if you go into exile and just separate your life from doing anything and say it's a totally personal thing. It's cowardly in that sense. But you can go into exile and work very hard for the same beliefs. Even more so than somebody could, possibly, by being in prison. Or doing anything in this country. You can in effect go into exile in this country, by just obeying the laws to whatever degrees you have to. It's a cowardly thing to not act on your beliefs, not doing what you believe in, and I think there's a lot of ways you *can* do something about what you believe in. It doesn't matter whether you're in prison, or in the Army, or in exile. Each person has to do it their own way. But that's where I see the cowardice come in, not doing something about what you believe in.

WAYNE   What you're doing in here is saying that the government doesn't any longer control your life out of fear. That's what the draft does. It frightens or it coerces you into doing certain things that might be against what you think by holding over your head that you come to prison. And so if I say, "OK, I'm going to hide out, I'm going into exile," it doesn't seem that I'd be getting above that fear principle. They're still controlling me, they're still making me do something that I wouldn't normally do. Out of fear. In a sense, then, if you say you'll accept what they'll do, their ultimate punishment, sending you to prison, then they actually have nothing more to hold over your head. Except killing you.

NICK   Isn't that what prison is?

WAYNE   Yeah.

NICK   Killing you for a particular amount of time.

WAYNE   It's an attempt to do it. I feel that's what the challenge of the place is, not to be killed while you're here.

CARL   It isn't exactly killing. It sort of numbs you.

BEN   That's the problem, when you get your emotions all pent up and can't release them in here.

WAYNE   I don't know how many guys I know in here that want to get out and make it and take off to the hills or have their little farm someplace. Just have people leave 'em alone. This one guy is 25, talks about, Jeez he's tired of fightin' and he says he feels he's old at 25. He just wants to toe the line till he can find his little niche. He's afraid if he gets too much time in here he'll never make it. He feels like he's on a razor blade in here. You can go either way, really, no place to grab. Someone told him, I think it was a case worker, "About the only thing you can do now is tape up the nerve endings." You know, he's afraid he's going to blow his cool and hit somebody and get thrown in The Hole and have to stay. He's an eight-year bank robber, and he's got about forty-two months left.

BEN   The government becomes a real thing in here, an opponent. And they're fighting against it, struggling in this prison. It does the same thing to me, and I want to fight against it. That's it. I can't be a pacifist any more!

WAYNE   The thing goes deeper than that. We recognize it goes beyond the judge, back into the government, back into society. When I was riding outside, on the truck out to the farm, and saw all the people riding around in their cars, *real* people with colored things on their bodies, and a gas station with red and white pumps, and a restaurant, I kept looking at people coming up behind the truck in their cars, and I kept thinking how much in prison you can be out there. I looked at the guy, the gas-station attendant was in there, and thought how in prison he can be with that job. I've been thinking how similar this kind of experience is to experiences I've had on the outside. Just as imprisoning. Just as threatening. And I said to myself, "You leave here, so what, you go back and you just continue the struggle out there that you recognize a little more clearly in here." The only difference is there's some other people out there. That's the thing you look forward to. And you can move around a little bit more.

NICK   What you're saying is that the yard out there is really big.

25

Interlopers

THERE was wide variability among the resisters as individuals, and there were often angry and bitter differences between
them. That they had made the same choice of prison was not in
itself enough to guarantee close friendship or to prevent acrimony.
Indeed, in the early months of the group's existence it seemed that
the opportunity for dispute—which sometimes rose to the level of
discussion—was all that held it together. Close friendships, to the
extent that they could survive in prison, were often deeper between
individual resisters and other inmates than they were between resisters themselves. Many made good friends among prisoners convicted of marijuana smuggling or bank robbery, the two groups
most sympathetic to draft resisters. Although some resisters had
arrived at Lompoc thinking that they might be special prisoners
because of their ethical interests and their noncriminality, those
assumptions were soon eroded by the guilt-inducing and leveling
qualities of daily prison life, which tended to blunt ethical sensitivity
and to blur individual distinctiveness.

But however close they were to other prisoners, the resisters
came to be closely identified with one another, and in relation to
me, as the group began to coalesce. This gradual cohesion produced
a kind of mental boundary around the group which set them off
from other prisoners but which also brought within it all men classified by the officials as "Selective Service cases." Jehovah's Witnesses,

who clearly were such cases but who were very different in character from the resisters, were consigned by them to a separate mental area with a boundary of its own. The protective and adaptive advantages of this mental boundary around the resisters exceeded its limiting effects until it was suddenly breached by two very unwelcome arrivals, new prisoners who were undeniably Selective Service cases, were clearly not Jehovah's Witnesses, and yet were not at all the kind of men the other resisters wanted associated with them. Though neither of these new men actually joined the group in person, their presence in the prison strongly challenged the group's definition of "resister" and evoked the deep anxiety of each man in the group. These new prisoners personified characteristics of which the resisters had often been suspected or accused, and they embodied issues with which the resisters still had to struggle: homosexuality and cowardice.

John Doe arrived at Lompoc with a conviction for draft evasion, but he walked in with a notably feminine gait and his prison haircut did not conceal that his hair had been frosted and streaked. His relatives had hidden him from the draft and the FBI for several years, hoping to maintain a complicated family equilibrium. No psychiatric consultation had been requested at the time of trial and none had been ordered by the court. Terrified at the prospect of being raped, he requested to see me therapeutically even before I could ask him to come in to discuss the group. He was no less apprehensive at the prospect of having to compare the circumstances of his arrest and conviction with those of the other Selective Service prisoners, and he immediately declined my invitation to meet with the group. His presence quickly became known in the prison, however, and though the group was relieved that his challenge to their self-esteem would remain indirect, they were still concerned that the prison staff and inmates would seize the opportunity to further equate resistance with effeminacy or sexual deviation.

Neither effeminate nor frightened, Robert Smith arrived a few weeks later, and when I saw his name and offense on the daily announcement of new arrivals, I routinely asked him to come to my office to discuss his joining the group. He was a little more guarded than some prisoners facing a psychiatrist for the first time; he would not discuss his refusal to report for induction and he was adamant about not joining the group. Since I regarded draft refusal as a private matter and membership in the group as voluntary, I didn't press either issue and told him that he was welcome to join the group in the future if he should change his mind. When I mentioned this to the group at the next meeting, they were a little surprised and some felt that they had been snubbed. Eager to find out more about the new man and to include him in the group, Mark Henley looked him up and spoke with him privately. Mark was shaken by their conversation, and by the time he discussed Robert Smith in the next group meeting he was eager to keep him out. In fact, he had already excluded him psychologically by redefining him in his own mind as "not a resister."

MARK   First of all, he's not a resister. I talked to him, talked to him at length. Number one, he's not a resister. Number two, I don't think he's gay. He said, if it's true, he has a wife and one or two children. The reason that was brought up, about his wife and children, was that he said he wasn't going to risk himself over there, with a wife and children. He said he was against the war, as far as that goes, but he would serve anyplace else. I said, "We'll talk it over together in the group; maybe some other guys will talk to you if you're interested." He came up to me yesterday morning and said that he would prefer that he wouldn't be part of the group. He was quite adamant about it; he said in a very nice way that he didn't care to come to the group. It came about because he moved all over, that's how the charge came about. Dodging was what he was. And not for any real moral or political convictions.

LM   You mean he was a coward?

MARK   I don't know whether it's cowardice or not. He doesn't believe in the war. He was adamant about that. He was surprised that I asked.

LM   But from what you say, it was more because he was concerned about getting hurt or leaving his family than it was about the social, moral, or political reasons for being in the service.

MARK   Some things you'll get killed for, some things you won't.

LM   Well, that's one view, but what I'm pointing out is that he said he didn't want to get hurt.

MARK   A funny place to come with that attitude. But he seemed to be straight in every other way. Coward or what, he's straight, I think.

There had been many silences in the group. There would be many more. What consumed the next two hours was utter silence.

It was not until a week later that Mark found the voice to articulate the feelings of the group. In that silence there had been anger at the new men for forcing the issue by their presence, shame for themselves for being embarrassed, and fury at me for mentioning it. However strong their tolerance or resistance to homosexuality (and no resister in this group cooperated or was raped), the inherent conflict and daily challenge were undeniable. Nor had their choice of imprisonment completely resolved their conflict over imputations of cowardice; cowards could be found at Lompoc, too.

MARK   I got to thinking why I didn't want to call him a coward. I got to thinking, in a way it's because he's one of us, in that he refused the service. Sort of like what's-his-name, the one who's gay. It's sort of like he reflects on all of us. In actuality he doesn't, because we're not known as a group inside the institution and I doubt that they're thinking, "This one's another one who's a coward." There's no real connection in the mind of the population or the staff. There is among *us*, and that's what counts. And it's like he's one of us, only he didn't come here for moral or political reasons; he came here because there's a big yellow streak up his back.

LM   I think this group does exist as a group, not only in here in this room but in the minds of all of you. I don't know about the rest of the population.

MARK   It was the straw that broke the camel's back. It was bad enough to have a homosexual come in on a Selective Service beef, but to have a *coward* was the final straw. In a way it's worse than a homosexual. I can understand a homosexual being a resister, one who won't take the cop-out of going down and doing the physical and saying, "Yeah, I'm a homosexual, you don't want me anyway." I can see someone keeping quiet about that during the physical and then just refusing. I can even see a homosexual refusing for actual resistance reasons, rather than [Doe], who didn't want to leave his mother.

NICK   Doesn't it occur to a coward that he might get hurt in prison? I went through a period, after refusing, wondering just what is the measure of myself. Asking myself, are you kidding yourself or something? And I think this internal question, of am I a coward, is the really psychologically explosive aspect. After you do about six months' time, I think you could say, "No, I'm not."

26

"An Inmate with a Mustache"

T<small>HE</small> "psychologically explosive" issue of cowardice was one that was neither fully discussed nor fully resolved. Nick's prescription of six months' incarceration was sometimes not sufficient for some men to be fully certain of their motives; others needed no further confirmation than their having made the decision and faced its consequences. The issue would sometimes force itself into the open, but more often it remained in the background. But however confident each resister was of the truth of his beliefs and of the validity of his acts, that inner certainty was subject to the constant pressure of an environment and a social system which devalued discretion and placed a negative value on ethical sensitivity, and which forced prisoners to cooperate with that devaluation and negation. More specifically, the resisters' inner certainty was ceaselessly threatened by the attitudes and actions of many prisoners and employees. Many of them scoffed at the very existence of such a psychological dimension as moral courage, and they considered the resisters disloyal or craven in the most contemptible sense. Those who could concede the existence of moral courage, if not its importance, regarded the resisters as either foolish or sick and as fit subjects indeed for a psychiatrist's concern.

The attribution of cowardice and the denial of moral courage were added emphasis, so far as the resisters were concerned, to the general atmosphere of impersonal condemnation which every prisoner inhaled, an extra stroke of coercion through the arousal of infantile guilt which was the major psychic effect of the prison organization. For it is true that outer laws tend to become inner laws, that outer coercion can become inner coercion; and the laws which were enforced at Lompoc were not those of the nation or of ordinary human decency but rather the strictures of the prison rules and the imperatives of the inmate code. It was these laws which the resisters now had to resist—and they had to struggle even more against their own natural inclinations to follow them.

The prison rules, the inmate code, and the psychic changes of incarceration tended not only to undermine a sense of connection to life outside and the opportunity for association within the prison but also to erode the inner capacity to make attachments, maintain loyalties, and form groups of any kind. But in the clinic, groups did begin to form, however tenuously, and this was the result of the interplay of many elements: their therapeutic value, which was widely variable; the climate of relative openness, which was a change indeed from the secrecy of the rest of prison life and a challenge in itself; the moratorium on condemnation, at least from me. These slight encouragements applied to the resister group as well, but there were certain aspects of their group that were unique: there was the opportunity to compare with each other the problems of resistance to the draft and to prison, and the chance to explore and define, perhaps to resolve, the inescapable ambivalence aroused by imputations of cowardice. Each resister was able, as one man said, "to run a check on myself to see how I'm holding up, how much I'm giving in compared to the others, what things I'll stand up for in here and what things I'll let go by. I don't think I'm a coward, and I don't think anyone else in here is either, but some days it seems like everyone in this place thinks you are and says so."

It was indeed an Orwellian world in prison. Love was Hate (aggression tended to predominate over affection); Peace was War (the overall institutional quiet was kept through official overlooking of constant minor violence); Honesty was Theft (the rules against personal possessions were so absurd and the inmate code so forceful that everyone stole, and hardly anyone bothered to conceal it). The moral inversions which constituted necessities for prison survival could capsize any conscience. This was a particular problem for the resisters, sometimes an excruciating one, and another force in the consolidation of their group.

Innate character structure, reasonable guardedness, and the unreasonable suspicion of the prison climate retarded the formation of the group, but once it began to coalesce, it coalesced tightly. Though I had demonstrated trustworthiness, drove the right kind of car, and was properly disliked by the guards, such conditions only facilitated the formation of a more powerful bond: the close identification between me and the resisters, or better, among all the members of the group.

This cohesion depended on more than trust and on more than the clear perception that I was truly identified with them in their struggle to preserve both their beliefs and the integrity of the group; a more powerful element was the degree to which certain qualities were made over to me as the group's epitome, and the degree to which I was drawn into the group as its member. Under the extreme pressures of prison life, even resisters had to make ethical compromises; and during the period that these compromises were in effect, while they were living on a different ethical plane, I was often acutely aware that I was implicitly becoming the repository of certain qualities of some of the group members or of the group as a whole—aspects which were considered valuable, even essential, parts of themselves, but which were temporarily useless and were even impediments to prison survival. I was aware that it was even more my responsibility not only to contain what had been temporarily entrusted to me but to nurture it, to interpret what was happening, and to return it gradually.

Thus the group began to form over time, through a process that was mutual at some points, reciprocal at others. At times we were all identified with each other in relation to some other person or concept; at others, the resisters were identified equally with each other in relation to me. The shared idealism within the group, or its concentration upon me, helped the resisters to ward off their doubts and reinforced their grasp on their purpose: their refusal to go against their consciences, their not allowing themselves to be coerced by fear.

It was not just their ideals and beliefs that I was expected to contain and preserve for the resisters, but all those attributes, faculties, and identity fragments which had been eroded by incarceration. Moreover, I was not to be merely a passive repository of deferred ideals and suspended selves but an active mediator as well: I was expected to exercise those faculties which were lost, to establish continuity, to integrate and formulate what was happening, to endow with meaning what was becoming progressively meaningless. And in doing this I came to realize that the border of the group was the border of a shared identity; that the group itself served as a bulwark against the identity erosion of imprisonment; that the group was, among other things, an association to ward off overwhelming anxiety.

The most consistently stated or implied perception of me by the group was that I was a kind of "inmate with a mustache." They were, of course, never completely unaware that I was a psychiatrist, but in this special relationship, some aspects of which were unconscious, I was far more an inmate than I was a doctor, and this view was realistically supported by the group's observation that I was contained, frustrated, inhibited, and infuriated by the prison. It was no distortion for one inmate to comment that "Dr. Merklin's doing some time himself."

But in seeing me as an inmate with a mustache the group not only saw me as more inmate than doctor, they also felt that in possessing what was forbidden other inmates—a mustache—I also possessed particular advantages and power. I was a "special" inmate; I went home to an apartment at night yet I was still a prisoner; I was similarly incarcerated yet I was expected to know more about survival and to do far more than merely survive. Paradoxically, the accurate perception that I was "doing time" and showing it, rather than appearing omniscient and "neutrally" uninvolved with them, made it possible for some prisoners (and not only resisters) to see me as a suitable recipient of their temporarily disavowed better selves; and having thus made over to me that which was best in them, I could then be seen not only as their personification but as their paragon.

There was, as well, an element of denial in this idealization, for to the extent that I was an inmate with a mustache the differences between the group and me were minimized. To the extent that I was seen as different from them at all, it was as a benevolently superior fellow inmate. This tacit classification served to deny that I was both a psychiatrist and a prison employee and that I might destroy the group's identity in order to impose one of my own devising. Conversely, there were occasions when I was not seen as an inmate with a mustache but as one psychiatrist in a group of research psychiatrists of equal rank who were investigating prison life and its effects. In this situation, I was not drawn into prison; rather, we were all out of it, in a seminar with a common scientific goal but whose immediate benefit lay in the avoidance of the painful life at hand.

However much I admired the resisters, was grateful for their friendship, and was inspired by the moral charge with which they had invested me, I had to be careful lest I grasp too eagerly the role they had assigned me and overlook my responsibilities to them and to myself to point out the reasons why this particular perception of me was important and what realities this particular role both expressed and denied. However much I might have liked to have remained an idealized figure without examining the bases for that idealization, I could not have done so. Even if it had been desirable for me to have assumed the role of a superinmate, it would have been impossible, for the painful life at hand was affecting me as well.

During my time at Lompoc, I was anxious and depressed and, more than ever before, subject to sudden anger. On one particularly infuriating day an inmate clerk made a relatively small error, but it wrecked my appointment schedule for the next few days. My anger at him was far out of proportion to the error committed; it was more than ordinary anger, it was savage anger. This was not the first time I had taken out my frustration and fury on a relatively innocent person, nor was it the last, but it was the first time the resisters—who were waiting in the hospital corridor to go into my office—had seen me lose my temper. Instead of the usual shuffling, banter, and competition for the softer seats that preceded each group, I was met with silence. They were too surprised to say anything, and I was too ashamed. The stillness was finally broken by the pained voice of one resister who pointed out how excessively angry I had been and how disappointed he and the group were that I had violated their high opinion of me. He and others gently emphasized how much they expected me to bear for them while they were completely in prison and I was still relatively free. It was that pained reproach which bore home to me, much more than my clinical suspicions had already suggested, how vital to the group was their endowment of me with their better selves and how important I was as their trustee.

Over the next few months I became a little more adept at controlling my anger, but I slowly came to realize that there was yet another aspect of my relationship with the resisters. It was still important for them to attribute to me the "good" parts of themselves that were endangered by imprisonment, but to an only slightly lesser degree I had to contain their "bad" aspects as well. The experience of incarceration was arousing in the resisters, as it did in other prisoners, memories, feelings, and attitudes that had long since been repressed. This experience led them to feel that not only was the reality of incarceration bad but that they were also becoming more vulnerable to the uncontrolled assault of their own bad aspects and to the power of their own malevolent wishes. As soon as they began to sense the threats to their better selves from both the environment and their own destructive impulses, they had endowed me with those better aspects they wished to preserve, seeing me thereafter as a highly idealized figure.

But as the resisters' destructiveness mounted and their fear of it increased, that too had to be made over to me lest it overwhelm them. Because I was already felt to be superhuman, having been projectively identified with their good aspects, I was felt to be capable of taking on the bad ones as well. Having become the recipient of both their ideals *and* their destructiveness, I had the duty not only to contain them but to keep them apart. My responsibility, therefore, was to keep what was best in them from being debased by the prison and destroyed by their own destructiveness, and to prevent what was worst in them from being evoked by their incarceration and from being ennobled by their good instincts. Part of the reason for the resisters' shock at my temper tantrum, therefore, was their horror that I couldn't hold, that I couldn't "maintain"; that if I could not control myself, then I could not control what they had given me.

As time went on, the resisters were exposed to the basic fear which confronts every prisoner: the dread that he will be overwhelmed by his own impulses. To mitigate this fear and to allay anxiety, the resisters responded with unconscious psychic processes, partition and projection, which are universal but which are maximized by imprisonment. As this unconscious reorganization progressed, anxiety diminished, but the price for the absence of anxiety was all too often the absence of all feeling. The prisoners' world tended to be timeless, colorless, concrete, and populated with figures who were arbitrarily perceived to be either highly idealized or intensely persecutory. Subsequent events in the group reflected these changes in the resisters, inner revisions which were more extensive than I had realized.

After a year at Lompoc, I went on vacation for a few weeks. The group had become so well consolidated that they asked to meet in my office while I was gone. Another doctor opened my office for them and locked it when they left, but they met alone. When I returned, however, I had been unconsciously transformed. I was no longer the wholly good inmate with a mustache who was entirely within the group. The opposite and equally arbitrary attitude toward me now was that I was a hostile, watching guard, and that I was entirely outside the group. My voluntary absence—and even more my voluntary return—had been proof beyond denying that I was indeed not a prisoner. And, given the psychic inflexibility which now gripped the resisters, if I could no longer be an idealized inmate then I had to be a persecutory guard. The inner logic of their position dictated that if I was no longer an inmate like them and the bearer of their good selves, I must therefore be seen as a guard, someone utterly different from them, hostile by definition and the representative of all that they loathed in themselves. As I had been absolutely trusted, idealized, and incorporated, so was I absolutely distrusted, degraded, and expelled.

What is more, my absence had not been seen as a vacation but as a desertion. Over the previous months the resisters' access to what they had attributed to me, their better selves, had come to depend on my physical presence in the prison. When, during my vacation, this physical access was no longer possible, they were unable to think of me and what I represented as being present in spirit. My "good vibrations" had departed with me. Because of their concreteness, my departure appeared to deny them access to me and to their better selves, leaving them feeling depleted of all worth and of being at the mercy of their persecutors. It was not so much that I had gone away and left them but that I had absconded with all they valued.

This sudden, complete shift from one partial but absolute view of me to its opposite was not entirely a surprise, but I was taken aback and hurt by the ferocity of its manifestations. I was cheered somewhat by the intensity of the attachment it expressed, however negative its accent, but I was even more depressed over the degree of regression it represented. This polarized attitude was not learned or imposed, it was evoked or regressed to; it is a universal potentiality noticeable in children but residual in adults. It is a derivative of a basic mental constellation of early childhood, but it is also reflective of, and adaptive to, the isolated, helpless, threatened psychic situation of prisoners which recalls their early childhood perspectives. Nor was this mental orientation of utter inclusion and absolute exclusion limited to inmates. Its derivative was equally recognizable in the prevailing philosophy of prison officials: either "you're part of this institution" or "you're prejudiced against us."

27

The Challenge

T HE changes among the resisters were sobering in themselves, but the consequences of those psychic alterations reached
their most tragic when the group began to turn upon itself. For
several months the group remained stable in membership because
newly convicted resisters were being sent from court to the prison
camp at Safford, Arizona. This situation was attractive to the resisters at Lompoc. They felt they were becoming a social unit in a
place where cohesion was difficult, and they felt some continuity
where each day was usually crossed off and forgotten. But this
sense of continuity often lasted only for the two hours of the group;
many groups were later as easily forgotten and as hazily recalled
as individual days in prison. Furthermore, no departures meant no
envy of the men who were leaving and no guilty mourning for
themselves. No arrivals left them free of disturbing changes in the
social fabric of the group. This quiet period encouraged the resisters in the belief that as they remained static in number, so they
remained stable as individuals; that no turnover meant no overturn
of their view of themselves; that as the group remained unchanged,
so they would emerge from prison unaltered.

The next man into the group would have had difficulty entering
its closed situation even without his burden of an anomalous and
upsetting sentence. Imprisoned by a well-meaning but uncertain

judge, Ned Farley arrived with a term of three years: six months in prison and two and a half years suspended. If he refused another draft call during his suspended sentence, he would be returned to prison. Ned Farley was different from John Doe and Robert Smith; he did not threaten the group with homosexuality or cowardice, but his arrival undermined the group far more seriously. In contrast to Doe and Smith, the rest of the group saw Farley less as an interloper than as a hidden persecutor ("he's from the CIA"), or as a foreign contaminant ("he's a germ, a virus"). Ned's short sentence only emphasized the length of time all the others faced. The others were envious and resentful; they questioned Ned's sincerity and wondered aloud whether he had made a deal with the court.

True to form, the resisters did not express their anger directly. Mark Henley could tolerate Ned only in elaborate jest, and the rest of the group usually ignored him as if he were invisible: they "shined him on." Although he joined the group, Ned was never allowed into it, and this realization profoundly disturbed him, undermined the validity of his conscientious objection, impaired his belief in himself, and complicated his time at Lompoc. When we talked privately he spoke of his exclusion and of how he hadn't felt guilty until he joined the group.

"I was making a point yesterday and I don't think I got it across very well because I have to speak from the vantage point of being short, being here only a short period of time, and looking at everything that way. It pisses me off because I can't tell about my experiences here any way other than humorously and defensively, waiting for them to say, 'That's because you aren't here very long, you're getting out, you're not doing your time anyway.' I don't know how I would do two and a half years; I think I would do it, it would be possible. I can remember guys going home, when I was in A & O, and I felt, 'Gee, I wish I was going home.' I'd feel the start of the frustrations: 'I can't go home, there's nothing I can do about it, I have to start thinking a different way.' I see this happen to them more often and in a deeper sense because they can't say, 'At least

I'm getting out in a couple of months.' Lots of them are kind of defensive. Like talking with Henley; he seems the most preoccupied with the difference in sentences and therefore everything I say is always invalid. This is always in joking, but it gets to the point where I don't think I've been able to carry on a serious conversation with him. At first I thought it was because I hadn't been here very long so I didn't press it, and now I'm leaving and I don't see any opportunity for establishing any kind of rapport.

"I really don't know why it is that out of all these sessions we've had, I never once made the point of giving my viewpoint or that I felt defensive about being short. I certainly thought about it, and each time it was easier to say to myself that I'll do it some time later. I really felt I wasn't entering the discussion, that I was more of an observer, which perhaps I am. I felt I was being rejected by the people in the group. Sometimes I would dread seeing Henley because if I wasn't in the mood for joking, I would take offense at what he said.

"I didn't feel like I copped out until I got *here*, until I joined the group. I didn't feel that way at the time of the trial or afterward. When I came here I thought six months was a lot of time. Seeing how long other people were doing, I realized it wasn't that long compared with these people doing longer, and I started questioning how I felt about my sentence. My mind is completely muddled on that. I'd like to be out, I feel I'd be more productive outside. On the other hand, I could do my time, the whole time here, I know that."

Still, other resisters did not fully accept the fact that Ned had a short sentence until he was actually gone and his absence could not be denied. They were silent for most of the first meeting after his departure and the comment was terse:

NICK   We haven't even begun to talk about Ned's leaving.
MARK   We have to first decide that he actually got here.
LM   Well, in a sense, he was, to rephrase what's been said before, a walking reproach. It stirs up more feeling now that he's physically not here; until this week he was only

potentially leaving. Now he's actually gone; it's an accomplished fact that he did get out this morning.

MARK They were saying in here, about someone like him, "You were short when you drove up." And every time I'd look at him I'd say "short."

LM To yourself or to him?

MARK To myself and sometimes to him. I used to constantly ride him about his time.

The subsequent arrivals of men with split six-month terms forced the long-term men to restrain their mounting anger even more. The situation, as it evolved, raised new issues regarding resistance, cooperation, and the degree to which prison life, often unawares, could influence mental functioning and behavior. Jay Bowman was the next man to arrive with a six-month sentence. He traveled from court shackled to Ben Post, whose sentence was eighteen months. Despite their deep individual differences, their shared bondage kept them friendly and their joint arrival united them in the eyes of the group despite the difference in their sentences. On the day of their entry into the group, few others spoke; the two of them dominated the two hours with questions about prison routine and court and county-jail gossip. The long-term men were either elaborately uninterested or a little more openly irritated than they had been when Ned Farley arrived.

LM One thing I noticed about this group today was the relative silence of the older people in the group. The absolute silence of some of them.

MARK Well, you asked a specific question of the new man.

LM Yes, but I didn't ask him to spend the entire time on it. What I do feel is that it has to do with some of the issues that were discussed, and the lack of enthusiasm of the discussion has something to do with duration in prison.

BEN I don't necessarily agree with that.

MARK No, it's true, oh, it's *true*.

BEN Well, who I am personally is different from someone else; the prison won't have the same effects on me as it will on someone else.

MARK   We'll see eight months from now.

BEN   When I came in here, I came in perhaps with a different attitude than other people did.

MARK   I think I was silent because I felt a lot of nostalgia listening to you. I was looking back twenty-two months and listening to you speaking. I could have talked very similarly to the way you're talking, twenty-two months ago.

BEN   But you won't now?

MARK   No, I won't now.

BEN   Do you feel differently now?

MARK   Yeah. I have very little feeling for community. I'd rather reserve judgment till I get out, because I think that a lot of what I feel now is due to being locked up. It's a change brought about by being confined.

LM   Mark and Ralph probably the least of the older people, but everyone else looked really bored. If it wasn't boredom, that's what it looked like. You didn't look interested in what was being said.

CALVIN   Yep, that's right.

MARK   If you listened now to Ralph and Nick and me talking in the cell block, you couldn't tell that we were COs from what we were saying. When a lot of the COs were coming in last summer, one of the first things I'd ask them was, "What are your reasons for coming here? What kind of a CO are you?" I'd really want to know. Now I'm not interested. That's what it comes down to, I don't give a shit. When I had visitors up and they were talking about what was going on outside, they said, "Do you like the visits?," and I said, "It doesn't make any difference," and they looked sort of aghast or, you know, strange. When I was here the first six or eight months I would've been interested in what was going on.

CALVIN   Yeah, I was tuned out, I was just thinking about all the broken windows around here, saw your window was broken too. [The broken windows around the prison were the result of a riot. The window in my office was

broken accidentally by a member of the hospital st
I was completely off. You know, there's a lot of brok
windows around here now.

Six weeks later, Joe Cox arrived with a similar split sentence.
The pressure of two such men in the group increased the resentment and the tension.

LM	No one has acknowledged the new man.
BEN	I thought Nick was vetoing him.
LM	Nick was what?
BEN	Vetoing him. Since he had so short a sentence, Nick was jealous and was vetoing his appearance in the group.
NICK	Just like I vetoed the last two.
LM	We ought to discuss that. I think the group's feeling about new group members ought to be considered.
RALPH	I think you ought to go and get a court order, Bud [the author's nickname], that would authorize you to take all of our sentences and throw them in a big bowl and divide us out an equal share.
BEN	He just wants it to be unfair but impartial.
LM	How is it partial now?
BEN	I don't know; somehow it's partial in giving people different amounts of time.
NICK	The idea of having this other fellow in here *is* upsetting, I might add. He has six months, and two years suspended. Not that I'd be completely pleased with *that*, but I'd be much happier than with what I got. I suppose I'm upset in the same way that Ralph, with a Youth Act, is often upset at me. Because Ralph has more time, more worry, and more hassles. I think specifically we're all ignoring him. It's upsetting to think that he's only got another three and a half months to go.
MARK	You can't get into a conversation with a person that's that short. I mean I tried, I tried to get into a conversation with Ned Farley.
RALPH	He said, "Excuse me, I'm on the run. Just passing through."

JOE   How many resisters are in here? Just what's in the room?

CALVIN   That's all.

JOE   I expected more.

CALVIN   We all did.

RALPH   You know, since you've been here there hasn't been a
(*to* LM) suicide. We're overdue for one, it's been two years now.
          Maybe the guy that follows you will have several.

CALVIN   There've been attempts, lots of attempts.

RALPH   That was meant as a kind of compliment. The suicide
          statistics and various psychotic elements that I have con-
          tact with in here assure me that we're long overdue. Some-
          body has to do it just to fill the quota.

LM   What do you mean that we're overdue for a suicide?
          What use does suicide serve to the rest of the people in
          the institution? From what you say, there's a need for it
          that's not being met, and its not being met is being felt.
          Psychotic or not, it's still there.

NICK   Well, I don't know, the administration may think about
          it and decide that the place is not pressing enough punish-
          ment for the inmates if they're not committing suicide,
          not meeting the quota.

RALPH   It's actually a feeling on the part of the administration,
          and some of the inmates overhear them discuss it because
          it's a nice morbid topic. "Long overdue, long overdue."
          Mrs. X in the office, for example. When I first came here
          she told me that lots of people had strung themselves up
          in their cells. "Just the other day so-and-so took his life."
          She talked about it like it was great.

NICK   She probably remembers all the suicides in the last twenty
          years as though they were yesterday. My boys!

LM   Why are they saying it to you?

RALPH   I don't know. It does seem morbid. I couldn't see any
          personal meaning at all.

LM   Well, the feeling that there should be a suicide soon sug-
          gests to me some kind of sacrificial quality.

RALPH   There not being any virgins around to sacrifice, the next

best thing . . . what's the next best thing? A Selective
Service case?

LM   I think for the Selective Service case coming to prison is
something of a sacrifice. In that respect I think it parallels
the situation.

NICK   They're still screaming for their quota, so the [inmate]
population and the administration don't accept that.

LM   I don't mean to imply that that's my interpretation of
what the population is saying. What you hear on the
compound does seem to be a logical, if that's the word,
extension of the bloodthirsty quality of the general population, of the need to relieve tension through violence.
I wonder maybe if your bringing it up in here *today* has
something to do with your feelings towards the new man.

RALPH   Why don't you elaborate?

LM   Does it need elaboration? A guy that comes in with a six-
month sentence?

NICK   Kill that son of a bitch!

RALPH   If we killed Joe, that son of a bitch, that would be murder.
So it wouldn't be the suicide thing. It *would* be a sacrifice.

NICK   Is prison everything you thought it would be?
(*to Joe*)

JAY   I wonder if they'd shoot a CO if he tried to escape from
the farm.

CALVIN   They'd shoot anybody if he was a convict.

BEN   If you try to escape you're not a CO any more. It's a new
crime.

JAY   I don't think they'd shoot us, Ben.

NICK   I'll tell you why, Jay.

JAY   Because, because, it'd be an almost *political* thing.

NICK   Take off, find out. We'll come visit you in the hospital.

CALVIN   Experience is the best teacher.

JAY   I'm short already, only a few more weeks to go. I'm trying to take it up for Ben.

LM   How is it that you feel they wouldn't shoot a CO for trying to escape?

JAY   I mean, it'd look bad somehow.

CALVIN   From which end? Your end or theirs?

JAY   It'd look bad to me if I was outside. Oh, you know, it'd look bad in the papers.

NICK   It probably wouldn't be put in the papers. They don't print all the escapes.

JAY   They don't?

NICK   You could make the papers real good, Jay, if you got killed escaping.

JAY   Be a good deal, a bid for sympathy for prisoners.

BEN   Send him to the psychiatrist.

JAY   Seriously, do you think they'd shoot you? I'm not necessarily serious about escaping. I'm serious about thinking about it.

CALVIN   You're serious about thinking about it because you're a CO and you don't think they'd shoot you?

JAY   I don't think they would.

CALVIN   They don't think, "Oh, that's a CO, I'd better not shoot him"; they just shoot you.

JAY   Yeah, but they don't have guns, they don't have guns out there.

CALVIN   When there's an escape, they have guns.

NICK   Just escape, you'll see what happens.

LM   Your idea is that they would miss you at work and then the officer on the farm would call the guy down here and say, "It's Jay, he's a CO, don't pack a gun"?

JAY   Right, they wouldn't shoot a CO.

CALVIN   The sheriffs and all don't know you're a nonviolent man. They just know that you're a convict and you're escaping.

After ricocheting from job to job in the prison, flirting with the idea of escape, and painting peace slogans on farm buildings, Jay was sent to The Hole for laziness. In Jay's temporary absence, the problem of the short men was at last openly discussed.

LM   I wonder if any of you have felt that Jay's being among this group had anything to do with his going to The Hole.

RALPH   Well, yeah. I think his being in the group accelerates his understanding of prison. You can be somewhat naïve and stumble through your first six months not really sure about anything. It may seem like the case worker's a cock sucker, but until you get in a group and you hear that everybody thinks the case worker's a cock sucker, then it's kind of like official.

LM His first six months are his only six months.

NICK I think that's a very important part of this.

RALPH Oh, yeah; well, everyone envies his position. I mean having only, well right now he has forty days to go. There isn't much they can do, whereas the person with a Youth Act is in just the opposite position.

NICK I was agreeing it's the shortness of his time. Not only that, the fact that Ralph and Mark both complained that they had been given a great deal more time and they had been punished a great deal more, and that the person who is short, then, is expected to hassle the system more than Ralph can expect to hassle it because he's too vulnerable.

RALPH I don't think being short is a cross somebody has to carry. I mean there is an *advantage* to harassing the system, harassing these hacks. There is an advantage in saying, "I'm not going to work today"; it's something to do with dignity.

NICK It is an advantage, Ralph, that you have essentially not taken part in.

RALPH I got off the farm. It was a medical reason, but I got off.

NICK True, but you didn't say, "I'm not going to work, send me to The Hole."

RALPH I did, I said both those things. He said, "You want to go to The Hole? We're not going to let you go." I have to be more cautious, I can't flagrantly violate the rules.

NICK Why not?

RALPH I've got to outmanipulate them so I've got a defense.

LM I don't think it's accidental that the man with the shortest sentence went the furthest in terms of resisting in prison.

RALPH Maybe you're a bad influence, Doctor.

NICK   He's got the most encouragement, he's got the least to lose.

RALPH   Yeah, he's got encouragement, the system provides that. We may simply reveal it to him or make it more clear.

NICK   Whether you suggest he has a cross to bear or not, there is this aspect, that you expect him to hassle the system more than you feel you're able to. You even have expected *me* to hassle more.

LM   The idea seems to be that the man with the shortest sentence should do the things that the men with the longest sentences can't do because the prison would punish them more or they would do harder time if they did the same things.

RALPH   I don't like the way you word that. If I had a smallish sentence, and I was then in the position you were describing, I wouldn't say yes or no to the short guys. I don't think you really try to *pressure* them, the shorter men; you simply tell them why they should do it.

LM   But why him, why the man with the shortest sentence?

RALPH   Well, because they can be less abused, there's less room for retaliation by the hacks.

LM   Yes, so the man with the longest sentence, then, can't do those things because he would be abused more.

RALPH   Well, I don't think that is completely true. As I said, you can do these things but you have to be very careful; it's mostly manipulation.

LM   Another thing that's occurred to me is that the man with the shortest sentence may be expected by those with longer sentences to go to The Hole because he experiences harder time for a shorter period and equalizes the "easier" time that the rest of the people serve over a longer period.

RALPH   I disagree with that. If I had an eighteen-month sentence, I would go to The Hole. I'd rather not work here. None of the jobs are the least bit interesting, none of them entail any real responsibility. I'd rather go down to The

Hole. You'd get into A-Rest [Administrative Restriction, the "upstairs" part of The Hole] after a few months at most.

BEN   When you get down to eighteen months, are you going to go in?

RALPH   The only thing bad about it, if I went to The Hole, it might be used against me at the parole hearing.

BEN   You're screwed.

NICK   Isn't it true, Ralph, that you are not getting individual treatment, that you're treated like any other Selective Service case? You're expected by the system to do twenty-four months regardless of what you do while you're here. You're not going to do any more time than that whether you do it in The Hole or wherever. Then in fact you really don't have more than twenty-four months regardless of how you behave or whether you cooperate. Therefore wouldn't it have been just as sensible to have said, "Well, I'll do my twenty-four months, or whatever's left, in The Hole because I'm going home whether I behave well or not"? Or do you not trust the system to treat you equally, regardless of how you behave?

RALPH   I wouldn't be surprised if they kept me longer here than two years.

BEN   I know it's been on *my* mind a lot about going to The Hole. One day goes on to the next and nothing ever comes up, so I don't do anything. I've sort of gotten into a rut while I've been here. Wake up one morning, drag myself to work, work if I feel like working, work a little bit if I don't. Come back for lunch, drag myself back out if it's sunny. I've gotten to the point where I don't respond to words any more. If I decide to do something, I don't respond to the hack. I may look at him, but I never give any emotion to him. When I first went there I sort of tried to respond, but it's pointless.

RALPH   Especially if you work hard, they expect you to work harder the next day.

BEN   Right. I immediately got the reputation of being a hard worker but it wasn't because I worked hard. You're going to chop that tree anyway and I felt like doing something, so OK. So by my responding to them they would give me a worse situation. So I don't respond to them. If I feel like working hard, well fine, and if I don't, I don't do anything. There have been some days when I did almost nothing and the guard saw me doing nothing. I'm not sure what he thought of me because usually I work pretty hard. But still I've gotten into a routine. It's hard to actually suddenly say, "Well, the time's right now, I've got to go down to the lieutenant and tell him I'm not working." Maybe that day'll come.

RALPH   If I could go back in time I wouldn't even take alternative service, which I would have then, because I look at that now as supporting Selective Service. I think the longer I'm in here, the less I'll do.

LM   That does seem to be the trend. The shortest people should do the least in terms of cooperation. The longer you have to go here, the less you do to fight it.

BEN   My first three months here, I was trying to understand where I was, what is it, and all of a sudden I said, "Man, why am I cooperating?" For the last month I've been thinking about it all the time. It's continually in my head. What am I doing here? Why am I doing this? Why am I working? It's been plaguing me since then, but at first I was trying to understand the situation around me here and whether to work or not.

LM   What did you understand about the situation?

BEN   I've come to feel that the prison does almost nobody any good. It makes one more inclined not to work or cooperate. When I first came here there was a possibility in my mind that this institution might be serving some purpose and that my not cooperating with the prison would not be to the same point as that of not cooperating with the draft. I happen to be here, and it wasn't right for me to be here, but perhaps someone else's being here was right. My not cooperating could interfere with that person's correction or something, so I acted different. But first I wanted to *see*.

LM You mean if you didn't cooperate you might interfere with the rehabilitation of some real criminals, is that what you mean?

BEN Well, a real criminal or someone this place might do some good. I haven't seen much good being done, if any. For the most part, I've seen it's a training school for further criminal activities. And general hostile views and embitterment about life that really build up here. The very institution itself is something not to be cooperated with; it has no real basis for existence, really, because it's not serving the purpose it was set up for.

RALPH You see, he comes to the same point of view Jay does and nobody pressures him. I think everybody will come to the same conclusion unless they're insecure or they're dullards.

BEN The thing is, I'm not sure. I don't really mind working at some times, but sometimes I do mind. Just the same with Jay. Maybe they gave him half-assed jobs because he was a half-assed worker. He would have gone right back where he was working before, because his intentions were never to go to The Hole. It was to play the game of seeing how little he could do *without* going to The Hole. It was testing their powers.

Moved by his personal response to prison, prompted by Jay's action, and encouraged by the group pressure, Ben made up his mind to refuse to work and went to The Hole. By the next group meeting, Jay had returned to work and Ben was escorted from The Hole by two guards.

RALPH For refusing to work? They have to escort you for that?

LM Did they clean you up before they brought you down here?

BEN   Clean me up? No.

LM   You look remarkably neat for being in The Hole.

BEN   Oh, I keep myself neat.

CALVIN In The Hole? Neat in The Hole?

JAY   Oh, yeah. You can go take a shower on Saturday or Sunday.

BEN   They gave me a towel, so I cleaned up. One end of the towel is for a washcloth and the other for drying.

NICK   So what do you think of The Hole, Ben?

BEN   It's fine.

NICK   Seg or A-Rest?

BEN   Seg.

NICK   Downstairs?

BEN   Yeah. I was upstairs for one day. I didn't like it as well as downstairs.

NICK   Really?

BEN   So much noise and all that upstairs. People talkin' to you.

RALPH You just refused to work?

BEN   Yeah. I decided that I'd sit it out.

LM   Eighteen months?

BEN   For the rest of my time, yes.

JAY   No! Oh, Ben, you need some exercise.

BEN   I get plenty of exercise. I jump around.

LM   What made you feel that you couldn't work?

BEN   I don't feel that my being here in prison is justified. I don't think there was anything wrong in the offense I committed, so any form in which I cooperate with my imprisonment is, I think, wrong. My not cooperating is not going to hurt me in any real form, and I don't think my being in The Hole is going to hurt me any at all.

NICK   For how long? Eighteen months?

BEN   How long? We'll see.

JAY   They can't keep you down there but seven days, I don't think.

BEN   Well, I'd rather be down there than in A-Rest.

JAY   You can't read down there, can you?

BEN   They give you a Bible.

JAY   You ought to take a pencil back with you and write in there, put it in your hair or something.

BEN   How'd you get it there?

JAY   They accidentally gave me one.

LM   What is it that appeals to you about downstairs?

BEN   What appeals to me about it? It's fairly quiet.

LM   Quieter than upstairs?

BEN   Right, yeah. And upstairs the guy in the cell next to me kept talking to me. I was approached from one cell to the next, but I went to the Adjustment Committee the next morning and was moved to Segregation so nothing ever came of it. You know, by homosexual-type characters. It was interesting because he kept carrying this out by passing me notes for hours on end. He was a very intellectual-type person and he talked to me very precisely. He was one of the weirdest characters I've ever met.

LM   What sort of notes was he sending?

BEN   First he asked me if I would "walk with him," that's the way he put it, and that we'd be friends and all this stuff, and implications of my being a sissy. He didn't even see me; I think he was in the next cell down from me. So I said no to this guy and he sent back another message. Finally he said that he was going to have to be more persuasive, he was going to have to be violent, and so tomorrow morning he would attack me. He wanted to know if I was going to snitch.

NICK   How did you refuse to work?

BEN   I went down and told Mr. X that I wasn't going back to work, that day or any other day in the future.

LM   How did he talk to you?

BEN   He just asked me why, and I explained, that was all. No hassle really. I mean there would have been a hassle if I'd tried to make a hassle. I was very calm about it. Actually I was very surprised that I was able to talk as well as I did.

LM   Cooperative about not cooperating?

BEN   Yes. And fairly clear about my not cooperating. The guard at work had said for me to report to I Block door where he'd meet me. So I went down there and told the guard. He couldn't believe it, he hadn't heard anything about it. He told me to sit there. He said it was the first time in the six months he'd worked there he saw anyone having a hard time getting *into* I Block. I went to the Adjustment Committee the next morning and I made my points clearly to them too. It went very smoothly, although Mr. X, he wanted to make it clear that I was going to suffer in The Hole. I was going to become grubby and mangy down there and very uncomfortable. At least so far I haven't found that; I mean, they gave me a towel and soap, and my toothbrush and my comb.

JAY   They told you that if you went to The Hole you'd get dirty?

BEN   Basically. Resting in your own excrement was what they said. The main point they stressed was that there are inmates here who are caring for you, and other people who are caring for you, and you've got to do your part, you're part of this institution.

LM   They said that there were people in this institution who were caring for you? How did they say that they were caring for you?

BEN   Fixing my food for me, y'know, this type of thing. But mainly they implied the inmates were doing it.

LM   And you were supposed to reciprocate that by working?

BEN   Right. That was my part.

JAY   Should take a pencil, you know. Give you something to write. They won't give you one if you ask them.

BEN   They've been pretty cooperative so far.

JAY   They won't give you a pencil. You got to smuggle a pencil in.

BEN   It doesn't really make any difference to me whether I have a pencil or not.

JAY	Give you something to do.
NICK	Is that their attitude, that you're not allowed to write letters in The Hole?
JAY	They let me write one, then they sent it back to me. They didn't give me a pencil and paper any more.
BEN	Maybe something was wrong with it.
JAY	I mentioned I was in The Hole, and said derogatory things about the institution.
BEN	The walls are really slimy. I've been walking around in my bare feet to get as much grub on them as I can and washing them off in the sink.
JAY	You really think you're gonna stay there the rest of the time?
BEN	Sure gonna try.
NICK	You seem more at peace with yourself.
BEN	I feel much more at peace with myself since I've gone there.
LM	What do you do?
BEN	Well, there are things you can do that don't need anything.
JAY	I mean it's the environment, it's like a dream, something you can't explain, just something you experience.
BEN	I get exercise by doing what you might call creative dancing. Actually there's a limit, and I've got that Bible there.
JAY	There was a couple of guys trading a sissy when I was down there.
BEN	Trading what?
JAY	Trading a sissy. She was upstairs. *It* was upstairs.
BEN	They asked me if there was any pressure on me to go to The Hole. I don't know if they meant homosexual pressure that I was trying to escape, or pressure from this group.
RALPH	Well, you raised the issue last time, Dr. Merklin. You almost suggested that people with the least amount of time had a kind of obligation to go to The Hole.
LM	It seems to me that that was my interpretation of what you and the group were saying.

RALPH   Yes, right. Well, anyway, I brought it up and you gave it that interpretation.

LM   I think that's different from advocating it.

RALPH   Not much; it's an idea.

LM   I could discuss many ideas and not advocate them.

RALPH   Well, since this is such a naturally attractive idea, I think bringing it up constitutes advocacy.

LM   Why it's attractive is something to be discussed, since it never came up until recently within the group.

NICK   What's your position now, Ralph?

RALPH   I think going to The Hole would be beautiful.

NICK   And in a year you haven't made it?

RALPH   Oh, I didn't say *I* was going to The Hole.

LM   How does my discussing The Hole mean advocacy of it and your saying it's beautiful and not going . . .

RALPH   For obvious reasons, going to The Hole is attractive; for the reason that it's so restful, there's no harassment from hacks. It's like B Unit [the honor unit, in which there were no guards] in that sense. There's no responsibilities. There's no fascism down there. If they hand you a tray you can kick it out. Where are they going to put you then?

NICK   In the strip cell.

RALPH   Big deal.

LM   One thing that I'm curious about is, you say that going to The Hole would be beautiful, but you don't consider that as advocacy for going to The Hole.

RALPH   Well, going to The Hole by itself is beautiful. Going to The Hole if it has repercussions of keeping you here longer is ugly.

LM   And therefore for Ben it's ugly?

RALPH   That's silly.

LM   It could keep Ben here longer.

BEN   Not all six years, as Ralph is, on a Youth Act.

LM   True enough. Is that how the group interpreted what I said last week about going to The Hole?

NICK   No. I didn't; in fact I thought you were a little noncommittal one way or the other.

JAY Maybe you were just trying to bring this pressure by the big-timers out into the open so that we wouldn't feel, so that we would be able to be objective about it. What I mean is, you see, I feel terribly guilty about leaving after five months. My conscience really bothers me something awful. And they don't say anything to ease my conscience. They don't say, "Oh, it's OK, your leaving after five months." More or less, "We forgive you."

LM The idea of group pressure occurred to Ben because when the officer asked about pressure, he thought of the group.

BEN Yes, that's true. Actually I was more cynical during the last month when I was realizing what was happening to me. That I was being pushed around, and that I really shouldn't be working. That was really more the effect it had on me.

LM You were feeling more uncomfortable?

BEN Yeah. I'd go to work and I'd be thinking about how I shouldn't be working while I was shoveling. One day I almost did nothing, but that was only one day. When I went to The Hole they said, "You have really good work reports."

NICK Ralph says you won't get any more time, but stick your neck out too far and you might find someone who wants to give you some. They could frame it very easily, charge you with obstructing the functions of the institution.

RALPH That's not a crime; a riot would be. Your big offense was refusing to work. Work wasn't one of the provisions of your commitment. This wasn't so many years of hard labor.

JAY It was explained to me that working was a privilege, it made your time pass easier or something. They were telling me they were trying to help me. Man, there ain't no sense in rottin' down there. I'm serious.

NICK These people fuck you around enough without your helpin' 'em.

RALPH There's a dignity down there, there's a sense of dignity down there.

NICK They can't deny you a visit, can they?

BEN I've had two since I've been down there, and then they denied me a third one. They said if you're not going to cooperate you don't get any privileges. They took me upstairs, gave me a shave, got me all ready to go for my visit, [then] Mr. Glenn [a prison executive] said, "Put a hold on it, I'll check this out." I was sitting there for about ten minutes, hadn't heard from Glenn yet, and in walked Lieutenant Russell. He said, "What're you doin' in here sittin' there?" and the hack says that I'm waiting for a visit, waiting for an OK from Glenn before I have to strip. Lieutenant Russell said, "I flat deny it right here; send him downstairs." That was all I heard of it till Glenn came by and told me why a couple of days later. He said, "You don't cooperate, you don't have any privileges."

NICK You gonna quit eatin' too?

BEN If you eat too much you get fat.

LM Does being in The Hole decrease the problem of bad vibrations?

BEN Oh, sort of; it gives you so much time to think of what you're missing that it bothers you sometimes. You have so much time to think about it that it really gets to you after a while.

JAY My ribs got all tired from rolling on that bed after a while, all crunched up.

BEN I'm getting where I can sleep pretty good now; I don't sleep well, but it doesn't bother me that I'm not sleeping well. I go to bed as early as I can and sleep as late as I can in the morning.

JAY You been doin' set-ups and push-ups and things like that?

BEN Not too much; there's no motivation to do anything down there. In the mornings I don't get to do any exercise at all because I'm cramped up. I swing my arms around and move my shoulders because they're so stiff and aching. After a while it'll feel OK and I sit there and wash my face, and I feel OK so that by afternoon I can take a nap.

JAY   Actually, I see no hang-up in going back to work. If it's gonna mess you up, like you said; there's nothin' wrong with being down there as long as it doesn't mess up your health or something. Your head, that's what I mean, your head.

RALPH   You've got the group to go to; after six days of fucking your mind, they give you one of health.

BEN   Can they deny me to come to the group? I was worried about that.

LM   It has been done. I called Glenn just now and asked them to bring you up and he gave me an argument. I told him that if he was concerned about your behavior it would be better to have you in the group than not in the group.

BEN   The last time when I came back from the group, Lieutenant Russell came by and said, "You're not crazy, are you? What are you going to that group for? What's wrong with you? Nothing wrong with you."

NICK   He thinks you gotta be nuts.

BEN   Yeah, so I said, "I guess you don't understand much about group therapy." He says, "Oh, yes I do."

RALPH   "That's what we do with our most severe disciplinary problems: put them in the group."

LM   What did he say he understood about the group?

BEN   I never got that. I should have questioned him about that. He's hard to talk to because he aggravates you. I mean, he's trying to aggravate you.

LM   So you're as sensitive to his bad vibrations in The Hole as you would be outside?

JAY   The only things you look forward to down there is your meals, you know, three meals, and when the hack comes walkin' by, or the doctor might walk by.

BEN   I don't know. I watch the sun through the window so I know exactly when things are going to happen. I can't see the sun, so it all depends on where the shadow lies. If the sun's between the middle section and the top section of the windows, that means it's breakfast time. When it

	gets down below the bottom window, that's when the work whistle is going to ring.
LM	Some men in The Hole say they're getting half rations. Was that your impression?
BEN	It all depends who was serving. Sometimes the plate's full, sometimes it's just a little bit. It all depends who's there.
LM	Do they give you utensils?
BEN	Just a wooden spoon.
LM	Do you get enough water?
BEN	The water's pretty ratty; in the morning it stinks.
NICK	Do they shake you down every time you go back?
BEN	Oh, they usually do, yeah. I have a thing with that shaking-down bit. What it's saying is, they don't trust you. They have no reason *not* to trust me.
LM	You won't work, that's one reason they don't trust you.
BEN	Oh, that has nothing to do with your honesty.
LM	To them it does.
BEN	To them, I know.
LM	Anyone who doesn't follow the rules is not "part of the institution," and if you're not "part of the institution" you're not trustable.
BEN	*They've got to learn that not everybody's in here because they're not trustable.*
LM	From what you said earlier today, it seems that the difficulty you're having now has to do with your feelings about what you're missing.
BEN	Yeah, right, about spending time, and I think maybe after a couple of months you get used to it, getting your mind into a pattern as long as it's not too messed up. When I get mail I don't react very well to it. I was doing pretty well down there until I got a letter from home. I'd been thinking about things going on there, the things they're doing, and it really got to me that I wasn't going to be there. Everything going on without me. I got depressed after a while.
NICK	Come on, why don't you just tell them you want to go into industries and get good time?

BEN	I don't want to do that, man.

BEN   I don't want to do that, man.

NICK   Why not? You can get a job in the cable factory. If you
        feel better staying in The Hole, go ahead, but if it's hurt-
        ing you . . .

RALPH   The option to leave is yours every day.

NICK   I can see being in A-Rest, but that Seg, man, is just
        a dungeon. It'll kill you off physically and mentally. When
        you leave here, you could be pitiful.

BEN   We'll see how it goes.

NICK   If you feel you're doing some good, I can sort of under-
        stand it.

JAY   The only people you can talk to is the guards down
        there, and they know they're keeping you down there for
        no reason at all, and you're right, and they won't admit it.

NICK   They're just following orders, they don't know anything.

BEN   That's what Glenn says when he comes down. "We're
        not the ones that put you down here. We're just holding
        you here. Why aren't you cooperating with us?"

RALPH   That shows you how guilt-ridden that cock sucker is, you
        just know he's got to break some day.

NICK   I can't make a moral judgment for Ben. All I can tell
        him is that I don't think he should stay down there if it's
        going to hurt him.

RALPH   Unless you drop out and go to The Hole, become a
        human being. It's probably the solution to the puzzle, the
        right answer.

LM   Part of the reluctance to give advice doesn't have to do
        only with moral questions. I think it has to do with part
        of the code, which is, you don't give anybody advice.

NICK   I gave him advice, I told him what I thought he should do.
        I said it first and then I went back and lightened it up.

LM   So it wouldn't seem like an order.

NICK   Yes.

RALPH   You've already conformed, you're already the docile
        citizen of the totalitarian state, and every day you become
        increasingly worse. When he comes up with an argument
        that's basically humane . . .

NICK   I don't become worse, Ralph; I just take a look at reality and act accordingly.

RALPH   You're reacting to force. You're reacting to the force here.

NICK   There's a time and place for everything. You can't shovel shit against the tide all the time.

RALPH   You mean this isn't the place for action? Look at Post; he's been in The Hole and he has every one of the arms and legs he had last week.

NICK   How will he be six months from now? How will he be if they decide that he won't have the benefits of the group? No visits? No communication with the outside? Why don't *you* do it for the next four years, then? Is there some little stretch, that if you did it, you would be a worse human being?

RALPH   There is such a thing as an excess, I'm sure.

NICK   Oh, I see. And the excess is where it starts hitting *you*.

RALPH   The excess is where it goes beyond a two-year period. Two years is cool; two years and one day, fuck it.

BEN   Why did you resist the draft?

NICK   Because I felt I had to.

RALPH   You're very defensive about it.

NICK   If we must talk about it, my feelings are still the same. I have to point out that my relationship to prison and resistance is quite different. I refused induction the way Ben went to The Hole. There was nobody there telling me, "Well, it's all right," "It's been done before," and that sort of thing. I was all by myself, and uh, I can certainly agree with you, it's not easy to, under those circumstances especially, I mean if there was one other person, and you're not all by yourself, you can stand up much easier.

BEN   When I started draft resistance, it was the same way with me. By the time I got to trial I knew lots of people. They sort of magnetated.

NICK   I didn't have any contact other than through the news, which is no contact, really.

STEVE   By the time I refused, I was so far into it that I had the feeling of frustration that I wasn't doing enough. It wasn't just refusing, it was *how* you refused, whether refusing was *the* thing to do. It wasn't a question of whether it was right or wrong, it was whether *this* was the thing to do. You know, could you be more effective some other way? It wasn't as scary as that for me.

BEN   It wasn't scary for me, either. I knew exactly what I was doing.

NICK   Well, I'm glad you guys did, because I still remember very clearly going into that induction center and wandering through, and even then in my mind, I'm divided, I don't want to stand up and, all alone, this, you know, you don't do that. You know that it's the right thing to do, but having the nerve to stand up and say no. I'm wondering, how can I do it? When I finally did it, I expected that immediately there would be five sergeants jumping on me, taking me to a back room, beating the hell out of me, clapping me in irons, putting me in jail, I'd never be seen for five years. The most shocking part was when they just turned me back into the streets of Oakland. You know, you've done it, and it's over, and there you are standing in the streets of Oakland. You don't know a soul.

RALPH   It's worse than being in the Army.

NICK   For Steve it wasn't a question of whether he should or he shouldn't; it was how to do it best. In my case I just barely managed to do it, so I did it very poorly, from lack of planning. Nonetheless I feel satisfied that I was just able to stand up and do it; if I didn't do it very well, at least I did it.

BEN   Are you more sure of your position now that you've taken it? Do you see now that you've done the right thing for sure?

NICK   Oh, sure.

BEN   But before, you were scared?

NICK   As hell.

BEN   But you could have looked for a loophole, found a 4-F or a 1-Y.

NICK   And lost my moral integrity for doing so. If you're going to The Hole for your moral integrity that's fine, but at what point do you begin balancing your mental health and your moral integrity?

BEN   I don't think I'm really in danger about mental health.

RALPH   I think you're more in danger for your mental health out here in the population. They treat you like an animal, you act like an animal.

LM   If the system treats men as animals, how are you more of an animal if your cage is bigger, let's say as big as the prison, in which space you can move about relatively freely?

BEN   You're a trained animal when you're in the prison. You're like the animals in the circus.

JAY   I really felt like I was becoming an animal in The Hole. You know, you look forward to your meals; it's the only thing you look forward to, that meal comin' in. And you grab at it, you sit down on the corner of your bed. I felt like I was becomin' an animal in The Hole because, you know, you run over and you set it down on the washbasin, you take your spoon and you shovel it, shovel it right into your mouth, slurp it right up, and wolf it down.

BEN   *I don't do that.*

JAY   You don't sit down there and grab it?

BEN   *No, I don't.* And I only eat a little bit of it. I don't eat it all. If I ate it all it'd be bad for me; I'd become very obese after ten months in there.

RALPH   One thing, though, you can act like a human being down there. If they come down and give you the slop you can take the fuckin' thing and push it out, out of the fuckin' cage, and let it go on the floor.

BEN   I can say what I want to because they can't do any more to me. *I can do what I like as long as I'm in The Hole.*

RALPH   What kind of force are they going to use on him now? Are they going to start playing sounds that'll drive him insane? Are they going to start dropping water drops on his head? They've already got everything taken away from him now.

BEN   They can take me down to the strip cell and give me one blanket and a mattress and that's all, or they can give me nothing if they want to.

LM   This raises the point that was touched on before, that people who are here for short terms are more expected to go to The Hole because, since they were here for short terms, being in The Hole wouldn't be all that difficult. If you're there for a short time, it's bearable. If you feel that being in The Hole is a more human way to do time, does it seem to you that the people who go to The Hole are doing more human time, or are less dehumanized, than the people who are here for a long time and must adapt and be trained animals or some other kind of animal, outside of The Hole?

RALPH   Yeah.

LM   So in a sense people who are in The Hole are doing easier time.

RALPH   Yeah, and at the same time they're bringing to the consciousness of the administration the human factor. They're protesting. They're in effect saying, "Fuck you, I'm a human being, I don't want to be stripped at the rear sally port. I don't want the rest of your shit." And they scratch their heads and wonder what gave this guy the idea he was a human being.

BEN   Whatever they do to me physically, I'm not going to give in. They can take away this and that but I'm not going to give in. I'm still going to say, "Well, I think this is right and I'll do it." Maybe it would be easier if they just shot me and got it over with. The point is, by going back to work I'm not being right; I'm just being blah, apathetical.

RALPH   You're going back to being regimented.

BEN   Whenever I *do* something then I'm *being*, I *exist*, man. Perhaps it would be right if I refused to cooperate at all. Not take food or anything. I couldn't convince myself to take that position. I don't know why. But I finally got to the point where I said to myself, "Well, I have to take this step of not working. I'm not going to do what's wrong, and I'll stay apathetical until I know what's right."

NICK   You're living in a real world with real people. They live and they die and the ideal is to stay alive as much as you can. You have to balance that against other ideals, like doing the right things.

LM   It seems what Ben is saying is that he's more alive by staying in The Hole than by being apathetic and being part of the code and being dehumanized outside The Hole.

JAY   In a way you're being apathetic to the needs of other people by being in The Hole because there are certain people who possibly need you. People outside. Me.

BEN   What can you possibly tell people if you aren't doing what you think is right?

28

Victimization

IF the presence of the men with six-month terms—the "short" men, as they came to be known—was a severe shock to the other resisters, it soon became no less a tribulation to the short men themselves. Each man, no matter what his sentence, was forced to question again the value of his act of resistance, and therefore his own worth. However circumstantial, this development imposed a further burden on each man's sense of identity, a self-perception already eroded by incarceration. For some men, this was the crucial test of their entire imprisonment, for it threatened to undermine not only their personal sense of honor but also the more temporary though more immediate identity of "resister"—an identity whose principal value was the degree to which it warded off the full acceptance of the identity of "convict." For however much the resisters believed—and insisted—that they were just like other prisoners in the day-to-day aspects of their imprisonment and in their responses to it, they also believed that they were still distinctive men acting responsibly, that they were men who had gone to prison for principle, that they were inmates but not convicts.

Throughout the previous months, despite the severe effects of incarceration, an important though largely implicit function of the group had been the delineation and acceptance of the shared identity of "resister." The membership of the group had been stable for a long while; and however much the absence of change stimulated the belief that prison was not changing them, it also provided a period in which the resisters came to know and to trust one another, to know and to trust me, and, despite individual differences, to become approximately equally identified with each other and in relation to me. If the presence of the short men was the crucial test of each man's integrity and was a threat to the temporarily shared identity of "resister," it was also the crucial test of the group in which we met and of its value as a bulwark against anxiety.

The manifest disparity in sentences aroused envy and anger in the long-term resisters. More evident than these strong feelings, which were quickly denied, was the resentment, silent at first and later outspoken, that the short men were getting away with something; that if they had not been exactly devious or dishonest, that if they had not actually conspired with the judges in their sentencing, they were at least not quite so pure in conscience as were the resisters with longer sentences. In voicing these resentments, the long-term resisters seemed to be paralleling the opinions of those in the general public who felt that all resisters were shirking their patriotic duty; they appeared to be re-enacting in the group the public censure to which they themselves had been subjected.

Moreover, the resisters' lingering anxiety over imputations of cowardice was reinforced by the presence of these men who were getting off so lightly, who would not have to test their bravery even in prison, and who would be leaving—with time off for good behavior—well before Nick Manos's formula (six months in prison means you're not a coward) had elapsed. Also, the arrival of these new men with their easy sentences aroused the fear that they might not be resisters at all but agents sent to infiltrate the group. Finally, the psychic changes of incarceration had left the long men intolerant of variety and suspicious of diversity. There had been an implicit agreement within the group not only on the identity of resister but also on the range of acceptable sentences for resistance. The wide disparities in sentence aroused the idea that there might be wide disparities in conscience as well. They seemed to feel that the new men would become equally and fully identified with them and with me and that with their light sentences and lesser consciences, they would thus devalue the consciences of the long men, weaken the fabric of the group, and diminish its importance by diluting the intensity of the shared identification in idealism on which every member of the group depended.

The anger of the long men toward the short ones was considerable, and it was intensified by the thousand other angers of prison life. But it was as much a character trait of many resisters as it was an axiom of the inmate code that anger should not be expressed directly. The anger which led other prisoners, in crisis, to physical assault or self-mutilation was discharged by the long men upon the short men. Their murderous anger was at first denied completely. It was later expressed toward Ned Farley in jest and in his relentless psychological exclusion from the group. Jay Bowman and Ben Post were greeted with elaborate indifference, Joe Cox by the announcement that a suicide was overdue. All of these short men, and those who followed them, were encouraged to redeem themselves in The Hole by doing shorter but harder time. Faced with inequality in sentencing, the long men suggested that it be made up in suffering; confronted with men who claimed to be resisters yet were to be incarcerated only briefly, the other resisters demanded concrete proof of their integrity by a dramatic act of resistance in prison and by the most extreme form of incarceration.

In expelling the short men to The Hole, the long men were meeting the threat to themselves and to the group in their own way; they were establishing their own system of justice and standards of equity and demanding compliance with them. Only by going to The Hole could the short men justify being called resisters, for only by this means could they achieve the degree of suffering which the long men had come to consider requisite. Because of their own suffering and pain, the long men were incapable of seeing the short ones as "just other resisters," as equals. Although the long men were identified closely with each other and had tacitly agreed on a rather flexible definition of what constituted a resister, they were inflexibly bound to this agreement and psychologically unable to tolerate not only the difference in sentences of the short men but also their individual distinctiveness. By imposing a single solution on all the short men, irrespective of their individual qualities or circumstances, the long men were acting in grisly parallel with the Parole Board's position of requiring that all resisters serve a two-year prison term for "parity" with the term of military service.

Moreover, the short men also represented the other resisters' disavowed wishes for a shorter term for themselves, for the whole thing to be over with, or to have never happened. These unspoken wishes heightened the conflicts among and within the long men which had been aroused at the prospect of having the short men meeting with them in the group, of associating with them in the general prison population, and of being identified with them by other prisoners and guards. As they had learned to respond to inner conflict by partition and projection, so now did they deal with the short men by the same means. In expelling the short men, the other resisters were purging them in every sense of the word. To relieve their anxiety and to justify their suffering, they treated them as no better than the worst in themselves.

In sending the short men to The Hole, the other resisters were clearly using them to moderate their own anxieties, trying to relieve an intrapsychic conflict by interpersonal means. But there was more to this than scapegoating; for in exploiting the short men to relieve their own anxiety, in victimizing them to mitigate their own sense of victimization, in using them as a means to restore their own equilibrium, the others were taking a vindictive—and psychopathic—revenge.

However understandable this may be, the vengeful wish and the psychopathic means were the manifestations of a "conscientious regression," a deterioration in moral functioning which was widespread in prison. For many resisters, the conscience which had been an inner governor became a tyrant; that which had been an adviser became a vigilante. As the resisters' aggression mounted, so did the demands to control it, arousing in them a moralism as excessive as the drives it was to check, and imposing on the group a moral dictatorship as absolute as that in which they lived.

For their part, the short men soon felt all the guilt the long men wished on them. They had not sought any advantage in sentencing but soon felt as if they had. Even before going to The Hole, they were living in doubled isolation: from the prison population and from other resisters. Going to The Hole was attractive to some of the short men, not only because it would relieve some of their guilt but also because it would get them out of the general prison population. At the same time, some felt that by going to The Hole they would be more valid prisoners for being deeper in custody; that they would be more accepted by the group because they were acting for it; and, since they had no time which could be taken away from them, that they would also be more free to protest.

Group pressure alone, however, could not have forced the short men to go to The Hole unless such action was also personally in character. Though the short men complied with the demands of the others, though they took upon themselves the burden the others decreed, each also went to The Hole because he was so inclined, and each went in his own way. Jay Bowman went with despair and flamboyance and stayed briefly; Joe Cox quietly waited, quietly went, and quietly stayed; Ben Post pondered and deliberated until he was sure it was right for him and he resisted further when he got there.

But when the short men actually began to go to The Hole, responding to the wishes of the others, the effect on the long men was unsettling. It was one thing to deny their anger and the presence of the short men by acting as if they were not physically present in the group or that they were not leaving soon; it was quite another to see their angry wishes being carried out. As time went by, and as the short men began to talk of their life in The Hole, the long men became uneasy. They began to feel guilty (some more clearly than others) for sending them to The Hole to risk psychosis or worse. When some of the short men became celebrated in the general prison population for their refusal to work and their persistence in The Hole, the long men began to wonder if, by their noncooperation, the short men did not appear to be the better resisters. And, having been fearful that the short men would disrupt the group by becoming equal members in my eyes, some long men now came to feel that the short men were becoming "more equal" because I was seeing them every day in The Hole.

Ultimately, the conflict over going to The Hole recapitulated for each resister, whatever his sentence, the conflict over refusing induction. It was often said in the group that each man's decisions were his own, that his degree of cooperation was up to him. Did resistance stop at the prison gate? Did one refuse to work at any job, or did one refuse only to braid cables destined for the Air Force? Did one work at all? Many of these issues came to a head around the figure of Ben Post. He refused to work, though it meant The Hole; he refused to have his body searched, though it meant no visits; he refused to be thought dishonest, though it meant further suspicion. As Ben acted as his conscience demanded and his character decreed, as he acted on what was best in himself, so he activated, unintentionally, what was worst in others. His account of his noncooperation, of his being "torn down and frisked," and of his determination to prevail over the effects of The Hole inspired respect at first and resentment later. Did his personal moral vision suggest to the others their relative myopia? Did the "inner light" of his convictions appear to outshine their own? Did his willing resistance reveal their grudging collaboration? The implied exposure of their relative compromises by Ben's more absolute action aroused shame and anger among other resisters. As the intensity of this situation began to build, I wondered to myself if Ben Post was not also Billy Budd, and I feared that he would meet a similar fate.

In the next group session, Ben recounted his refusal to submit to a strip frisk, and he went on to describe the guards' assault which followed.

NICK Their authority is based on overwhelming physical strength.

RALPH Right.

NICK And it *is* overwhelming physical strength; when sixteen or twenty of those guys grab you, they have you.

BEN They *don't* have you, that's the meaning.

NICK   They probably could as well yank *you* in pieces as your pants or your shorts.

RALPH   So what? Let's get back to the basic point, Nick, the thing about dignity, the thing about principle versus the force that seems to cause you to tremble or be so fatalistic. What about when you were in the induction center, when you were thinking about refusing, that they might just drag you off anyway and throw you in a stockade and kick the shit out of you until you finally cooperated?

NICK   For all I knew, that's precisely what they *were* going to do.

RALPH   But it wasn't important?

NICK   Certainly it was important.

RALPH   It wasn't so important as to cause you not to refuse.

NICK   I had to refuse anyway.

RALPH   Why did you have to refuse?

NICK   Because of the principles involved.

RALPH   OK, so you can have a principle but Ben can't?

NICK   No, I'm not saying that Ben can't.

BEN   Well, what was the principle involved in your case?

NICK   There are religious principles involved which I'd just as well not get into because they're too complicated.

BEN   You mean about killing or fighting or what?

NICK   Killing, fighting, the whole thing. From the political side of it, the problem of freedom, equality, the problem again of authority that has overjumped its bounds.

BEN   But has it overjumped its bounds in here?

NICK   It has, I agree. I'm inclined to believe that a direct confrontation here is ridiculous. Their reaction to us is that we're young kids and we just don't know what we're doing; we're just rebelling against authority because we're young, not because of any principles or ideals which they can see and understand.

BEN   The only real way you're ever going to get across to someone is by your *example* and not by your words. I might tell Glenn the way I feel about frisking, and I might tell him the way I feel about having me as a slave here; and if I don't *do* anything about it and go on just letting him know, then I haven't said anything to him. The only way you've said anything to him is by the way you *behave.*

NICK   Have you spoken to him?

BEN   What d'you mean, have I? He knows my position. He comes and sees me every week.

NICK   Are you making any headway?

BEN   Well, I think the fact that he can come down to The Hole and see that I'm perfectly happy there, this partly proves my point.

NICK   If you're perfectly happy in The Hole, I think you're nuts.

RALPH   For principle, Nick.

NICK   Principles in terms of whatever takes you to The Hole are fine; to be perfectly happy there is ridiculous.

BEN   Not *perfectly* happy, but relatively happy.

NICK   Relative to what?

RALPH   To out here.

BEN   I'm doing much easier time down in The Hole than I was out in the compound. The time is even going faster, which may not seem reasonable, but it is.

NICK   I'll accept the pain of struggling along out here.

RALPH   For what seems to be a shorter period according to you and the calendar.

NICK   For what *is* a shorter period of time in terms of what most people call reality.

BEN   You're just trying to get it over with. The way I feel about it is, while I'm here I'm not asking the time to go by as fast as possible because I've still got just as much time when I'm not here. While I *am* here I want to be *living,* and to be *living* I can't be a *slave.*

NICK   Can you be an animal locked in a cage?

BEN   I'm not an animal locked in a cage.

NICK   You think you aren't, but you just said a few minutes ago that you are perfectly happy locked in your cell.

BEN   Well, OK. Physically, that part of me is locked in a cage. But my conscience is free. When I was in the compound it wasn't. My conscience was a prisoner of the authority of the institution. I had to compromise my conscience to be able to walk around on the grounds here, to go out to work. The whole thing was a compromise of my conscience. I was physically slightly freer and my conscience was partly a prisoner; it was a compromise position, part prisoner of conscience and part prisoner physically. I've decided my conscience is much more important than my physical being, and I'm willing to let my body be completely a prisoner and my conscience not at all.

NICK   So you compromise your physical being in terms of your conscience?

BEN   Yeah, I compromise. The alternative to that would be to have been killed. I haven't got that far. I still have a slight amount of freedom physically within the space of my cell. I can do exercises and eat.

NICK   What you're saying is that you compromise at a different point.

BEN   I've compromised at a lower level. No, not compromised; it's not a compromise at all. There's no compromise. It's a force situation. I haven't got the physical power, but I have the powers of conscience. They can't in any way (except maybe through torture or make me go insane and I lose awareness of my conscience or something), they can't rule my conscience in any matter. I'm the one that has to put my conscience in prison.

NICK   You have made a separation between your conscience and your physical freedom, and you're determined that your conscience must be kept free even at the expense of extreme limitation of your physical freedom.

LM   Are you saying that because his body is in The Hole, therefore his conscience is equally diminished?

NICK   Yes.

RALPH   I think his feet are less significant than his conscience. I think his feet, his arms, and his hands are less significant than his conscience.

LM   Is that what you are saying? That because he is physically in The Hole and therefore his conscience is restricted to the same degree that his person is, his body?

BEN   I'd even put my, my, my, my, my conscience above my mind; my mind, you know, I'd rather go in*sane* than not follow my conscience.

NICK   But it seems to have a relationship. By putting yourself in a situation where nothing bangs against your conscience or you don't have anything probing at your conscience, you are not facing the adversity that should be faced. Of course in another sense you're hitting it head on.

LM   Are you saying to exercise your conscience you must test it daily in situations such as being in the population, and that to avoid being in the population is to avoid testing your conscience with behavior or experience?

NICK   That would seem to make sense.

BEN   OK, so I *was* in the population and testing my conscience. I reacted to the test in the way my conscience told me. And I got thrown in The Hole.

RALPH   Do you think he ought to go out again to the sally port and wait till they call his name so he can have another reaction?

NICK   You don't think that they [the prison staff] ever went through a situation where they had to deal with a situation where their own conscience upset them, or in something that they were supposed to do, they had a distinct feeling against it, and perhaps in some cases did follow their conscience?

BEN   I don't know. They might have, they might not. If they have a conscience, I don't know how developed it is.

NICK   Their conscience, let's say, due to the hammering of reality, is compromised.

BEN   What hammering of reality? Of the powers that be, you mean? That's only a very small aspect of reality. My being in prison is not that important a thing, really, in the total aspect of my total life and all my life's going to be. Eighteen months in Lompoc Segregation is *nothing,* it's only slight, but I'm making it a positive thing instead of a negative thing.

NICK   Isn't it eighteen months of death, really?

BEN   No, of living. I'm living whereas before, I was dead. When I was in the compound I was compromised.

NICK   I see, and to be compromised, then, is to be dead.

RALPH To be dying.

BEN   To compromise is to be partly dead.

NICK   And aren't you then dying completely? Certainly in terms of the rest of us all week long and to the rest of the population, you are in fact dead. Because you're certainly out of touch with us, you're not reacting with us.

LM   What you're saying is that Ben, by going to The Hole, in a sense assigns himself a social death?

NICK   Yeah, I don't mean physically, but he dies socially. It's a form of suicide.

LM   Whether that's true or not, it's a different position than he was in before. In The Hole he is not out of prison, obviously. Nor is he out of prison in the minds of the people who know him or in the minds of the guards. He's very much *in* prison, even more so, in that he's known to everybody instead of being one of twelve hundred faceless people.

RALPH You want him back?

NICK   I want him back, right, which is why I'm talking to him now.

RALPH Oh, no, you're going to take a *position* on whether or not he should stay in The Hole?

NICK   That has very little relationship to it since Ben is aware he's going back. No, what I'm getting at is you said that life in here, inside the prison, is merely the same thing that's on the outside of prison except it's condensed.

BEN   Very condensed.

NICK   Very condensed, much more immediate, and in many ways much clearer, more simple to deal with. When you get out, are you just going to lock yourself in a room?

BEN   No.

NICK   The simplest solution and the one that provides you with the most peace of mind would be to carry it to the extreme and die. Put you in a box, put you in the ground, and no one will bother you any more, no one will bang on your conscience, no one will ask you to do anything that you don't want to do or compromise your conscience in any way.

BEN   I don't understand what you're saying. I don't find it makes sense at all. I might as well die?

NICK   Certainly. Aren't these physically, socially, deaths?

BEN   What I'm doing is *living*, Man; . . . it's just the opposite of dying. Dying is compromise. The people out in society who don't follow their conscience, that are just nine-to-fiving, are the people that are dead.

NICK   I think you're probably living more than they are, but you're still, as far as prison is concerned, 70 per cent dead.

BEN   I'm dead to them because *they're* dead, not because *I'm* not alive.

NICK   Well, your terms for living apparently don't involve anybody but yourself.

BEN   I'm one organism.

NICK   It doesn't involve reacting, being involved with other human beings?

BEN   Yeah, but eighteen months of limited involvement makes up for, I mean, it's just a small thing, I mean by not being involved now it makes it much easier for me to be involved later. If I don't follow my conscience, then how can I relate to other people on the basis of, say, tell them to follow their conscience? Do you follow your conscience in *every* situation or just some situations? I've gotta set this example, gotta say something, gotta follow the way I believe. If I believe that I should follow my conscience and live on that level, then I've got to do it, I can't compromise.

LM   Set the example for what?

BEN   The example of my beliefs. That people should follow their conscience. Set an example that it's not only possible but also the repercussions of following your conscience are acceptable. I think that's why my brother ended up turning in his draft card and placing himself in the situation he placed himself in, because he was going around telling other people to stand up for their conscience and work in the resistance. He couldn't really speak to other people because they'd say, "Well, what are *you* doing about it?" He could answer, "Well, nothing; I'm a 1-Y and I don't need to worry and I can tell *you* not to worry about it."

NICK I agree with your determination about the draft. I think this is again a limited area of opposition to authority. Whereas you are involved here in a complete . . .

BEN   There's only one authority as far as I'm concerned; the government hasn't got any authority, it only has power.

NICK Well, you're making a religious argument now.

BEN   It's basically a religious issue, I think.

NICK Do you think that you needn't have any relationship to the world you're living in?

BEN   What? The government isn't the world I'm living in. It is a power that exists in it.

NICK No, but it's certainly the power that exists in this world.

BEN   On a physical level. There's more than a physical level.

NICK What I'm trying to get at is, you deal on two levels, one being reality, the world as it is. In the other with ideals, the world as we would like it to be.

RALPH Maybe he's made you uncomfortable, maybe that's good.

NICK Well, I have concern for Ben. I believe last week we did mention depersonalization in here. I suggested that it would involve loss of personality, and I think that if you isolate yourself in a cell, and again it's you who are doing it and not just them, when you could be out reacting and dealing with people in a larger reality, then you're hurting *yourself*. I think this is painful to me, yes.

RALPH   Even though he says he's dying out here but he's alive in there? You don't accept his personal impressions of what's happening. You impose your own.

NICK   Disagreeing with what he's saying, yes.

BEN   Well, perhaps it's something like this. If I considered myself separate from everything, that I had no feeling of belonging somewhere, then I probably would feel depressed. I mean I wouldn't be able to put up with the situation in The Hole otherwise.

NICK   Yeah, I see what you mean.

BEN   But I don't. I have a feeling that I'm not alone in a larger sense. On a level of conscience I'm not alone. I feel there's people out for me, people whom I'm close to. I have that assurance that there are other people who feel the same as I do although they haven't been put in the same situation I have, or haven't reacted in the same way, but *would*.

NICK   I understand that, but . . .

BEN   There's a unity between us in our conscience; that's why I believe all consciences are basically a unity and that by making your conscience more sensitive everyone's conscience is going to come to a simultaneous point of agreement.

NICK   That's all well and fine, Ben, but you'd better face reality; namely, that these people here aren't interested.

LM   The point which seems to be sticking here is that you all have recognized the unjustness of the law, the draft law, by going to prison rather than complying with it, but you've also recognized the validity of the law by putting yourself in the custody of the law-keeping authorities, the Federal prison.

NICK   I do that because I feel that this will help to change the law, and apparently it has.

LM   All right, but what Ben is saying is something different; no one questions the law part of it. What Ben is talking about, and Ralph, is the matter of conscience in relation to law. All of you have obeyed your conscience rather than the law or you wouldn't be here. The question is, once you're here, where does your conscience meet the law? The law says that you must abide by the prison rules. Ben feels that his conscience dictates that he can't abide by the prison rules, that his conscience is being compromised by abiding by the prison rules, where you feel that your conscience is not. That seems to be the major issue. Ben feels that his conscience is more intact, more freely exercised, by being in The Hole than it is when he's in the population. But I don't think it's just conscience. Ben was saying there was more hassle living in the community, in the prison population, than there was in The Hole, and that he had to put up with bad vibrations and his own feelings of disgust or anger or anxiety when he had to live with the rest of the people in prison. Yet when he was in The Hole at least *those* feelings were no longer making him uncomfortable. Also, his feeling that he was compromising himself no longer made him uncomfortable, and therefore he says he's doing better time in The Hole. Everyone *else* in the group feels that doing better time is being in the community, in the prison community. That doesn't say that any one point is any more valid than another.

NICK   Now can I ask Ben, do you feel that you are doing the most you can for the ideals that you are seeking to live up to by staying in The Hole, and would you continue to do that, for instance, since you suggested you would come back to prison presumably again and again and again? Do you think you would be doing the most you can for your ideals that way, or wouldn't you do more for them by maintaining the biggest amount of freedom that you can and being also free to work for your ideals?

BEN   No, I don't think so.

NICK   If indeed you had faced the choice of, for instance, living here in the population and dying, which would you choose instead of going to The Hole? If the choice was between living in a concentra-, in the institution as it is, or being shot.

BEN   You mean when I went out and I refused to be frisked, if they were going to shoot me if I refused to be frisked?

NICK   Right.

BEN   I guess they would shoot me. It may take me a while to build up the courage to take that position, but I'm sure once I got to that position I, I would take it and I'd get shot.

NICK   There shouldn't be any question of courage. If you had the courage to go to The Hole, you should have had the courage to stand up *immediately* and be shot in the event that you're going to be frisked.

BEN   There are animal fears in a person which sometimes they can't control, and I don't think, and I don't think I'd be possessed by that. I think I probably would stand up and get shot anyway, yes.

NICK   If you had to face, for instance, the choice. If Mr. Glenn walked in the door right now and said, "Ben, you're going out into the population to follow the rules as best you can. If we have any more trouble with you for which we have to throw you in The Hole, instead of throwing you in The Hole we're taking you out to the rifle range and we're going to have some target practice."

BEN   I'd say, "Let's go have some target practice."

RALPH   Next question.

NICK   Well, you've got a lot of guts, I'll say that.

RALPH   It's not guts at all. Convictions.

BEN   I mean, it's a matter of living.

NICK   I see you have a commitment to death; have you a commitment to life?

BEN   Yes, that's what it is.

29

The Hole

Despite the pleas and threats of the group, Ben returned to The Hole. His commitment to life and his commitment to principle left him little choice. In going to The Hole as in going to prison, his survival depended upon his ability, however limited in range, to act independently, to exert active direction and conscientious regulation over his life, even if that exertion meant further physical and psychological constriction. Like other resisters, Ben had come to prison in good conscience, only to discover there the forces and power of bad conscience—in himself and in others. He had refused to work after protracted consideration and in good faith with his principles, but also in protest against the bad faith he found in the prison and felt rising in himself. He had gone to The Hole as the consequence of his refusal to work but also—in making the decision—to impose self-control upon the "bad vibrations" he was feeling and the psychic destruction they threatened, to remain in touch with the inner guidance of his conscience rather than yield to the outer demands of the prison staff. It was the "tenderness" of the ideals in that conscience—the ethical sensitivity that Ben would have died to maintain—that was being blunted by his life in prison, and it was that conscience which Ben hoped to nurture and restore to wholeness in the isolation of The Hole.

If sensitivity of conscience was most important in Ben's desire to remain in The Hole, his character was particularly well suited for the experience. He had a great capacity for re-creative withdrawal and a greater tolerance for solitude. By his embrace of the ethic of the organized draft resistance of "I'm in for you, you're out for me," he was closely identified in altruism with that movement; he could resolutely accept the psychic death of imprisonment knowing that others were living fully for him. Through his sense of continuity in faith and principle with his family, his past, and his anticipated future, he felt he could withstand the isolation of the present and draw strength from those sources in his struggle for confirmation.

Nonetheless, I was worried. I was well aware that Ben felt it his responsibility to set an example to his parents, to his brothers, to the group, and to his own conscience; yet I feared that he would be made an example of by the prison executives. I spoke with him on my daily visits to The Hole and saw to it that he came to the group every week. But as the weeks passed, I noticed his eyes glazing, his speech blocking, his attention wandering, his concentration diminishing. His laughter often seemed forced or too loud, more of a shudder of tension than an expression of mirth. He insisted that he felt all right and that he was "more alive" for acting in accord with his beliefs. I thought of asking him to come to the hospital even though it offered only slightly less monotony than The Hole, but I also knew how profoundly important his stand was. As with other prisoners who went to The Hole in protest (by no means were they limited to resisters), I was not eager to suggest hospitalization when going to The Hole meant so much as an affirmation of courage and integrity and when it did not seem to pose an overwhelming psychological threat.

Although I was worried about the early signs and the grave possibility of Ben's deterioration in The Hole, the way in which he looked after himself constituted a virtual manual of psychological survival. Against the boredom and inertia, he read the few books he was permitted and forced himself to think about them. Against the idleness and torpor, he devised a regimen of exercises and "creative dances." Against the timelessness and monotony, he kept track of the sun's movement by watching the shadows on the bars, and at the same time exercised his orientation toward both immediate reality and an existence beyond prison in which time was a meaningful dimension. Against the smothering "presentness," he thought often of the future, not only as hope and escape but as practice in long-range planning and in dealing with distant situations. Against the isolation, he tried to engage the guards in conversation, thought often of his family and friends, wrote letters whenever he could, and thought over the events in the group between meetings.

Against the intense pressures of ravenous—even cannibalistic— instinctual pressures, Ben exercised judgment, reflection, discretion, and control. He watched his diet, not merely to avoid gaining weight but also to restrain his mounting instinctual voracity in the face of massive deprivation. In arranging his days, measuring his time, scheduling his activities, organizing his thoughts, composing his letters, summarizing his reading, concentrating on each thing as he did it, limiting his urges, containing his impulses, and deferring to the greater satisfaction of persevering in conscience, Ben was doing more than I thought was humanly possible. He was surviving in The Hole.

But that survival required more than psychic exercise. Against all the pressures, what once was exercise became work, and after psychic work there eventually came psychic exhaustion. What once was fluid and spontaneous in him was now blocked and automatized. What had been purposive activity slowly gave way to the diffuse discharge of tension through motion. As time wore on, the changes in Ben became more manifest and more alarming. His eyes, which had been blue-gray and incandescent with a quiet moral gaiety, were now gray-blue and opaque. What had been a genial smile was now a grimace. What had been a laugh and then a shudder was now a gasp. His tone of voice was no longer even but flat. Where once he walked, now he paced.

I had been reluctant to impose my deep personal concern or my clinical impressions upon Ben while he carried out his moral struggle, and I was painfully aware of his preference for physical death to a compromise in conscience. Yet I was afraid that the severe psychic disruption he was experiencing in The Hole, the psychic death he was confronting, might eventually render him inaccessible to the very voice of conscience he prized so highly. I finally suggested that he come to the hospital. He agreed, but I am sure that my relief was greater than his. We talked of much in the next few weeks. We spoke of Ben's family and their farm, of the people and the land he loved, and often we sat in silence.

"Being in The Hole, there's a kind of slowing down. It's the slowness of it. I'm not really suffering, I'm going into deprivation. When I talked to you last time I wasn't really depressed, I was just down. I was sort of upset, things were sort of loose. I'm always thinking to myself, tearing down my ideas and trying to build them up again. Being here in prison, and especially in The Hole, it's hard thinking in terms of people. It's hard even for me to talk about it in a way. Just interrelating with people is difficult. There's no problem once I'm with them again, but when I'm not with people I have a hard time thinking about them. When I first came here I used to think about people on the outside a lot. But I have a hard time now, a hard time thinking about them at all. I have to be with people to have a feeling about them; if they're not right here, they don't exist any more. I'm momentarily paralyzed. I feel that I'm doing prison now, and when I'm doing it I have a hard time thinking. I think about the outside, but I don't think about it in terms of people. Prison makes you forget about community; I used to think of our farm as a little community, but now I think of it as isolation.

"Being in The Hole, I've had to learn how to deprive myself of things. I've always wanted to keep things simple, but being in The Hole—that is the real level of simplicity. I sometimes get to thinking of simple things, like working on the farm, but mostly when I think about the farm I think of *doing* things there, stacking rocks and things. I know it means more than that, and sometimes the values are there, but I can't get to them.

"After a while all you can feel is the vague sensation of wanting to cry, or yell, or sing—something like that—and you can't relate to any particular thing. It's just a vague, general thing of wanting to jump up and down or run across a field. The feelings still keep coming every once in a while with no particular thing to provoke them. No particular thought, just a feeling with no connection. You get suddenly upset, it's just a chain reaction, and you want to cry, but you don't. I don't know why, I don't usually hold back about anything like crying, but I do get the feeling and I can't.

"I was saying last time that in here they were closing off the poetic aspects in people's hearts. That's the thing. That really is, I think, the thing. You can't let out your feelings. I was trying to think of some way of working on this, how to release those feelings, how to keep on having them. I don't think I ever was much in tune with art things, but I think this is the situation where you need them, where you have feelings that you've got to let out—if you had some way to release them it would help."

As these excerpts from Ben's conversations suggest, his life in The Hole had begun to influence his mental functioning. He was becoming progressively less able to keep people in mind unless they were physically in front of him. When he thought of his home, it was as an isolated and a depopulated territory. It was more difficult for him to think conceptually. He was losing the capacity to concentrate upon his own thoughts or to use them for communication with others and with himself. His perception was slowly ceasing to register and his intelligence to assimilate. At the same time, he was losing touch with his emotions and with the ability to invest what he did feel with significance.

The destruction of perhaps the most specifically human qualities —introspection, reflection, symbolization—which had begun in the general prison population accelerated in the ultra-confinement of The Hole. The degeneration of the faculty of symbolic integration— the linking of thought, feeling, and action; the ability to appreciate metaphor and abstract representation; the capacity to differentiate between the literal and the figurative, between denotation and connotation—which was widespread among prisoners was particularly notable in Ben. He could think of routine tasks on the farm, but he was no longer sure of the lifelong beliefs they had represented, or whether they *were* representations of values or only chores. The very ability to recognize those values, to coordinate them with symbolic actions, and to enunciate them had been impaired. Because of this inner disjunction, Ben was losing contact with the very convictions which had brought him to prison and for whose validity and protection he had gone to The Hole ("sometimes the values are there but I can't get to them"). By this loss of inner coherence, Ben was less able to connect, not only with himself but with those beliefs which were the sources of his life and growth.

There was yet another dimension to my concern for Ben. Soon my two years at Lompoc would come to an end. I had no idea who would replace me or indeed if there would be any replacement. I knew that when I left, the group would terminate, at least in its formal sense, and that Ben would go back to The Hole. For most of the time remaining we talked together, at whatever pace was possible, and I spoke and listened with a particular goal: to reawaken and strengthen in Ben, for the long months to come, his sense of the past and future, of the present as well as the absent; to help restore those connections which would help him sustain a sense of continuous life. A few months later my term at Lompoc expired, but Ben's determination did not. On a day that was very clear but not very bright, I left the prison and Ben returned to The Hole. He stayed there until his time ran out.

PART FOUR

Afterword

30

In Conclusion

What happened among the resisters was hardly unique. They were treated with contempt and callousness equal to that given other prisoners, and they responded with equal pain and courage. Under intermittent but galling supervision and subject to a confusing barrage of insult and indifference, the resisters were pressured, as were other prisoners, to think of themselves as not only errant and insignificant but as entirely bad and of utterly no consequence; as not merely numbers but ciphers. This "subtlest form of violence," as Ben Post described it, often had devastating effects. By resonating with the repudiated, disavowed aspects of the self which have persisted unconsciously, the plodding contempt of guards and officials forged a deep liaison with prisoners' own capacities for self-contempt, for the activation and realization of their own negative identities, and therefore for their unwitting cooperation in their own dehumanization.

In their encounters with judges, marshals, county jails, guards, case workers, psychiatrists, and other prisoners, resisters ran the usual squalid gauntlet of inmate experience and they suffered the usual psychic—and sometimes physical—assaults, the same extreme challenges and the same constriction in the range of possible responses. If their consciences were particularly prone to the threat of deterioration—from the sensitive to the irritating to the vindictive—the resisters were also exposed, in every dimension of their character structures, to the major effect of incarceration: the erosion of one's own identity and the imposition of the identity of convict.

Though all the resisters were proud of having accomplished what they set out to do in going to prison, none denied the psychic costs of their months in custody. Most of them felt that the results of their incarceration were deeply penetrating and at least potentially persistent, that no one so immured in Lompoc could remain immune to it. Encapsulated in space, they soon felt isolated in time; restricted from those who meant most to them, they gradually lost touch with themselves and their world. They felt neither sameness nor continuity; inner links and outer ties were progressively weakened and ultimately broken. Their inner lives, like those of other prisoners, came to resemble a psychological no man's land, an inner terrain at once dangerous and barren. This mental state was the result not only of regression but also of a disarticulation of previously well-linked mental agencies and their recombination in a more simplified and fixed configuration, going beyond identity erosion to true character destruction. Among resisters as among other prisoners, an adaptive premium was placed on those qualities which were as controlling, punitive, and finally as automatized as the prison regime. Inner tyranny complemented outer despotism; inner monotony, outer routine.

Survival was all too often purchased by the sacrifice of the abilities to experience directly, to feel strongly, and to think clearly. The adaptive raising of an inner barrier against potentially noxious sensations and imagery left many men without the vitality this defense was meant to protect. The need for a sense of autonomy could often find expression only in the "games" and puerile hassling so prevalent among prisoners and staff; and it was the excitement of these momentary flings that made perversity so appealing. To exist meant stagnation but to thrive meant psychopathy.

The inner lives of resisters and other prisoners were not characterized by stability but by rigidity; there was no sense of a fluid equilibrium but rather that of a brittle pseudo equilibrium based on inner partition, easily shattered by the rage it barely controlled.

The inner lives of prisoners reflected the psychosocial climate of the prison: there was timelessness without permanence, enclosure without security, noise without communication, quiet without peace, life without vitality.

This is an atmosphere of living death. Indeed, the surrender of basic rights upon incarceration has come to be known as "civil death." Beyond civil death, there is a state which might be called social death; it is a state not merely of isolation but of the inability to connect with, to care for, and finally to imagine a world beyond the cell. No aspect of imprisonment was more effective in promoting this state of social death than was the dominant group ethic of the inmate code, a precept which was, paradoxically, one of isolation: Do Your Own Time. Beyond social death lay the inner impoverishment of what has been called psychic death. The atmosphere of death is so palpable in prison that it is hardly a surprise that the slightest review of prison literature suggests the same theme. Even the titles announce it: *Memoirs from the House of the Dead, Darkness at Noon, Soul on Ice.*

The imagery of death, darkness, and suspended animation expressed in these titles was repeated almost daily by prisoners in and out of the psychiatric clinic in their descriptions of themselves as robots or zombies or as turning to stone. The state of helpless inactivation was repeated in outspoken fears and in dreams of cataclysmic destruction by flood, nuclear accident, or earthquake. But whether they occurred in waking thought or in dreams, the images of death were often too urgent and potentially overwhelming to be borne. Many prisoners stopped dreaming or, more correctly, stopped remembering their dreams. These dreams were frequently banished from waking memory through an unconscious censorship whose apparent goal was to limit not only the intensity of the imagery of such dreams but first the imagery and then the dreams themselves. For other prisoners, after they had been impaired in their ability to abstract, to symbolize, and to appreciate metaphor, this imagery ceased to be symbolic and became literal. In both instances the intensity and force of the imagery of death led to the death of imagery.

It was common for prisoners at Lompoc to feel that they were in a concentration camp, "a psychological Auschwitz," as Ralph Lombardi expressed it. The reader may not need reminding that the practice of rehabilitation at Lompoc was not so horrible as what was perpetrated in Nazi death camps, that leaving Lompoc even at the last possible mandatory release date was not quite the same as never leaving Auschwitz. Indeed, when compared to concentration camps or even to more regressive American prisons, the Federal Correctional Institution at Lompoc constitutes a subsidiary horror.

The reader may need reminding, however, that his perspective is not that of the prisoner. For men who had undergone the psychic changes of incarceration and were more likely to equate the helplessness and inactivation of psychic death with physical extermination, the resemblances between a concentration camp and the prison were often more evident than the differences. Inmates in both situations were immersed, to different degrees, in a process they could not sufficiently grasp, control, or resist. That the specifics and the contexts differed was not so important to many prisoners at Lompoc as was their realization that the inner experiences were comparable, that they were experiencing psychically what others had undergone psychically *and* physically, and that the two modes of experience were equivalent.

Although they had been subject to the inactivating effects of imprisonment, the resisters differed from other prisoners in this respect: they would not return, or be returned, to prison. Their felony convictions did not exempt them from reclassification by Selective Service. But none would accept a second draft notice, and few felt that they would return to prison. This change in attitude represented for some a significant revision not only in conscience but in character; not only a value reversal but a profound identity change. At the time of their initial resistance, their decisions were based on the assumption that moral principle and self-interest were identical, that they could act in no other way and still be recognizably themselves, that they were "exerting their beings" at a time of historical, national, and personal crises in the hope of resolving them.

Imprisonment had altered the resisters' assumptions of the congruence of moral principle and self-interest; some had difficulty recognizing themselves in any form; some felt that they had put themselves in the custody of a government they had trusted, only to discover that the government was far less trusting and trustable than they had imagined, that it was not suffering from a few benign and localized illnesses but from a malignant, generalized, and possibly fatal condition. In following their consciences to Lompoc, the resisters found that they were punished as viciously as if they had had no consciences; and as a result, most approached their release from custody with a considerably diminished appreciation of the value of altruism. As a result of their isolation from their families and from society, and with their forced acceptance of prison life and its standards of behavior, they found themselves gradually alienated from their prior conceptions of their nation and its ideals and of their own identities and standards.

In serving their sentences this time, many resisters felt that they had completed their transaction with the government and with themselves. If they felt that they had been mistreated, they also felt that they had made their point to their satisfaction and that it did not require redefinition. They had seen the first draft notice as the product of an unacceptable, inhuman, but random system; a second notice could only be a specifically vindictive harassment, just as unacceptable, no less inhuman, and anything but random. As one man expressed it, "Coming here once hurts, but it is right; coming here twice means becoming a convict, and that's someone who's being destroyed." For others, it would not have to go so far as "coming here twice." Any government harassment would be sufficient proof that the government was indeed the police state it had seemed to be from within the prison, that the nation was no longer the America they still had hope of loving but a nation and a part of themselves they could only think of leaving.

These sentiments were still provisional; their realization depended on events in the future. But the resisters had at least one other advantage over other prisoners. Though they suffered and endured as much as anyone at Lompoc, they knew that they had come there voluntarily. However much they revised their expectations of subsequent imprisonment, they did not resent having come the first time. They had come to protest the war and the draft as well as to validate their perception of themselves as distinctive men acting responsibly. Their distinctiveness was eroded, their responsibility was undermined, and they took such psychological steps as were necessary for survival. Their inner identities were sorely tried, sometimes damaged, often compromised, and severely threatened, but they never entirely yielded. They did not recant.

The element of active decision, of having chosen what was necessary and of trying to keep on choosing once inside, in however diminished a range, was a major source of strength. It was hardly a guarantee of immunity to the effects of incarceration, but it prevented, at least partially, what was far more widespread among other prisoners: the assumption of the identity of the helpless victim. Having chosen to go to Lompoc, having needed to make the choice, having endured its consequences, it was much more difficult for the resisters to say, "I was violated." Indeed, it could be said that they resisted the pressures of imprisonment to adopt a masochistic relationship with their guards, with their nation, and with the strictures of their own consciences.

But to resist these pressures was to realize their power and their own vulnerability to them. In his paper "The Economic Problem of Masochism," Freud pointed out that "the masochist must do what is inexpedient, must act against his own interests, must ruin the prospects which open out to him in the real world and must, perhaps, destroy his own real existence." The resisters had gone to prison the first time for many reasons, but not to gratify their masochism. In the opinion of most of them, to return to prison would be to do the inexpedient, would be against their own interests, would ruin their prospects, and would, perhaps, destroy their own real existence. They would not return to prison for many reasons, but not the least of them was that they were not masochistic *enough*.

Because many resisters were caught between their inner commitment to responsible action and institutional pressures toward conformity and chicanery, their prison experiences were those of solitary men struggling for unity. Although personal solitude had been the preference of many, they found themselves threatened with an isolation beyond any they had contemplated. Having come to prison in good conscience, they were confronted in themselves and in others with the force and the consequences of bad conscience. Under pressure to ignore their own feelings and to avoid attachment, they combined and worked together for their own affirmation; they resolved that their time would be remembered and their grief not forgotten. In "exerting their being," they often approached nonbeing; in suffering physical limitation and psychic constriction they recognized better what in them was irreducible; in doing hard time they experienced rigidity but retained what was most enduring. In knowing voracity, they learned satisfaction; in confronting anger, they exercised control. In refusing the draft, they were refusing to be coerced by fear—and in this they epitomized the courage of a generation. In carrying through what they had done for principle, they pursued their search for a wider identity through the straits of a narrower one—to the discovery of a manhood more clearly their own.

31

Epilogue

Some time after I had left Lompoc I returned to California, this time to San Francisco, to give a paper at a scientific meeting. Some of the resisters were still in custody and others were constrained from meeting with me then by parole restrictions or budgets. But several did come to the city and we spent parts of several days talking together. There was no longer any problem as to who had a mustache or what it meant; there had been a dramatic increase in hair in each man in rough proportion to the amount of time he had been free. Although the group drew together quickly, I had no wish to convert what was basically an affectionate reunion into a research investigation. Any true follow-up, any worthwhile consideration of the longitudinal effects of incarceration, must await a more careful study than could be attempted in a few hours in Golden Gate Park.

There was a great deal of talk, of course, about the prison, of the riot that had broken out the summer before, and of the personnel changes that had followed it. Although the prison talk had not yet taken on the rosy glow of retrospective idealization, much of its tone was affectionate and even fond. In fact, there was a great deal more discussion of the prison among these men who were now free than there was of themselves and their immediate lives. But the prison talk and its tone were at the same time very much about the men and their immediate lives, in that the principal psychological task before them was that of integrating their prison experience into their ongoing lives without utterly repudiating it and thereby repudiating a part of themselves.

Like many other prisoners, these resisters had found that to leave prison was not to leave it behind. Many were struggling to reintegrate within themselves and with a world less simple and less controlling than prison had been. They were trying to restore the inner and outer links which had been disrupted by their incarceration and at the same time trying to preserve a link with their imprisonment, attempting to master it by harmonizing it inwardly with other aspects of their lives in order to more fully re-establish their grasp of freedom. This process of reintegration, involving the yielding of the identity of "heroic" resister or "destroyed" convict to that of "ordinary" citizen, occupied many of them. This reconstitution was often an anguished process, and one which, when operating in the context of the psychic damage of their incarceration, complicated their return.

Some of the resisters had been able, in Nick Manos's words, simply to "close the book" on their prison experiences and go home and back to school or work with little apparent difficulty. But the majority, including Nick himself, were unable to so completely wall off the full impact of their incarceration or to lightly dismiss or radically repudiate what had been, for all its pain, a profoundly important experience. The process of gradually working it over after the fact, even if it meant a time of inner discomfort and social distance, was deeply necessary as an act of restoration, repair, and mastery—for to forget the pain would have been to forget the purpose.

Both Mark Henley and Nick Manos described an initial period after release of dazed detachment and physical listlessness. They had watched television a great deal and found it difficult to concentrate their thoughts or focus their attention on anything more demanding. Mark had returned to school soon after leaving prison, but he had stopped after a semester, not yet sure of his bearings. Nick was working at what he felt was a marginal job until something better came along and until he himself was better. Ralph Lombardi did not receive a parole after the interview described in this book, but he did make it the next time around. On returning home, he found the bonds of marriage intolerable and he separated from his wife. After the divorce, he felt more at ease living with her. He was going back to school in order to work in psychology and he had recovered much of his wit. Wayne Foote had just been released and was still visiting his family. After an initial period of "feeling like a blank," Calvin Jones had gone back to school.

Ben Post had been out of custody only a matter of weeks, having spent the intervening months in The Hole. When his mandatory release arrived, he did not walk home. He had been offered a ride home from prison by a friend, but he could not find a reason, or the words, or the voice to refuse, and he had ridden home in silence, unable to say anything. He was living on his farm and cultivating his garden, but he hitchhiked to the city for the weekend. In the months after I left Lompoc I had had great difficulty thinking of Ben in The Hole because·of the anguish I felt. His occasional letters, though disjointed in content, had been optimistic in tone. Having tried to forget what I did not wish to recall, I was unprepared for what I should have expected. His face was impassive and his speech was halting. The stare had not left his eyes. He spoke in bursts, followed by long silences. He ate voraciously. There was warmth in the vigor of his handshake, but his palms were cold.

All the resisters were anxious about the possibility of government interference in their lives, particularly after their parole periods expired. Some were working or going to school, living clearly aboveground. Others were slowly gathering their energies, delaying a return to full life until they felt confident of living it—living at ground level; among those who were doing this more literally were Ben Post, tending his garden, and Joe Cox, who had returned to college, not as a student but as a groundskeeper. And one man had clearly gone underground. There were many influences which led to his assuming a new name and a different identity, but it was difficult for me to overlook the fact that Carl Bronson had been a six-month prisoner and therefore subject to the group pressure which influenced all such men. He had arrived at Lompoc relatively late in the group's existence and I did not remember whether he spent any time in The Hole. Though I did not think that the discrepancy of his sentence was the most important aspect of his decision to go underground, it did seem that he was saying, in effect and in part, "If I have been an incomplete resister and an insufficient inmate, I can be a genuine outlaw."

32

Prison Reform?

W<small>HO</small> can contemplate the idea of prison without dread or the prospect of making a statement on prison reform without futility? Every book written about prison life is itself an argument for prison reform, and if one adds to such books the number of tracts, polemics, essays, and editorials specifically addressed to reform, the bibliography is as overwhelming as the problem. Most of this literature is well-meaning, much of it is repetitive, and most of its conclusions and recommendations are obvious to any thoughtful reader; yet little has come of it.

"The road to hell is paved with good intentions." In the fifty years since George Bernard Shaw borrowed the phrase, in use in some form since the twelfth century, it has remained a truth and become a truism. It is no accident that it appeared in an essay on prison reform, one which was to introduce a study of British prisons which itself had been prompted by the experiences of conscientious objectors incarcerated during the First World War. Most of what Shaw observed and decried in 1919 still persists, from the determined naïveté of judges who prefer not to know the consequences of their sentencing to the resistance of the public to meaningful change in the treatment of "moral inferiors."

Well-intentioned prison reform has resulted in institutions such as the one at Lompoc. That prison was reasonably clean, reasonably airy, and reasonably maintained, but it was unreasonably violent, unreasonably organized, and unreasonably administered. The practice of overt physical brutality was transferred from the staff to the inmates—I did not see a single official bastinado in the two years I worked there—and the staff assumed the practice of psychological brutality even more oppressive for its relative subtlety. Unremitting inmate violence at a Federal institution such as Lompoc was all the more remarkable since most of the offenses for which the prisoners had been convicted were not desperate acts of violent men but rather impulsive or (rarely) specifically calculated ones involving interstate illegal transactions. The daily assaults did not seem to be the consequences of the uncontrollable aggression of unusually violent people but rather the acts of ordinary men whose ordinary capacity for violence had been provoked by life in a particularly violent institution.

In their efforts to improve physical conditions and liberalize procedures, reformers have replaced the lash with the "invisible fist" of administrative force, grotesque physical torture with the dehumanizing pseudo efficiency of processing. As a consequence of reform, the prison staff at Lompoc was not composed of bizarre, drooling sadists but, for the most part, of glumly isolated men who were barren, gloomy, empty, pale, and above all profoundly bored. But the high-minded motives of reformers have not put an end to the high-handed treatment of prisoners. Prisons that have been thus reformed have not been improved; they are no less evil for their change of form from the lurid to the banal. The reduction of official physical brutality has only exposed the psychological brutality that has always been at its heart.

Improvements in physical conditions and the addition of staff who can at least appear to be rehabilitative tokens have not promoted the prison's attainment of its "mission" to deter criminal behavior or to protect society. The incidence of first offenders is always rising, as is the recidivism rate; most prisoners, no matter how long they have been in custody, are eventually returned to a society that is then more than ever in need of protection. Most importantly, the cosmetic changes that have taken place in the name of reform have not facilitated genuine rehabilitation because they have not interfered with those aspects of imprisonment which undercut rehabilitation most effectively and which prison officials regard as most important: punishment and custody.

At present, the public seems to be getting what it wants; the appearance of improvement and the practice of confinement. This situation does not encourage rehabilitation; indeed, it increases the need for it. Any rehabilitative approach—short of the use of electrical appliances—depends on a meeting of minds, yet a prison therapeutic interview cannot help but be soaked in shame and cloaked in distrust. A rehabilitative attitude implies a belief in the potential for change; the power of the correctional attitude ensures stasis. If a criminal act is due to impaired relations with others or with oneself, the correctional practice is to impair them further; if it is due to impulsiveness or aggression, then these tendencies are channeled into even more intense and grotesque forms of expression. If a rehabilitative attitude connotes recognition of individual differences, a variety of social relations, a range of ethical relativism, and a commitment to life, correctional practice is based upon the eradication of individual distinctiveness, the disruption of emotional ties, the imposition of a hypocritical moralism, and the assignment of civil, social, and psychic death.

It was abundantly clear that immersion even in a reformed prison such as Lompoc made every inmate a likely candidate for psychiatric treatment, but the emphasis of those rehabilitative efforts I tried to make was not upon "criminality" or character disorder, but instead was focused by necessity upon the urgencies of the here and now, the stark immediate problems that were inflamed, if not engendered, by the stress of imprisonment. Such therapeutic gains as may have been made during my tenure at Lompoc I regard as fortuitous in their occurrence and only palliative in their effect. It is true that there were no suicides and that individuals and groups gained something from their contact with the medical staff, but in considering the impediments to treatment raised by the prison staff and by the gradual psychological deterioration of the medical staff, I am convinced that such therapeutic benefit as there was came about because the medical staff made an intense effort to resist identification with prison authorities and to remain open and accessible to prisoners, and were seen to be doing so. There were limitations upon these efforts, however, and the degree of therapeutic benefit seemed far more related to the fact that the doctors were themselves members of a mutually sustaining group—a development that was again as fortuitous as it was beneficial.

Even if imprisonment did not impose such extensive psychic damage, it is doubtful that any institution which forcibly restrains its inmates can be truly therapeutic. The prohibition of meaningful human contact between prison staff and inmates; the psychic processes which lead employees to view prisoners as inanimate, unchanging, and interchangeable; the specific diminution of moral consciousness which prison employment requires (and which leads to the unquestioned acceptance of psychopathy and of various forms of human experimentation)—all these make it unrealistic to expect the prison staff to maintain a rehabilitative approach. In view of the psychic changes of imprisonment, it is similarly unrealistic to expect a prisoner to view any prison employee as a therapist. It is far more likely for any member of the prison staff to be seen as a hireling of the prison system and to be distrusted and devalued accordingly.

For all these reasons, it appears that the goals of custody and treatment are irreconcilable. It is not so much that custody and treatment are incompatible, or even antagonistic, but that they are complementary; that is, one can advance only at the expense of the other. Although treatment, ideally, should be able to mitigate custody, the sadistic attraction of having power over others gives custody the advantage, and the adversary role of custody debases the ally role of treatment.

Under these circumstances, it is self-deception for a therapist to believe that he can "work from within" or that he and his associates will somehow be an influence for good upon staff and prisoners while working for the prison administration. It is worse than self-deception for a therapist to believe that he is incapable of being manipulated and to deny that he probably will be manipulated. It is still worse to believe that symptomatic relief or slight behavioral change while in prison represents true rehabilitation (particularly when the simulation of change may flatter the therapist into recommending release), for it is very easy to believe that something is happening when in fact very little is. Until prison psychiatry (and its associated disciplines) recognizes its own limitations and the constraints upon its effectiveness, it will continue to be a farce played out in the midst of a tragedy.

If prisoners have scant access to treatment in custody, still less does incarceration bring an understanding of justice or a sense of equity. Although there is an elaborate system of codes, rules, transactions, and arrangements, it does not go beyond *quid pro quo* to an appreciation of shared values, cooperative endeavor, and mutual respect. Because of the institutional pressures and their psychic effects, it is not always a failing of the inmates that there is no honor among thieves.

It is not so much injustice which characterizes prison life, though it is certainly prevalent, as nonjustice. All the prisoners tend to be identified with each other by the staff. If an offense occurs in the institution and a clear culprit is not readily available, any inmate may be punished since they are all felt to be the same by the staff and therefore equally culpable.

Viewed as inanimate, unchanging, and interchangeable by the staff, and subject to the oppression that follows from such an attitude, inmates tend to see the prison staff in the same light, and with the changes in thought that follow prolonged incarceration, the total equation of the prison and the state is widespread. After some months in government custody, it is not difficult to view the state as the agent of one's destruction; with gradual impairment of abstraction, one is more likely to replace the metaphor "America *as* prison" with the certainty of "America *is* prison." For both the reactionary and the revolutionary prisoner, whether he identifies with the oppressor or the oppressed, prison and world may become one, no longer related but synonymous. The lessons of imprisonment—the experiences of wielding oppression and of yielding to it, the conversion to absolutism, and the attractions of psychopathy—are a powerful and frightening combination. Thousands of prisoners of every origin have honed their militancy while doing time; now that many others, some of them "not usual jail material," are going through prison, that rage can only be growing.

That, perhaps, is why there has been more interest of late in prison reform. To protect their children, their property, or their country, many thoughtful people have urged changes in prisons, even their abolition. But such institutions will not be torn down; the society which prefers the glacial isolation of its prisoners, and which requires their conversion from offenders to enemies, will not suddenly relinquish the fear of torrential anarchy and destruction which that frozen isolation is expected to contain. Having imposed on prisoners the void, the public will not suddenly choose what it takes to be chaos.

If the public has not acted precipitately to change prisons, it does not appear to have been out of respect for prudence. Indeed, it might be asked whether, after the outrage over the latest prison scandal dies down, there is not a more abiding and powerful wish for as little reform as possible; whether prisons really are *supposed* to change. At its founding in 1870, the American Correctional Association issued a declaration of thirty-seven principles, of which thirty-one have yet to be realized. Though these principles are unexceptionable in moral terms, they appear, in correctional terms and after a century, to be not so much reasonable objectives, noble ideas, or visionary notions as Utopian concepts in the narrowest sense; that is, to be realized nowhere and never.

Much has been written of the public's wish for vengeance, suggesting that the demand for retribution has been the principal impediment to meaningful prison reform. Indeed, the physical improvements in prison can be viewed as the kind of superficial amelioration which convinces the public that things are not so bad in prison after all and that its retributive urge has been tamed. But what has not been reformed is the psychological effect of incarceration, and what may not be so well recognized is that the public wish for the isolation of prisoners, the determined innocence regarding the fate of the guilty, may well be the limiting factor, the basic resistance, to prison reform. No inner dynamic is so intense as the wish not to know the unpleasant; it is this need for exclusion from awareness which has impeded reform, has required physical and psychological banishment for prisoners, and supports the public's comprehension of its own safety.

It seems that prison employees have received an implicit mandate to allow in custody what is not tolerable to the public in consciousness or in freedom. In addition, it appears that their attitude toward prisoners as inanimate, unchanging, and interchangeable is not so much their particular response to the unique requirements of the special world of prison as it is—in the dynamics of its psychic elaboration—the nucleus of the general public's attitude toward prisoners and of the public's image of its own security. For if prisoners are viewed as inanimate, unchanging, and interchangeable because they are required, on a deeper level, to contain not only their own attributes but those which we have attributed to them, then it appears that they are indeed convicted for what they do but that they are often kept imprisoned for what they represent.

The wish for the isolation and immobilization of prisoners is well expressed by prison buildings, many of which antedate the 1870 publication of the Declaration of Principles of the American Correctional Association and which, unlike those principles, are still in daily use. These gloomy, oppressive structures have a remarkable capacity for survival, one that goes beyond the quality of their construction or the persistence of evil. Though rebuilt several times after riots, Newgate Gaol occupied the same London site from 1188 to 1902. Never in need of reconstruction, the Eastern State Penitentiary in Philadelphia was opened in 1829 and operated continuously until 1970. It was reopened soon after due to "overcrowding" in the suburban prison built to replace it. In fact, it seems that these depressing buildings remain in use because they meet a need greater than mere detention. The mass of prison buildings manifests the idea of seclusion and immutability; the weight of the buildings embodies the psychic stasis of the prisoner, as if both the buildings and their populations were the permanent, inorganic receptacles of society's unwanted attributes. Prisons are forbidding because they contain the forbidden; their dismal appearance announces that their *genius loci* is death.

To point out that prisons are incapable of correction is not to deny that there will probably always have to be places of detention for those whose illegal behavior is otherwise uncontrollably assaultive, well organized, or persistently predatory. Such people constitute a small fraction of the population of most prisons, and for them a good case can be made for incarceration as both punishment and detention. Custody is what prisons are good at, and that is what they should be limited to doing. But if prisons can be limited to those who must be confined for the safety of the general public, then they will become even more difficult to manage and they will be in need of even more reform and more sensitive administration.

It may seem that I am advocating that prisons give up the pretense of rehabilitation, and that is exactly what I am advocating. What might be gained, in addition to a more equitable system of justice, would be a measure of honesty in the prison administration and, no doubt, a measure of relief among prison staff. With the open acknowledgment that the prison's goals are limited to punishment and custody, the pretense of rehabilitation need not be maintained in order to deny those goals, and the staff could then implement what they came to prison to do: keep the institution secure.

To suggest that prisons give up rehabilitation is not to recommend consigning prisoners to a regressive institution or to deny that prisoners will still be in need of treatment; rather, it is to signify that far greater therapeutic benefit could be obtained from outside resources, with prisoners going to existing rehabilitative facilities or with the necessary personnel coming to the prison as needed. In both cases rehabilitation could be carried out by men and women who need not be under the thumb of prison administrators, who will not so readily be seen by inmates as agents of the prison staff, and who will be better able to preserve confidentiality, the dignity of the prisoner, and their own self-respect.

If prisons were to be reserved for punishment and confinement, those who the court thinks need treatment should have the chance to get it without ever going to prison. To develop such a program would require an expanded probationary system to ensure adequate supervision. But supervision should not be confused with rehabilitation, for it is doubtful that the same person can be both supervisor and therapist.

Treatment, therefore, should be undertaken, not in grandiose new custodial facilities, but through the expansion of existing therapeutic agencies. The men and women in such work would require low enough case loads and high enough salaries for them to get to know the people they work with, feel worthwhile themselves, and not be tempted to compensate for overwork and underpayment by seeking gratification from the people they are supposed to help or by degrading them into mere subjects for case reports. Placing such a program in the cities will enable it to operate where the men and their problems reside and where the best staffs can be recruited. By placing such a program in the community, a wider scope of treatment would be available, far greater a range than the improvised programs (or the rigidly overstructured ones) imposed in prison. A wider range of therapists would also be available. Nor should every man be considered in need of treatment in its narrow sense; brief counseling, job training, and education may be more important than any form of psychotherapy.

It should be emphasized that therapeutic measures often succeed only to the degree that they are voluntary; few measures can undermine treatment so well as a "sentence to psychotherapy." It must also be kept in mind that psychotherapy carries no guarantee of success. The faith of many officials who think it would be better if only there were enough mental-health workers is indeed touching. No one would deny that there is a desperate need for them, but it must be acknowledged that some problems are resolved only by the passage—or the serving—of time, or after prolonged treatment or no treatment, and that some are not resolved at all. To have the courage not to rely *solely* on the illusory security of incarceration is only to have the nerve to fail at a lesser rate.

Life in an institution may seem attractive in its apparent simplicity when viewed from outside, and life may often be no less imprisoning for its less visible walls, but the rehabilitative programs of most prisons are antitherapeutic operations at their most cynical; they are base practices concealed by baseless claims. The broader range of an outside program would do far less violence and at least make possible the likelihood that an offender would be treated as human rather than inanimate, capable of change rather than unchanging, individual rather than interchangeable. It would support the basic moral principle that human life should be respected—a principle on which all rehabilitation depends and which incarceration specifically denies—and in doing this it would not only reform but would put an end to what has been incorrigible in the practice of corrections.

This book was begun because of my personal sense of revulsion by the force with which incarceration erodes the identity of every prisoner and employee, exploiting one's inner capacity for division, and imposing isolation from community, other, and self. I do not think it unseemly, then, to end it on a personal note.

The shriek of the four-o'clock work whistle terminated most groups, as it did most other activity in the prison. The inmates shuffled back to their cells to be counted, and the counters changed shifts and went down to the prison lobby to wait inside the door, not free to go home to their own compound until the senior officials led the way out. There was a brief gasp of silence and sunlight then, as if the shrill sound of the whistle had momentarily chastened the shore birds and military aircraft and restrained the smutty sea fog already sliding in to impose an early night. In the muddy brown office, acrid with the smell of Union Leader tobacco, I often thought, in those few quiet minutes, of the men I had come to know and of a question Camus had once asked. I regret as I write now, as I did then, that I can only repeat it: "To force solitude on a man who has just come to understand that he is not alone, is that not the definitive crime against man?"